Rhenish Capitalism

T0300208

Rhenish capitalism is an ideal-typical model of capitalism which is characterised by a bank-centred financing system, close economic ties between banks and companies, a balance of power between shareholders and management and a social partnership between unions and employers. The West German economy of the 1950s to the 1980s is the prime example of that model of capitalism which contrasts with the liberal Anglo-Saxon forms of capitalism. In accordance with recent debates about Varieties of Capitalism, the authors argue that research on capitalism should pay more attention to change over time. This book also claims to put the firm into the centre of analysis.

The empirical contributions uncover the differences between French and German corporate governance practices comparing two European automobile producers (VW and Renault); analyse legal debates and practices of corporate control in post-war Germany; show the tension between national corporate governance and increasing internationalisation by reference to four major West German producers of chemicals, pharmaceuticals and fibres; and explore the opportunities encountered by German big banks vis-à-vis their customers from big industry. Furthermore, they show that coordinating culture in the supply relationship of the German automobile industry came under pressure at the end of the boom and stress the importance of communication processes as a basis for interest coordination in Rhenish capitalism.

The chapters in this book were originally published as a special issue of the journal *Business History*.

Christian Marx is Researcher at the Leibniz Institute for Contemporary History in Munich, Germany, where he is working on a collective biography of the top management of the German central bank (Deutsche Bundesbank) in the two post-war decades.

Morten Reitmayer is Researcher and Supernumerary Professor of Modern and Contemporary History at the University of Trier, Germany.

Rhenish Capitalism

New Insights from a Business History Perspective

Edited by
Christian Marx and Morten Reitmayer

Routledge
Taylor & Francis Group

LONDON AND NEW YORK

First published 2022
by Routledge
4 Park Square, Milton Park, Abingdon, Oxon, OX14 4RN

and by Routledge
605 Third Avenue, New York, NY 10158

Routledge is an imprint of the Taylor & Francis Group, an informa business

British Library Cataloguing-in-Publication Data
A catalogue record for this book is available from the British Library

ISBN13: 978-1-032-19315-1 (hbk)
ISBN13: 978-1-032-19317-5 (pbk)
ISBN13: 978-1-003-25863-6 (ebk)

DOI: 10.4324/9781003258636

Typeset in Myriad Pro
by codeMantra

Publisher's Note
The publisher accepts responsibility for any inconsistencies that may have arisen during the conversion of this book from journal articles to book chapters, namely the inclusion of journal terminology.

Disclaimer
Every effort has been made to contact copyright holders for their permission to reprint material in this book. The publishers would be grateful to hear from any copyright holder who is not here acknowledged and will undertake to rectify any errors or omissions in future editions of this book.

Contents

Citation Information

The following chapters were originally published in the journal *Business History*, volume 61, issue 5 (2019). When citing this material, please use the original page numbering for each article, as follows:

Introduction
Introduction: Rhenish capitalism and business history
Christian Marx and Morten Reitmayer
Business History, volume 61, issue 5 (2019) pp. 745–784

Chapter 1
The concept of social fields and the productive models: Two examples from the European automobile industry
Morten Reitmayer
Business History, volume 61, issue 5 (2019) pp. 785–809

Chapter 2
Corporate law and corporate control in West Germany after 1945
Boris Gehlen
Business History, volume 61, issue 5 (2019) pp. 810–832

Chapter 3
Between national governance and the internationalisation of business. The case of four major West German producers of chemicals, pharmaceuticals and fibres, 1945–2000
Christian Marx
Business History, volume 61, issue 5 (2019) pp. 833–862

Chapter 4
Financing Rhenish capitalism: 'bank power' and the business of crisis management in the 1960s and 1970s
Ralf Ahrens
Business History, volume 61, issue 5 (2019) pp. 863–878

Chapter 5
Supplier relations within the German automobile industry. The case of Daimler-Benz, 1950–1980
Stephanie Tilly
Business History, volume 61, issue 5 (2019) pp. 879–897

Chapter 6

Confrontational coordination: The rearrangement of public relations in the automotive industry during the 1970s
Ingo Köhler
Business History, volume 61, issue 5 (2019) pp. 898–917

For any permission-related enquiries please visit:
http://www.tandfonline.com/page/help/permissions

Notes on Contributors

Ralf Ahrens Leibniz Centre for Contemporary History, Potsdam, Germany.

Boris Gehlen Department for Business History, University of Stuttgart, Germany.

Ingo Köhler Institute for Economic and Social History, Georg-August-University *Göttingen*, Germany / Hessian Economic Archive, Darmstadt, Germany.

Christian Marx Leibniz Institute for Contemporary History, Munich, Germany / Modern and Contemporary History, University of Trier, Germany.

Morten Reitmayer Modern and Contemporary History, University of Trier, Germany.

Stephanie Tilly Department of Economic and Business History, University of Cologne, Germany.

Preface

While many voices predicted – or once again longed for – the end of capitalism with the global financial crisis of 2007/08, the capitalist economic system once again proved to be more resilient than expected. The financial crisis led to significantly weakened economic growth almost everywhere in the world. According to the IMF, the real gross domestic product of the economically developed countries shrank in 2009 for the first time since the Second World War, and trade in goods also fell sharply. At the same time, public debt increased in many states. However, capitalism remained as an economic system. There was a lack of a tangible alternative despite all the prophecies of a post-capitalist era.[1]

The central banks provided massive amounts of money to the financial market to counter the debt crisis and to support the real economy. And many countries launched extensive economic recovery programmes and laws to stabilise the financial markets, because in a world that is becoming ever more closely interconnected financially, only appropriate regulation that sets incentives to preserve the system can prevent the next huge financial crash.[2] These measures stabilised capitalism, which had spread globally after 1989/90.

The breakthrough of globalisation, the spread of multinational companies and the increase in global interdependencies led to processes of hybridisation and harmonisation. Nevertheless, divergences between different forms of capitalism remained. In the light of these persisting divergences, an analysis of Rhenish capitalism from a business-history perspective is more than appropriate to show long-term development trends of the capitalist economy – in continental Europe and especially in Germany. The following contributions place the enterprise at the centre of the analysis and thus provide inspiration for further company-centred research on capitalism.

August 2021
Christian Marx and Morten Reitmayer

Notes

1. Paul Mason, *PostCapitalism*: A Guide to Our Future, London 2016.
2. Adam Tooze, *Crashed: How a Decade of Financial Crises Changed the World*, London 2018.

Introduction: Rhenish capitalism and business history

Christian Marx and Morten Reitmayer

ABSTRACT
This article examines the emergence and development of the comparative analysis of capitalism and recent debates about Varieties of Capitalism (VoC). We argue that the VoC-approach should pay more attention to change over time, and only claim to put the firm in the centre of analysis. Hence, we propose another, more historical, analytic framework, which is based on the VoC-approach and historical institutionalism, and which fits better to an analysis of Rhenish Capitalism, i.e. the German case, from a business history perspective. Keeping in mind this research agenda, we outline the history of the German economy in the second half of the 20th century.

1. Introduction

In light of the economic and financial crisis since 2008, the debate on the *Varieties of Capitalism* (VoC) is more relevant than ever. Germany is not only by far the largest economy in Europe and was the world's leading export nation for a long time – frequently considered as a model for other countries – but has also been characterised as the most significant example of a Coordinated Market Economy (CME) with a high degree of consensus and cooperation. Several approaches for the comparative analysis of capitalism refer to institutional arrangements and constraints, while the room for manoeuvre of individual agents remains an open question within these studies. However, institutions always enable and limit management strategies at the same time.[1] It is the aim of this special issue to learn more about this field of economic action and its dynamics at the level of the firm and to connect our results with the comparative analysis of capitalism.[2] In the 1990s, the VoC-approach, which claimed to go beyond several concepts of institutionalism and to stress the importance of strategic interaction, received great attention, but empirical work it inspired only rudimentarily elaborates the behaviour of economic agents. This is why the articles of this special issue aim to demonstrate the importance of the economic enterprises' role and action for the empirical analysis of modern capitalism in its different varieties.[3] As it is essential to integrate the studies of this special issue into a larger context, we outline here the history of comparative capitalism research, the precursors of the VoC-approach as well as its criticism, and propose an advanced version of the VoC-concept in a more historical way with a set of five key arenas or fields of action. In line with other authors such as Wolfgang

Streeck or Kathleen Thelen, we assert the importance of a historical–institutional approach to explain changes in modern capitalism over time, but suggest opening its perspective by examining economic agents more closely. In a subsequent step, we then outline the history of German capitalism and changes in the second half of the 20th century in these five arenas.

2. The development of comparative analysis of capitalism

Modern capitalism has always been a much-discussed issue, not only in Germany, but in all Western states. With regard to our purpose – of qualifying the concept of *Rhenish Capitalism*, and in this way, reflecting on the VoC-approach – it is worthwhile to examine whether these discussions tried to distinguish several national (or, regional, and so on) 'types' or 'models' of capitalism, and by what criteria they did so. Especially in order to consider and to appreciate the originality of the VoC-approach, and to explain its epistemological success, it seems useful to embed it into the broader context of the history of economics. Interestingly enough, focussing only on the academic discourse, the scope of these debates has narrowed significantly since the downfall of communism. During the late 19th and the first half of the 20th century a wide pluralism of criticism and defence existed. Yet after 1945, there remained for some decades only the confrontation between (Soviet) Marxist hopes and demands for overcoming capitalism as a whole, and the claims for defending the capitalist system of production, which was thought to function the same way in every capitalist society. Finally, during the 1990s and early 2000s, there was a powerful discourse claiming all those economies which had not yet fallen in line with the Anglo–American model of capitalism would inevitably have to do so within a few years. These prophecies aroused contradiction. One such argument was the attempt to prove that there were two different types of capitalist production, published by Peter A. Hall and David Soskice – provoking the VoC-debate in the late 1990s and the first decade of the 21st century.[4]

2.1. Precursors of the VoC-approach

The idea that different types of capitalism could coexist is not that new. Prior to and even after 1914, the so-called 'older' and 'younger' historical school of (German) economic science (*'ältere' und die 'jüngere' 'Historische Schule der Nationalökonomie'*) were open to quite different attitudes toward capitalism. While all of them advocated a vigorous social policy be introduced by the German state,[5] they had quite different ideas of its purpose. These economists were convinced that the agents' motives for capitalist production were in the deepest sense determined by economic, political, social, cultural, and even psychological preconditions, that institutional arrangements were heavily influenced by cultural forces and therefore of historical nature – in other words, that the modes of capitalism would vary from country to country.[6] Some of these economists, such as the very influential head of the 'younger historical school' Adolph Wagner, one of the famous so-called '*Kathedersozialisten*' (a group of bourgeois academic economists suspected to be more or less Marxists and supporters of the Social Democratic Party) were looking for a kind of 'state socialism' in Germany, where economic competition and entrepreneurial profit were to be constrained by law and administration.[7] His colleague Gustav Schmoller claimed that there were stages of economic development for countries to climb, but he defined these stages (in the strictest sense) by non-economic factors, such as ethics (*Sittlichkeit*) and the fair distribution of wealth.[8]

Others, such as the even more influential Werner Sombart and his followers (most prominently the so-called 'revolutionary conservatives') predicted a relative downturn of capitalist production itself, and an upspring of different forms of mixed economies. In the German case, Sombart really hoped for a 'German Socialism', where the technological and economic dynamics of capitalism were to reach an end.[9] To sum up: some very prominent German economists were not only critical of capitalism during the first third of the 20th century (especially to the liberal Anglo–American style of economy, politics, and culture[10]), but were deeply convinced that different and distinct forms of capitalism were in existence, because capitalism was at heart a historical phenomenon – and every country had its own history. Sombart explicitly talked about different 'styles' of economic action (*Wirtschaftsstile*).[11] Accordingly, German capitalism was expected to be deeply regulated by the state at least, if not authoritarian and (some thought: therefore!) oriented to public good, helping to structure society by social estates (*Stände*) performing high quantities of production and great technical innovation, but with a non-commercial (and in particular a nonconsumption-oriented) attitude. In their point of view, the varieties between different forms of capitalism were deeply rooted in the norms, ethics, and goals of economic agents, and in the purposes and the depth of regulation by the state. Capitalist logic was uniform, its execution by different peoples was not. These older German voices which had claimed the superiority of a distinct and outspoken non-liberal, Prussian–German mode of production, a would-be synthesis of '*Preußentum*' and industrial capitalism, had ceased after the defeat of Nazi Germany and the triumph of the Fordist US mass production system during the Second World War and after.[12] In other words, their capacity for historical comparison was buried by the discipline's trend towards mathematisation and to developing models – and because such comparison was explicitly (and not only implicitly) politically charged.

Interestingly enough, these ideas were not only superseded and replaced but forgotten. Though the history of economic thought does not hesitate to trace back the roots of economics to medieval scholasticism, some modern textbooks do not even mention the German historical schools at all. The study by Ernesto Screpanti and Stefano Zamagni does not allude to the German historical schools in their own right, but only to describe the moment when they were made 'outdated' by Carl Menger and the Austrian School.[13] Roughly speaking, the same can be said for authors such as Heinz D. Kurz, or the Penguin History of Economics.[14] Karl Pribram, a follower of Menger, claimed that the historical schools' approach of combining history, culture, ethics, and psychology to find economic laws to be true 'nonsense'.[15] In this perspective, the German historical schools of economics were no more than aberrations from the mainstream of economic thought.[16]

Nonetheless, the crucial point here is that the assumption of a historically and culturally determined capitalism – and therefore the possibility of different capitalisms existing at the same time – was contradictory to the rising claim of methodological individualism and universal, eternal, and exact economic laws, which had been the main trend in European and US economics since the late 19th century. Clearly, the methodological eclecticism, the permanent references to non-economic factors, and the insistence on the relevance of the state (most of these researchers held academic chairs for political science (*Staatswissenschaft*)) were not helpful for a successful establishment of economic science as a distinct academic discipline, and thus less attractive outside Germany. In any case, the idea that different variants of capitalism could and would exist at the same time disappeared from the economists' research agenda for about 80 years. In light of this, the general excitement and surprise about the very idea that varieties of capitalism could exist might have been a little bit smaller if familiarity with the history of one's own discipline had been greater.

After 1945, the idea that democracy and capitalism would necessarily be connected to one another overrode competing approaches. Despite the ideological confrontation of the Cold War, reflected too in the black-and-white thinking of political and economic theory of the day, some observers noticed existing differences among the capitalist societies of Western Europe and the USA. In 1965, the British economist Andrew Shonfield laid down the foundations for more subtle analysis of the varieties among modes of capitalist production.[17] His book became a classical study in comparative economic history. Shonfield pointed out that France, with its investment promotion of certain industries within *planification* after the Second World War, had an entirely different economic system to Germany, which he called an 'organised free market economy'. Though Shonfield pointed out that West Germany, like the United States, was swimming aside from the mainstream of modern capitalism (defined by extensive and intensive economic planning as well), he stated that the long-term economic purposes in West Germany were set by powerful arrangements between industrial associations, banks, large corporations, and sometimes also trade union representatives, and state officials. In other words, while planning in France was the prerogative of government and state administration, its functional equivalent in West Germany was corporatism. The French government did not renounce playing a decisive part in the management of the companies concerned. This large sector of state-influenced companies in France required a long-term coordination of governmental economic and industrial policy. In this way, Shonfield observed and conceptualised the so-called 'mixed economy' in several capitalist societies, and distinguished these economic models from those with a lesser degree of public intervention. Shonfield, however, was looking for an explanation for the advent of what he called 'modern capitalism', and found it in the growth of economic planning and more or less direct intervention of the state. His intention was to explain the differences in the economic performance of Western European countries and the United States, notably between continental Europe, where economic planning and the state played a prominent role, and the Anglo–American model, where these features were more or less absent. Thereby he distinguished between old-fashioned and 'modern' capitalism. Nevertheless, this did not imply the use of stage models and teleological approaches, and so he opened the door for the comparative analysis of capitalist societies, and in the long run, for the idea that different varieties could co-exist at the same time.

Economic discussion during the following two decades was dominated by the search of explanations for the end of the great international postwar boom, and by the new interest in non-Fordist models of industrial production (i.e. forms of production beyond standardised mass production).[18] Interestingly enough, these debates were also the intellectual origins of the so-called French Regulation School, which took into account the role of companies and identified different modes of regulation, the institutions of which created a stable arrangement for a while. Economic transactions are therefore not only part of the market but also take place within companies, through the state or networks.[19] With regard to our question about the intellectual roots and the development of 'Rhenish Capitalism', and the historical roots of the VoC-debate, it is noteworthy that studies of the 1970s and 1980s, mostly carried out by sociologists, advocated the idea of regional clusters of industrial production, in other words, they distinguished regional more than national differences. At the same time, political economists began to use the concept of 'corporatism' as a tool for the comparison of advanced capitalist societies, and thus began to outline the West German case vis-à-vis less corporatist societies, for example France.[20]

This is not the place to portray the complicated debate on this aspect at length, but one of the political and economic threads was the distinction between pluralistic countries with a fragmented labour movement, and corporatist countries with centralised trade unions, in which interest groups assumed state functions.[21] While smaller unions were able to follow only the interests of their members, national centralised unions had to rethink the macro-economic consequences of their demands. Conversely, German governments of all political colours acknowledged the privileges of the centralised unions. If employers' organisations and trade unions had agreed on a reasonable wage agreement for example, governments were able to extend these moderate wage settlements in other economic sectors. Social scientists labelled this consensus – with state involvement – with the term tripartism.[22] (West-)Germany was portrayed as an almost ideal type of a corporatist society because of its highly institutionalised system of integrating all kinds of social – but especially economic – interests, passing through all stages of the concept since the late 19th century.[23]

Again, the economic performance of societies as a whole was one of the vanishing points of these comparisons. The other, the still open debate on the future of democratic institutions – mostly pushed forward by political scientists – in a world of powerful interest groups. Though the intellectual roots of the term 'corporatism' or 'neo-corporatism' were much older, the 1980s and early 1990s saw the debate on corporatism reach new heights.[24] However, since West Germany was comparatively well-off in economic terms during the 1980s, this debate in Germany was focussed on political rather than on economic issues. On the other side, it was this economic stability which made West Germany attractive for foreign observers. One of them was the French economic politician and publicist Michel Albert. In 1991, only one year after triumphal German Unification, Albert shaped the term 'Rhine Capitalism'[25] in his book 'Capitalism against Capitalism', comparing the neo-American model of a capitalist market economy with the capitalist market structure in some countries of continental Europe.[26] Through this confrontation, Albert tried to highlight the positive aspects of co-operation between the state, capital, and labour, which attenuate the negative side effects of unrestrained capitalism – the Anglo–American model. At the same time, his distinction between different forms of capitalism was intended as a recommendation for the transformation of the French economy in the sense of the Rhenish capitalism ('France needs the Rhine model').[27]

Albert stated that Rhenish capitalism had found its ideal type in West Germany, and that it was characterised by financial issues, which were determined by banks rather than by stock markets, by close economic ties between banks and enterprises, by a more equitable balance of power between shareholders and management, and by a social partnership between unions and employers. These features have to be outlined more precisely, but we want to use these topics as a heuristic starting-point to examine to what extent we can confirm Rhenish capitalism by analysing empirical material. It is remarkable that Albert diagnosed these aspects exactly at the time when German capitalism came under pressure and the effects of the economic turbulences of the 1970s – increasing international competition, the return of mass unemployment, and rising public debt – prevailed. Although Albert's objectives were mainly political – to convince the French elites, the public, and the voters to rearrange the French growth model by adopting some German features – his book prepared the ground for much more subtle explorations into the diversity of contemporary capitalism, and sometimes even its historical roots. This turn towards a historical perspective is the reason why we have chosen his term 'Rhenish Capitalism' as the title of this special issue – even though Albert (as Shonfield) did not pay much attention to the role of companies as initiators of institutional change.

The collapse of state socialism and the renaissance of economic vitality of American capitalism since the 1990s changed the economic scene. The search by East-European transitional societies for the best way to recast their economies into a capitalist mode, the sluggish growth in Western Europe, and the performance of those economies which were shaped by 'neo-liberal' institutional arrangements all put heavy pressure on the state-driven, corporatist and/or social-democratic economies in Europe and Japan. Yet the economic slump and the end of state socialism also initiated a new discussion on the existence of different and distinguishable models of capitalism. Albert's expression 'capitalism against capitalism', together with a fresh reading of Shonfield, prepared the way for this idea (hardly any publication in question refraining from referring to both books, accompanied by references to Gøsta Esping-Andersen's 'Three Worlds of Welfare Capitalism',[28] another classic publication on comparative political economy of the same era). Political economists soon developed advanced models and categories to analyse contemporary capitalist societies, such as 'Non-Liberal-Capitalism'[29] or 'French Statism'.[30] Significantly, while all of these studies tried to establish their own typology of capitalist societies, and indeed often used the term 'Rhenish Capitalism' frequently (in most cases only in their introductions), they in no way employed it as an analytical framework or explained the role of companies within it.[31]

At the same time, the fundamental question arose whether there was any possibility of modes of capitalism which differed from the Anglo–American style existing at all. In a way, the idea of different types of capitalism found its loudest expression at the very moment when all these types were threatening to vanish in the distance like the backlights of a passing train. In particular, this is related to the fact that capitalism has no permanent and stable form but is fluid and can change over time. Was adaption to the Anglo–American model of capitalism necessary or even inevitable, with all its consequences: the strengthening of employers' power, weakening of trade unions, cuts in social security, less political intervention and more market within the economy, fiscal restrictions to improve economic competitiveness, and monetarist policies to reduce inflation? This question of the convergence of whole societies and economies towards the Anglo–American model was the big issue of the political and economic debates around the year 2000.[32]

Yet during the years when the American 'new economy' had its boom, a number of remarkable studies in the field of comparative political economy were published.

> 'Suddenly, the main question was whether Germany and Japan [these were those capitalist economies which seemed most opposite to the American model, C.M./M.R.], confronted with the political and economic challenges of economic internationalization, had to give up their distinctive institutions and the specific competitive advantages these seemed to have produced in the past, or whether they would be able to adapt and retain such institutions and restore their economic competitiveness without losing their social cohesion.'[33]

This pessimism defined the context in which *Varieties of Capitalism* was published, giving new hope to the 'pluralists' who advocated more – instead of less – welfare, stronger – instead of weaker – unions, more – instead of less – economic intervention by the state, and a larger – instead of smaller – contribution of the wealthy to the public financial needs, and who were looking for forces of resilience within the 'Non-Liberal' or 'Continental European' models.[34] Significantly, these hopes were met by macro (and not micro) perspectives on economic policy, approaches, models, and assumptions.

2.2. The Varieties-of-Capitalism-debate and some critical points

Peter Hall and David Soskice set a landmark in the comparative analysis of capitalism by distinguishing between *Liberal Market Economies* (LMEs), defined by a high stock market capitalisation, i.e. a high market value of listed domestic companies as a percentage of GDP, and relatively low employment protection, and *Coordinated Market Economies* (CMEs), defined conversely by a relatively low stock market capitalisation, and high labour protection. They did not claim that one type of capitalism was superior to the other, but that the two types differed with regard to their capacity for innovation and their distribution of income and employment. The VoC-approach combined the analysis of comparative capitalism with strategies of firms, so accordingly firms were identified as the key actors in capitalist economies which makes the approach very interesting for business history. Hall and Soskice claimed that firms have to deal with problems of coordination and differentiated five areas of strategic interaction: Industrial relations, i.e. the coordination between employers and employees (1), coordination between the single firm and its employees on an individual level (2), coordination of vocational training and education (3), corporate governance, i.e. the coordination between firms and providers of capital (4), and interfirm relations to suppliers and clients (5).[35] Central to the VoC-approach is the idea that these areas have to be 'coordinated', either by markets (as in the LMEs), or by non-market modes (as in the CMEs). In both cases, the firm uses the market, but in CMEs it prefers networks and collaborations, whereas in LMEs the firm coordinates its activity primarily via hierarchies and competitive market arrangements. According to Hall and Soskice, the characteristics of these areas are not distributed at random, since patient capital and long-term employment belong together for example, but institutional complementarities contribute to every system as a whole and reinforce the differences between LMEs and CMEs.[36] Furthermore, companies try to make the best of the institutional context, hence they confirm that context and behave differently in LMEs and CMEs. Technological developments and liberalisation in the international economy might challenge the system and create change, but there is no reason to expect full convergence on one model. However, these predictions about the future development of capitalism remain subject to discussion.

Here, Kathleen Thelen has made some key points, identifying three different trajectories of change under the common label of liberalization – *deregulation*, *dualization*, and socially embedded *flexibilization* – and suggesting that different varieties of liberalisation occur under the auspices of different social coalitions.[37] The authors of this special issue contribute to this perspective with case studies which focus on the institutional settings of long-term developments. Therefore, our approach to the debate does not cover every aspect. However, keeping in mind the idea of institutional complementarities, we assume that change in one area has consequences for the system as a whole, even though we know that some features can remain relatively stable whereas other dimensions can change dramatically. Thus, in contrast to the classic system-oriented VoC approach, complementarities should not be postulated as stable and fixed configurations in historical analyses.[38]

Hall and Soskice clustered the OECD countries on the basis of the five dimensions mentioned above. While the economies of the US, the UK, Australia, New Zealand, Ireland, and Canada represent the LME type, Germany, Japan, Switzerland, the Netherlands, Belgium, and the Scandinavian countries belong to the CME type.[39] Even though the authors did not argue that one type of capitalism is superior to the other, Peter Hall and David Gingerich have calculated that countries with institutional complementarities had a higher economic growth.[40] This conclusion was a warning for those countries which wanted to reform a single area, as reforms in one area always have an impact on other spheres. In the cases of France, Italy, Spain, and Portugal, it became even more difficult to attribute one of the two types to those countries. In France, the state took a much more important position, and employers and trade unions hardly worked together, organisations on both sides were relatively weak due to fragmentation. The associations exercised only marginally any macroeconomic coordination (as in Portugal), insofar France was liberal, vice-versa, the state – not the market – coordinated a lot of things that were exercised by associations in other countries. Italy (like France) lacked the strong co-determination and coordinated wage bargaining to be assigned to CMEs, however, Italy was no LME, because the capital market was not crucial for finance – as in Portugal. Like Italy, it was difficult to classify Spain, even the classification 'mixed market economy' for Spain was controversial, since the country was composed of different production systems and because of the economic policies under the Franco dictatorship which had put no market pressure on companies.[41] As a consequence, Hall and Soskice introduced a third type of capitalism known as 'Mediterranean capitalism', which was in particular characterised by a large agrarian sector and extensive state intervention. In these countries, the sphere of labour relations was marked by more liberal arrangements, whereas corporate finance was oriented to non-market coordination.[42]

This reflects a fundamental problem of the VoC-approach. With exception of the two leading examples of Germany (for CMEs) and the USA (for LMEs), the assignment is often difficult and can change over time. For a long period of the 20th century the Netherlands was a CME, but also showed many liberal characteristics at the beginning and the end of the century, and even the USA in the 1950s and 1960s, described as 'managerial capitalism', was more close to collaboration than to market liberalism.[43] Particularly, all Western economies experienced a crucial change in the 1970s due to the oil price shocks, the end of the Bretton Woods system, the saturation of markets for standardised products, and the emergence of the microchip. Companies had to react to these challenges, internationalised production, invested in marketing (in the broadest sense), implemented electronic data processing, and hereby initiated a change of the industrial system as a whole. Hence, the dichotomy between LME and CME and change over time were two of the most important points of discussion; varieties of firms and sectors within a national economy were the others. As a consequence, alternative proposals came to the fore. Bruno Amable proposed an alternative set of five different models[44], Robert Boyer, combining VoC with Regulation Theory, divided the world into four 'brands of capitalism'[45], and Bob Hancké, Martin Rhodes, and Mark Thatcher added two more models, mixed market economies and emerging market economies, to the VoC-approach.[46] As a result, since its publication in 2001, Hall and Soskice's VoC-approach has been widely adapted and discussed and more variations have emerged, but no consensus about the best framework has been achieved. The vast list of amendments, qualifications, extensions, additions, and exceptions to the original approach can only be touched on here.[47]

Despite its merits in demonstrating the existence of institutional varieties between advanced economies and in rejecting naïve assumptions of their fateful convergence, there have been three points of criticism which should be mentioned here. Firstly, though Hall and Soskice claim that their concept puts the firm into the centre of the analysis because it emphasises the importance of coordination at the level of the firm, the key elements of distinction between LMEs and CMEs are settled at a higher level, on the institutional level of national economies. Analyses in economic history should however pay more attention to the claim of Hall and Soskice about the importance of companies. Secondly, it was questioned whether the distinction between only two types of capitalism is really sufficient to catch the multi-variant reality of (advanced) capitalism. In other words: Do the similarities between the political and economic institutions, say in Germany, Japan, and Switzerland truly predominate substantially over their dissimilarities? Thirdly, does the VoC-approach enable us to observe and analyse historical change? It seems rather fixed over time, renders learning almost impossible, and downplays the impact of change in the world economy.[48]

Therefore, what we need is an approach which encompasses both institutional change caused by exogenous shocks as well as incremental change within institutions. Path dependence approaches tend to distinguish between institutional innovation and institutional reproduction – factors responsible for the genesis of an institution might be different from those that sustain it over time – and they often might be helpful to explain historical developments, however, particular institutional arrangements are resilient to huge historic breaks that disrupt previously stable arrangements. The distinction between causes of innovation and of reproduction is more convincing than functionalist constant-cause explanations or rational choice theories which see institutions as coordination mechanisms that generate or sustain equilibria, but even arguments of increasing returns have a rather deterministic view of institutional reproduction and fit better to explaining those mechanisms than the logic of institutional change. The literature on path dependence stresses the importance of exogenous shocks and turning points for institutional change and sees rapid change followed by long periods of institutional stasis (lock-in), whereas institutions often change on their own terms. Institutional survival is sometimes linked to elements of institutional transformation because institutions cannot survive for a long time unless they are adapted to changes in the social, political, and economic context in which they are embedded.[49]

In response to this criticism, the VoC authors themselves have stressed the limitations of their approach and suggested integrating issues of institutional change. According to Hall and Thelen, the persistence of institutions depends not only on their aggregate welfare effects but shifts in political and social coalitions that support or oppose institutional arrangements can affect changes in the form or function of institutions over time. Hence, the resilience of coordination or the change in institutions is not only a question of a Pareto-improvement in the context of strategic interaction but it can also be based on variation in the sources of support for different types of coordination. In this context, Hall and Thelen consider companies as initiators of institutional change which are as important as the state. The strategies of companies are conditioned by multiple institutions, conversely companies can change the character of one or more institutions. Thus, institutional change is one of mutual adjustment.[50]

We follow this amendment to the original approach and therefore combine the VoC-approach with the concept of historical institutionalism and the idea of endogenous institutional change. Institutions develop according to their own internal logic and in interaction with other institutions.[51] Douglass C. North has already drawn attention to the 'bounded change' of institutions.[52] Thelen has extended these ideas and proposes different concepts of how institutions might change, for example institutional layering and institutional conversion. Institutional layering means that institutional arrangements are renegotiated periodically in a way that alters their form while leaving other institutions in place. Thus, it combines elements of lock-in and innovation and stresses the flexibility and adaptability of institutions, whereas institutional conversion involves the redirection of existing institutions with one set of goals to new purposes, for example by incorporation of new groups or the shift from wartime to peacetime conditions.[53] These two modes of change are but two possibilities among many, institutional change as reaction to exogenous shocks would be another, as well as institutional drift.[54] Institutional drift occurs when institutions are deliberately held in place while their context shifts in ways that alter their effect. Hence, beside exogenous shocks we have at least three hidden forms of institutional change – by renegotiation or redirection of institutions or by new institutional effects due to a changing environment – which might help to explain how and in which directions institutions change.[55]

Wolfgang Streeck, one of the leading experts in political economy in Germany, stresses the importance of institutions and their history for the comparative analysis of capitalist societies and presents an analytic framework which fits well to the German case and overlaps with the VoC-approach to a large extent. We combine Streeck's analytic framework with previous ideas of institutional change to overcome the deficits of the original ahistorical VoC-approach. Historical institutionalism stresses how institutions emerge from and are embedded in temporal processes by emphasising the endogenous dimension, and it understands aggregate outcomes in terms of the actions and behaviour of individuals. We agree with these suppositions. This is the point where a historical approach, i.e. business history, can contribute to a more useful VoC-approach over time, since companies and their agents are essential for institutional change. Business history has to analyse the activities and strategies of individual firms, their managements, and their workforces as well as union leaders, business associations, politicians, and other agents who were part of the social field of action of companies.[56]

Furthermore, we agree with Gary Herrigel's idea that agents have creative options and choices within institutions and we propose to take these decisions seriously in relation to institutional change.[57] In contrast to political and social scientists who tend to stress power, path dependencies or other highly aggregated explanations downplaying the role of actors in those processes, we emphasise the importance of the company as a central economic organisation of modern capitalism. German capitalism did not break down by a single exogenous shock after 1945 – even though exogenous events and global processes had an impact on its development – but it changed over time. Hence, we need a concept of historical institutionalism which is open to endogenous institutional change caused by companies and their agents to explain the continued difference of Rhenish Capitalism in comparison to other forms of capitalism.

2.3. The institutions of rhenish capitalism

We choose Streeck's five 'institutional sectors' or 'trajectories' as a starting point for the improvement of the VoC-approach, and integrate historical institutionalism and a theory of institutional change into these key arenas of action, which are suitable for a comparative analysis of economic history and the exploration of varieties of capitalism. This approach incorporates the criticism of VoC and is appropriate to analyse German capitalism in a historical perspective, putting the firm in the centre of analysis. Streeck himself emphasises the importance of a micro-perspective describing the reproduction of capitalism which fits well with business history.[58] Based on this analytic approach, empirical studies – within and beyond this special issue – will show whether such a thing as Rhenish Capitalism existed (at a unique moment or over time) and, if so, how it changed over time. Different models of capitalism are not the product of a grand design or result of a functional logic, but the product of the past and ongoing re-setting. Capitalist systems as static equilibria are only wishful thinking, but institutional development and institutional change under capitalism are the outcome of a struggle between different agents.[59] The aim of the present volume is to analyse the institutional trajectories from a business history perspective in the period after World War II.[60]

Five fields of action, in which the firm must develop relationships to resolve problems of coordination, can describe the history of the German economy after the Second World War: (1) corporate governance, (2) vocational training and education, (3) industrial relations and collective bargaining, (4) intermediary organisations of capital and labour, and (5) social policy and welfare state.[61]

Firstly, according to Streeck, the most important single 'institution' that distinguishes the national economic models from each other is the system of corporate governance – the legal and practical regulatory framework for the conduct and monitoring of the corporation, including any relevant stakeholders.[62] This concept as developed by Streeck is the reason why the articles of this special issue are particularly devoted to this subject. For a long period of West German history, the model of corporate governance was defined by the political and social embeddedness of large corporations. That is, from time to time these large corporations were utilised by government for public issues (for example large joint stock banks have been repeatedly pushed to help industrial firms in severe crisis to avoid mass redundancies). But the majority of employees (about 70% in 1999) were and are still working for small and mid-sized family firms (*Mittelstand*), and even those companies became part of an evolving market for corporate control.[63] On the other side, politics avoided disturbing the banks' and industry's interest or at least tried to find consensual decisions and solutions. This relationship, completed by unions' representatives on the supervisory boards of large German companies, formed the backbone of (West) German corporatism. Some parts of German corporate governance (like the universal banking system or the corporate network) date back to the German Empire of the 19th century – described by some authors as 'organised capitalism'[64] –, other parts evolved or had to be readjusted after the Second World War. Several distinct features contributed to the stability of the German model of corporate governance: for example, patient capital was required to ensure long-term strategies of investment and incremental innovation in process technology, both necessary for Diversified Quality Production (DQP), which is and was the most successful profit strategy of German (large and mid-sized) firms on world markets.[65] Conversely, the German model of corporate governance has been frequently under pressure since companies in more liberal models of capitalism had more possibilities to search for basic innovations. According to Streeck, the German central bank (*Bundesbank*) shifted to a monetarist policy in 1974. It was a prominent turnaround in the economic history of West Germany. As a consequence, German companies had to react to the combination of hard currency policy and a high-pay wage regime and focussed even more than before on high quality production to capture further niches in the world market.[66] What has to be analysed in more detail is the development of the German corporate governance system over time. How did the relationship between companies and banks change in the course of the second half of the 20th century faced with the transition from the postwar boom to the 'Landslide'[67] since the 1970s, with increasing international competition or with the rise of new institutional investors in the 1990s? What did the entry of new managers, who advocated shareholder interests in particular and concentrated more and more on the performance of their companies while product orientation faded, mean for corporate governance?

Secondly, companies (especially those conducting a DQP-profit-strategy) rely on a well-trained workforce and face the problem of securing their workforce with suitable skills. This problem could be solved by a consensus about vocational standard-setting (in CMEs) or by institutions offering formal education with general skills complemented by in-house company training (in LMEs).[68] The German postwar vocational training regime had a high capacity to supply a comparatively well-qualified work force, which determined the companies' capability for the diversified production of quality goods. Significantly, its context and the qualification levels were fixed by government, employers' associations, and trade unions together – a core element of German corporatism.[69] Vocational training gave crucial institutional support for the country's high-skill, high-wage, high-value-added manufacturing economy and, as a consequence, had a determining influence on the competitiveness of German firms and their returns on the world market after World War II.[70] As the vocational training regime was the result of a broad consensus between the government, employers, and trade unions, it has to be questioned whether this relational triangle retained its structure or whether one party gained or lost importance since 1945. Companies had to rethink their willingness to participate when international competition increased and countries like Japan also began to produce high-value goods in the 1970s and 1980s.[71] Managers frequently made the accusation that wages were too high in Germany, especially in times of crisis. Hence, further research in business history has to examine whether the consensus about high skills shifted away or remained – particularly since the 1970s – and if a general trend across sectors emerged, even though traditional industries – like mining – were in severe decline while new jobs were created by the digital revolution.

Thirdly, the system of collective bargaining, located at the centre of industrial relations, determines the scope of mutual trust (or distrust) between employees and employers (particularly within companies), and thus influences the readiness of managers to invest. Furthermore, wages and productivity have an effect on the success of companies.[72] The West German combination of high competitiveness on world markets and high wages with only small wage spreads was based on a complex historical compromise on three different levels after 1945: Between liberal capitalism on the one side and its countervailing powers of Social Democracy and Christian Democracy on the other; between capital and labour; and between social traditionalism on the one hand and two alternative versions of modernism, i.e. liberalism and socialism, on the other.[73] This compromise was no timeless German rule as a glance at industrial relations during the Weimar Republic demonstrates. The compromise could be easily maintained as long as the distributive scope was big enough for all agents during the 'Golden Age',[74] but its historical conditions shifted in the 1970s when the internationalisation of enterprises increased, competition grew, and unemployment rose. For a long period of West German capitalism, industry-wide multi-employer agreements caused low wage spreads between higher and lesser qualified workers, between different regions, and between firms of the same sector. This regulated the labour market in a way that small and medium firms, especially in skilled trades (*Handwerker/Facharbeiter*) kept their interest in vocational training without fearing that their newly qualified employees would run off to the larger corporations which were able to pay much higher rates of pay. According to Streeck, the German model of co-determination solves a large part of the principal-agent-problem because of the unequal distribution of knowledge about production processes. It has to be asked whether this institution kept its character as it was installed under the influence of the Allies after 1945, if it was adapted to a changing environment, or if it changed on its own terms.

Fourthly, Streeck stresses the importance of intermediary groups, mostly trade unions and employers' associations, which help to coordinate vital fields of economic importance: first of all, of course, industrial relations and collective bargaining, but also for example, product norms, qualification levels and technical skills, working conditions within companies as well as the preparation and development of larger projects of varying public interest. This is also the field where Streeck diagnoses important changes within the German model. Since German unification, both employers' associations and trade unions had lost members constantly and to a significant degree. Their capability to coordinate diminished significantly. After 1991, many enterprises in the new eastern states of Germany had no interest in becoming part of a business association. Hence, economic and business history research has to explore if and why the high degree of organisation of trade unions and employers' associations was only attractive during a certain period of time in the history of West Germany. Did intermediary groups only change their character (because of evolving internal contradictions or the adaption to a changing environment) or did they more or less lose their role as major institutions of German capitalism?

Fifthly, the (West) German model of capitalism is shaped by the distinct form of its welfare state. Although it is widely accepted that the most important pillar of the German welfare state is its pension system, Streeck focusses on all those measures suited to easing tensions on the labour market as these are highly relevant for companies. For example, he demonstrates the importance of specific welfare measures (like early retirement schemes) which helped West German companies to overcome the economic obstacles of the 1980s and 1990s, but which were no longer available around 2000, due to financial bottlenecks.[75] It would be a worthwhile task to investigate whether German companies were able to maintain their competitiveness because the welfare state ensured a relatively small fluctuation of the workforce and softened social hardship in the case of job cuts – in combination with German codetermination and redundancy payment schemes ('social plans'). The latter factor, for example, of early retirement, gave companies an instrument of flexibilization of the rigid German labour market which was not necessary in times of full employment, but which could increasingly be used by companies in times of crisis. The same applies to other typical German modes of socially acceptable forms of flexibility such as working short time (*Kurzarbeit*). Hence, further research has to explore to what extent companies have benefited from these measures and to what extent they themselves have contributed to the shaping, maintenance or abolition of these welfare state regulations.

Finally, three points still need to be made. Firstly, returning to Streeck's starting point – the question of convergence of all advanced economies into one Anglo–American styled capitalism – his perspective on this problem seems to have been radicalised with time. While during the mid-1990s, the question was still open, after 2000 he claimed that the whole German model, 'Germany Inc', was in a state of 'liquidation'.[76] Finally, in 2013, he postulated that democratic capitalism as a whole was in crisis.[77] Secondly, it has to be noted that Streeck's terminology is rather loose with regard to the denomination of (West) German political economy. Although Streeck develops a pretty coherent 'institutional' model, its denomination changes according to his current interest: 'German Capitalism' to stress its uniqueness (vis-à-vis a vague Anglo–American style of capitalism), 'non-liberal capitalism' to demonstrate common features with Japan, 'Germany Inc.' to focus on the – changing models of – corporate governance of German large corporations. Thus, it is not possible to adopt Streeck's analytical framework completely one-to-one, quite apart from the fact that this framework is only partially designed to analyse the specific way in which firms make profits, even though companies are central to his five institutional arrangements. Thirdly, Streeck's concept includes the possibility of both endogenous and exogenous change of institutions. Looking at German history of the last 30 to 40 years, Streeck argues that change in one institutional field was not always balanced by change in others. Rather, all five institutional trajectories evolved in the same general direction towards a decline in centralised control and organised regulation and an increase in competition – in particular as a result of changing power relations between capital and labour. This evolution was not driven by one master institution, but each change originated on its own, albeit that these independent institutional developments became interdependent as relations of mutual reinforcement arose between them.[78] Companies were not only subject to these changes, but were often initiators of change and reshaped institutions. Taken as a whole, we have chosen Streeck's historical-institutional concept and the VoC proposition to put the firm at the centre of analysis. In this way, we get a robust analytic framework in order to investigate German capitalism from a business history perspective.[79]

3. The German economy in the second half of the 20th century

In the following, we outline the economic history of Germany after 1945 on the basis of the different fields of action mentioned above. However, we suppose that agents always have room for manoeuvre. Unlike many social science approaches, we do not postulate a stable institutional structure, but we assume a dynamic development of institutional change over the course of time. Thus, we call for a stronger sense of time and history, and an understanding of institutions as outcomes of complex social processes of negotiation.[80]

3.1. Industrial relations and collective bargaining

At all times, companies face the problem of coordinating bargaining over wages and working conditions. The German system of industrial relations addressed this problem of coordination by wage setting through regional industry-level bargains.[81] In comparison to Sweden, for example, there was never an intersectoral collective bargaining at the national level in West Germany. However, there was some intersectoral coordination as many unions followed a pilot agreement negotiated by a designated wage leader which increased the reliability of expectations for companies. Wages were typically negotiated by industry and due to high centralisation of national unions, regional wage variation tended to be low. The coverage of workers by collectively bargained industrial agreements used to be high and the industry-wide multi-employer agreement (*Flächentarifvertrag*) was a central component of West German capitalism up to the 1980s. Company agreements (*Haustarifverträge*) – legally possible – remained an exception. It was only in the 1990s, particularly in East Germany, that the industry-wide multi-employer agreement lost its importance – especially in the metal and electrical industry, whereas trade unions and employers of the chemical industry defended this principle until the early 2000s.[82]

Furthermore, in comparison to the USA or the UK, postwar West German wage setting was characterised by a remarkably low wage dispersion – both intersectoral as well as between small and large firms. As a consequence, the wage distribution between the different deciles remained moderate in comparison to other countries of the OECD in the postwar decades – even during the 1980s. Until the late 1960s, management and labour followed a wage policy which was orientated to the development of productivity. In contrast to Italy, France, or the UK without intermediating institutions between employers and employees, smaller countries like Sweden, Norway, Denmark, Belgium, Austria, or the Netherlands favoured the creation of central consultative institutions ensuring moderate wage rises in exchange for social security – quite similar to West Germany.[83] National centralised unions had to rethink the macro-economic consequences of their demands, and employers benefited not only directly from moderate wage developments, but this consensual relationship also increased planning security for the management and competitiveness of companies compared with LMEs. Unlike Anglo-Saxon LMEs, but also in contrast to France, German employee representatives were on the supervisory board due to legal regulations, demonstrated their willingness to cooperate and to compromise, and hence, created stable productivity coalitions with management.[84]

During the European postwar boom, trade unions and employer associations could reconcile differences easily; even if corporate earnings rose faster than wages, workers experienced real wage increases over the long period of the *trente glorieuses* pushing the conflict between labour and capital into the background.[85] Some authors argue that due to the liberal-conservative programmes of Western European governments with a tendency toward decentralised collective bargaining at the level of the firm, the growing strength of workers' representatives at company level has been weakened centralised bargaining systems since the 1980s.[86] According to Streeck, the centralised unified system of wage setting through industry-wide collective bargaining was fragmented increasingly in favour of individualised wage setting, company agreements and a growing non-union sector.[87] In this context, automobile companies such as BMW and Volkswagen pushed for more flexible arrangements, cut voluntary payments, demanded opening clauses for the industry-wide multi-employer agreements (*Flächentarifvertrag*), and often moved into the more flexible regulations of working hours – like the 'Benchmarking Production 5000 x 5000' at Volkswagen or the new conditions at the BMW plant in Leipzig at the beginning of the 2000s.[88]

On the company level, further remarkable differences between German industrial relations and those of its European neighbours become apparent. In comparison to France, where workers were represented by staff representatives (*délégations du personnel*), trade union sections (*sections syndicaux*), and works councils (*comités d'entreprise*), which could lodge complaints but had no negotiating mandate, the rights of German works councils (*Betriebsräte*) remained on a high level, even in the 1990s. The ineffectiveness of French works councils was mainly caused by the structure of the French trade unions, which had been split into six large competing unions since the 1960s. In France, social progress was instigated foremost by the state, whereas in Germany the willingness of trade unions and work councils to cooperate with management was responsible for economic modernization. As a consequence, France – in terms of industrial relations – was neither an LME nor a CME, or part of Rhenish capitalism. German representatives at the level of the firm were more similar to Dutch works councils. The Netherlands introduced modest legal participation rights after World War II, steadily strengthened the position of workers in the following decades, and can – in this field – clearly be categorised in the CME group.[89] Beyond this, the lack of works councils and the existence of enterprise unions in postwar Japan reveal – despite parallels in other fields – the differences between the German and the Japanese model.[90]

Precursors of the works councils had existed in Germany prior to the First World War – with the Works Council Act in 1920 they even gained relevance at company level. Hence, German co-determination was not only a response to the experience of the Nazi past. After the Second World War, in 1952, Adenauer's conservative government issued a new Works Council Act (*Betriebsverfassungsgesetz*) despite trade union protest. The background to the protests was the step achieved for the mining and steel industry in 1951, which secured full parity of employees on the supervisory board as well as a labour director (*Arbeitsdirektor*) on the executive board, whereas the Works Council Act only provided a third parity on the supervisory board. Nevertheless, the 1952 law gave extensive competencies to German works councils in comparison to other countries. In addition to the right of to be heard and of information, they had in particular the right of veto in social matters.[91] In the spirit of the late 1960s, the need for a reform of German co-determination grew. Within the context of 'More Democracy', a slogan propagated by Chancellor Willy Brandt, the Works Council Act was amended in 1972, and a new law of co-determination passed in 1976.[92] Even though the laws of the early 1950s were adopted under the influence of the Nazi past and Allied occupation, their predecessors point to the long-term path dependencies of the German system of industrial relations. This development was confirmed by the new laws in the 1970s. In practice, works councils became a balancing factor within the conflict field of the company and contributed to the diffusion of the principle of conflict partnership in West Germany.[93] At the same time, as is well-known, the spread was on the large-scale: While works councils became a general rule in large companies, small and medium-sized (family) companies implemented fewer works councils. In 2001, a further reform strengthened the formal rights of works councils, while on the level of the firm the institution of the works council has weakened since the 1990s. In East Germany, the degree of coverage never reached the level found in West Germany.[94]

Both endogenous and exogenous factors were responsible for this development – as well as for the weakening of collective bargaining. After the exogenous shock of the collapse of the socialist states, employers and employees in the new eastern states of Germany lacked the social practices of partnership for years. In West Germany, changes in industrial relations remained incremental and less visible until the 1990s – despite the economic turbulences since the 1970s. 'Free collective bargaining and the commitment to this principle, the strong position of banks as shareholders of industry and other components of the Rhine capitalism remained intact. The German unification was politically and legally an expansion of West Germany'.[95] However, the attempt to impose the institutional structure of West German postwar capitalism on the former GDR did not succeed completely. In the course of the spread of 'neo-liberal' ideas, not only West–East transfers took place, but changes in the post-communist world also reverted to the West. Philipp Ther describes these East–West transfers as cotransformations.[96] The free field of experiment in Eastern Central Europe was used by the pioneers of the 'Washington Consensus' to justify and to enforce changes in the West – especially in the field of industrial relations and the welfare state. While the introduction of new laws and the reform of existing laws concerning works councils and co-determination until 1990 may be explained by institutional change in the sense of institutional layering, this concept is hardly suitable for describing the time thereafter. By incorporating new groups – in East Germany – the institutional framework of co-determination began to totter, even if it was neither abruptly nor completely replaced. Additions at the European level, like the European Works Council Directive introduced in 1994, which was a result of trade union demands for a transnational European employee representation since the 1960s, did not reverse this trend, since the European Works Council had fewer rights than its German counterpart.[97]

On a meta level it could be argued that German co-determination minimised transaction costs by producing trust, and thus became an indispensable part of Rhenish capitalism.[98] Until the late 1990s, the combination of trust in co-determination, the willingness of strong unions (which were politically connected to regional and/or federal governments) to cooperate with employers for productive gains, a highly qualified workforce, and the absence from pressure of financial markets ensured a long-term and reliable 'partnership in conflicts' (*Konfliktpartnerschaft*), which enabled corporations to solve even severe crises in mutual accordance, i.e. without threatening the corporate governance compromise – very much in contrast to the French experience –, as Morten Reitmayer demonstrates in his article.

Co-determination is principally not a problem for companies, rather it can be a solution by providing organisational tools to handle conflicts. Nevertheless, due to the ideological turn to 'neoliberalism' in the course of the breakthrough of globalisation in the 1990s this model has been frequently questioned.[99]

3.2. Intermediary organizations: trade unions and business associations

Wage setting and co-determination hit business strategies and were always closely related to intermediary organisations of capital and labour that performed some quasi-public governance functions in postwar Germany.[100] Compared to Scandinavia or Italy, union membership was never high in Germany, although the Scandinavian states were also attributed to the CME type. It accounted for 35.4 percent of West German workforce in 1950, 33.8 percent in 1960, and 31.1 percent in 1970, and experienced – in parallel with the emergence of new social movements in the 1970s – a renewed increase to 32.9 percent in 1980, but then gradually decreased. In 1990, the level of organisation was 29.3 percent in West Germany, after reunification the decline accelerated, and in 2003, the level fell below 20 percent. In the course of the 1970s and 1980s, a change had taken place, which is described by the social sciences as 'selective corporatism'. Aside from specific conditions in Eastern Germany, persistent high unemployment and the increasing problem of the representation of interests beyond the borders of the nation state,[101] the decline of employment in the manufacturing sector and the shift towards the service sector with lower levels of unionisation was responsible for this development.[102] The level of organisation varied among the different unions as well as between subgroups within large industrial trade unions. Thus, the degree of membership and organisation varied not only over the course of time, but also in terms of the sector, the size of the enterprise, the employee group (*Beamte, Arbeiter, Angestellte*), age and gender. In general, male workers in large companies within the tradi- tional industrial sectors were organised to a higher degree. It is beyond the scope of this introduction to consider these developments in detail here.[103]

The importance of trade unions as intermediary organisations was maintained until the 1990s. In cooperation with companies and employers' associations, their policy took account of industry-specific conditions of competition, technical-economic rationalisation and inno- vation, and secured competitiveness. Nonetheless, the general trend of a decreasing level of organisation is remarkable as the success of the German growth model depended on the self-organisation of both employees as well as employers. A distinctive feature of associations relating to the enterprise is their functional and organisational differentiation between eco- nomic and employers' associations (*Wirtschafts- und Arbeitgeberverbände*) and the chambers of industry and commerce (*Industrie- und Handelskammern*). While employers' associations negotiated binding regulations with trade unions with regard to wages and working con- ditions – here the Federation of German Employers' Associations (*Bundesvereinigung der Deutschen Arbeitgeberverbände, BDA*) acted as an umbrella organization – economic asso- ciations coordinated the design of product markets and represented the interests of pro- ducers vis-a-vis political agents. Since its foundation in 1949, the Federation of German Industry (*Bundesverband der Deutschen Industrie, BDI*) organised more than 30 industrial associations, which achieved a high level of coordination for the German model of Diversified Quality Production. The chambers of industry and commerce constituted the third pillar of the German model of economic interests and assumed responsibility for products and train- ing standards. In contrast to economic and employers' associations, they were based on compulsory membership. All three types of organisation took on coordinating tasks, were agencies for a cooperative competition with numerous standards, and had an astonishing organisational stability until the 1980s. As the degree of organisation among economic and employers' associations has declined since then, their capacity to coordinate weakened as well, though here much more research must be done on the dimensions of this trend and its effects.[104]

Two articles of this special issue demonstrate the high performance of coordination as exercised by these organisations. By analysing supplier relations within the West German automobile industry from the 1960s to the 1980s, Stephanie Tilly underlines the importance of the German Association of the Automobile Industry VDA for establishing *trust* as the precondition for stable and robust relations between car-makers and their suppliers. Tilly demonstrates that especially the demand for original equipment (OE parts) – which required a high level of quality production – favoured this arrangement between corporations and intermediary organizations. However, Tilly also shows that the car-makers themselves (as in the cases of Daimler Benz or Volkswagen) even in times of economic downturn tried to establish a resilient consensus with suppliers.

Tilly concludes that this particular institutional setting of business associations, which helps to maintain stable and long-term relationships between individual corporations through the mediation of conflicts, the exchange of information and technical assistance, forms a distinctive feature of Rhenish Capitalism, especially if compared to the US automobile industry. Tilly's findings are in line with those of Ingo Köhler, who examines the profession- alisation of public relations in the West German automobile industry during the 1960s, 1970s and 1980s. During this period, car-makers had to face several serious challenges – two oil crises, demands for a marked drop in car pollution, and a new politics of public transport. To cope with these, automobile producers transformed their public relation policies from 'wine-and-dine' evenings for selected journalists (who were considered as uncritical dissem- inates of the firm's public images) and extremely asymmetric concepts of communication, to more elaborate forms of agenda-setting and (for example) a joint initiative of the auto- mobile industry, federal and local communities, the German Association of Car Drivers ADAC, insurance companies, trade unions, and churches to promote a programme to improve road safety. Again, the automobile producers' organisation VDA played a key role in these efforts. Köhler's most important contribution to this issue is probably his conclusion that the ability and will of all relevant groups of agents to participate in a well-managed consensus has to be part of the explanation for Rhenish Capitalism's enduring capacity for permanent renewal and regeneration.

In the metal industry, which was significant for the whole German economy, the employ- ers' association's degree of organisation remained stable until the mid-1980s, but it had dropped about 20 percent to 53 percent by the early 2000s. In East Germany, this trend was even more pronounced; here, the level of organisation of employers was below the 20 per- cent mark in 2008. However, this trend in the metal industry is not transferable directly to all sectors as the development in the German chemical industry shows, where the level of organisation remained constant at about 70 percent until the 2000s.[105] The trend on the part of the employers was caused by declining solidarity, aggressive outsourcing, international- isation and the creation of a membership without commitment to collective bargaining (*OT-Verbände*) – a kind of institutional layering – even though not all industries turned to this possibility until the 2000s.[106]

All these trends illustrate the stability of the West German system of intermediary asso- ciations between 1945 and 1990 and the institutional change in the 1990s. The German organization of capital and labour in times of the Cold War can be characterised by a rela- tionship of mutual interdependency – a relationship Albert described as co-responsibility.[107] By solving problems of collective action and coordination, this institutional arrangement created a competitive advantage for the production of quality goods and services by German companies. In the 1990s, a process of mutual destabilisation of economic interest organisa- tions – due to a declining membership and a loss of bargaining power – began, and both trade unions and employer associations found it hard to maintain their organisational capac- ities for coordination in times of high unemployment, increasing national debt, and growing international competition.[108]

3.3. Social policy and welfare corporatism

While the welfare state in West Germany has its roots in the 19th century, the relationship between the state, organised business, and labour had to be adjusted after the Second World War and as a result companies were directly involved. Although supporters of the 'social market economy' (*soziale Marktwirtschaft*), according to the minister of economic affairs, Ludwig Erhard, and the so-called 'Freiburg School' of economic 'Ordo-Liberalism', were not willing to promote the development of an interventionist state, they did not draw on other welfare state models. Consequently, classical fields of social policy expanded under the aegis of the social market economy despite all liberal rhetoric.[109] In contrast to Japan, which is also labelled as embedded or coordinated capitalism, the self-governing bodies formed the institutional backbone of the (West) German welfare state, funded by compulsory contributions from employers and employees, whereas the Japanese welfare state was especially based on large enterprises reconstituted as social communities (enterprise communities).[110]

During the mid-1970s, the West German welfare state experienced a fundamental change in at least two ways: Firstly, the overall expansion of welfare came to an end, due to the fiscal needs of slow growth and high unemployment, and the room for manoeuvre for new benefits became smaller. And secondly, the focus of the West German welfare regime, which until then had been aligned to the male industrial worker – the protection of other groups such as women and children was more or less derived from the former, depriving groups such as single mothers – shifted towards the 'new social questions'.[111] But the real break came in the 1990s. Following the mal-financed German unification, which put a heavy burden on the system of welfare production,[112] the scope for the established ways to smoothen lay-offs – that is the extensive early retirement schemes – narrowed significantly. This happened just at the time when high interest rates and an over-valued German currency (both announcing the advent of the *Euro*) led to a severe crisis of costs for German export companies. These companies tried to reach their benchmarks by cutting costs, i.e. by massive lay-offs, which in turn affected political decisions to change the institutions of the welfare state.[113] Under the auspices of triumphant 'neoliberalism', the consequence of these accumulated problems was a substantial adjustment of the German welfare state, known as the 'Agenda 2010', introduced by the centre-left government after 2000. Previously, early retirement and high unemployment benefits had guaranteed the limited resistance of employer associations to union wage demands, while trade unions and work councils tolerated industry-wide workforce reductions in the name of international competitiveness. From the 1970s onwards, employers and trade unions were compensated by the national insurance system for continuing to participate in the collective bargaining regime of the boom years.[114]

On the whole, however, the German welfare state has not yet fallen into the trap of privatisation. The continuing existence of a huge state administrative apparatus shows that no radical change has taken place in market terms and that path dependencies prevailed.[115]

3.4. Vocational training and education

Firms need a workforce with suitable skills while apprentices and workers have to decide how much to invest in which skills. This problem of coordination affects individual companies, but the question of training and qualification in general as well.[116] After the Second World War, the established vocational training system was reconstructed in West Germany building on pre-war institutions and practices, as Kathleen Thelen shows in her brilliant analysis of vocational training in postwar Germany. Key legislation of this period included the Skilled Trades Law 1953 (*Handwerksordnung*), which re-established legal foundations for the existence of craft chambers and their role in administering training, and the Provisional Regulation of the Rights of the Industry and Trade Chambers 1956 (*Gesetz zur vorläufigen Regelung des Rechts der Industrie- und Handelskammern*), by which chambers of industry and commerce officially regained their status as institutions under public law. These laws constituted no dramatic change and employers defended to a great extend the principle of employer self-governance, but employer chambers had to allow union representatives to participate in their deliberations on training.[117] After this period of reconstruction in the 1950s unions pressed for more democratic accountability in the area of vocational training, and as a consequence, the government passed the Vocational Training Act (*Berufsbildungsgesetz*) in 1969, which created a new structure for plant-based vocational training consisting of tripartite boards at the national and state level. It was a significant innovation as it created a framework above the chamber system in which unions were full parity participants. In the 1970s and 1980s, the content of vocational training adapted to changing economic conditions based on cooperation between unions and employers. Hence, corporatist self-regulation and collaborative social partnership kept the German system of vocational training up – even in periods of economic recession.[118]

Comparative studies on qualification structures have documented the success of the West German vocational system in a long-term perspective. It produced a rich supply of broad skills supporting the competitive strategies of German companies, based on quality.[119] Conversely, LMEs, such as the USA or the UK since the 1980s, lacked institutions that encouraged employers to invest in those skills of their workforce that were not only suitable to their own corporation.[120] In contrast to Germany, firms in the USA preferred standardised mass production technologies with low prices and wages that can be used by low skilled, mobile and replaceable workers. At the same time, the USA's education system also enabled top-level education and research.[121] Thus, the USA and other LMEs were characterised by a gap between a low-skill equilibrium with low wages on the one hand and very well-paid high-tech production on the other hand. This structure left only little room for business strategies based on quality production.[122] US corporate management practised a more aggressive recruitment policy, which reflects Albert's characterisation of the Rhenish model as more equitable, efficient, and less violent.[123] On the other side, the constant fluctuation of the workforce discouraged management to invest into broader qualifications. Therefore, training programmes of individual large enterprises remained islands of excellence in the USA.[124]

Conversely, German corporatist agents (companies, unions, and the state) together took responsibility for vocational training. As a consequence, training routes in West Germany up to 1990 were characterised by two principles: Firstly, qualification for the mass of the school-leavers remained the central task of the system. The German apprenticeship system absorbed half of all school-leavers. Consequently, the number of German school-leavers who found themselves unemployed was much lower than in the UK, but also unlike the rate in France. Secondly, the social status of manual skills (and the status of their owners) is much higher than in most LMEs, or France, for example. Apprenticeship combines competencies adapted to a special firm (or a special workplace) with those for a whole branch of industry. The workforce in Germany is less fragmented by professional divisions (such as the division between planning and supervision on the one side and execution on the other), and management (high and middle as well) has to have – and in reality very often has – not only authority through hierarchy, but also due to technical competence.[125] Since the 1990s, long-term trends like the rise of the service sector or intensified competition in high-end markets as well as the unification shock have generated a huge set of problems. As a result, many authors announced the demise of Germany's dual system of apprentice training, but in fact it has persisted to today.[126]

3.5. Corporate governance and corporate networks

Corporate governance highlights several issues of authority, control, and coordination within and between companies – like the allocation of resources, the access to finance, technology transfer or the different interests of investors, management, and workforce. The German system of corporate governance emerged during the late 19th century and was based on a bipartite governance system with an executive (*Vorstand*) and a supervisory board (*Aufsichtsrat*). The third body of German stock companies, the annual general meeting (*Hauptversammlung*) of all shareholders, elected the members of the supervisory board. However, the West German bipartite management- and control-system of corporate governance reveals its distinctive features only at closer examination. Combining some approaches from the sociologist Pierre Bourdieu and from the French Regulation School, Morten Reitmayer uncovers the differences between French and German corporate governance practices in his contribution to this special issue. Comparing two large European automobile producers, Volkswagen and Renault, during the 1970s and 1980s Reitmayer shows that the distribution of formal and informal authority, and of other social assets as well, within a corporation's 'field of power' can explain the firm's ability to find consensual solutions especially in times of crisis, easily recognisable in the strategy of avoiding large numbers of lay-offs without losing profitability in the longer run. In this regard, there were significant differences between West German and French corporations, not least due to the less rigid hierarchy within the executive board and its relation to the supervisory board of German corporations.

Stock corporation legislation only limited the scope for quite different models of corporate governance, as Boris Gehlen demonstrates with insight in his contribution to this issue. Though in theory, the supervisory board had to control management, in reality the corporate governance arrangements extended from a supervisory board as the de facto executive body to arrangements where it was a mere body of representation, with the majority of firms in between. The real form of corporate control depended on market structures, opportunity costs, and stock composition. Indeed, cross-shareholding became an important form of concentrated ownership after 1945. Since the equity participation of families and government decreased in postwar Germany, nonfinancial firms became the dominant shareholders. Their proportion increased from 18 percent in 1950 to more than 41 percent in 1996, the proportion of shares held by financial firms and foreigners increased as well from the 1960s to the 1990s. In the 1990s, share ownership by nonfinancial firms dropped, whereas insurance and foreign companies increased their shareholding. From the 1960s to the 1980s, family ownership lost importance among the large stock corporations but ownership remained relatively concentrated and families still took a prominent role, particularly for non-financial, unlisted companies and smaller firms.[127] As these factors changed significantly, the dominant arrangement of corporate control seems to have shifted from 'self-regulation' towards 'capital-market-control', though the size of this drift is still unclear.[128]

Christian Marx, who has analysed the strategies of internationalisation of the German chemical industry, shows in his article that, besides market structures, the shareholders' composition, and opportunity costs, there were additional factors of great importance which pushed for change in corporate governance: the supervisory board of joint stock companies acted – next to its control function – as a meeting point for directors of banks and other large companies until the 1990s. This structure enabled the exchange of important information, created a basis for trust relationships, and provided outside stakeholders with tools for corporate control. In contrast to an LME, West German managers had to secure agreement for major decisions from the supervisory board which included employee representatives and other managers as well as suppliers and customers. This structure facilitated consensual decision-making and the sharing of information and – as other institutions of Rhenish

Capitalism – generally remained intact in the 1970s and 1980s.[129] The transaction cost approach, which has been adopted in economic and business history in recent years, high-lighted this functionality of relationship in particular.[130] Trustful relations reduced transaction costs which could be incurred in the procurement of information and implementation of agreements.[131]

During the 1990s, the policy of the EU against price-fixing, as well as the difficulties of extending the tight woven network by interlocking board memberships between large corporations beyond national borders hampered the feasibility of firms limiting the loss of profits by hidden agreements.[132] To meet the shareholders' demands for higher profits, some companies decided to change their strategy towards shareholder-value practices and the commodification of the firm (or parts of it) itself by mergers, acquisitions and divestments.[133] Nevertheless in the longer run, most of those who focussed on their core competencies survived, even within a modified economic milieu. Clearly, Rhenish Capitalism permitted very different short-term corporate strategies, but favoured only certain ones in the long run.

American influences on the West German economy were obvious in many parts after 1945, but, for example, the technological influence of the USA on the West German economy took place very slowly and incompletely. Hence, despite transnational influences, the German model retained its specific features.[134] This was even true of the West German corporate network. It did not only provide firms with information and established trust, but also offered firms collective protection against pressure from minority shareholders and potential take-overs by foreign investors as well as socialist demands for nationalisation. It also guaranteed a low but steady return on investment which is frequently called patient capital. Here, Germany was close to the Netherlands, where hostile takeovers were also an exception until the 1990s.[135] Although the antitrust legislation of postwar Germany, which was encouraged by the US European Recovery Program, was supposed to counteract the concentration of economic power, the network of directorates formed itself again in the postwar era.

The close and risk-averse relationship between German banks and industrial enterprises and the main bank principle (*Hausbank*) were consequences of a shortage of capital and secured companies smooth access to the capital market and long-term financing options.[136] Access to patient capital made it possible to retain a skilled workforce through economic crisis. Conversely, due to this type of financing, banks were tightly bound to industrial com-panies because of long-term credits, stockholding, and the exercise of proxy voting rights. Finance was not dependent on publicly available financial data, so investors needed other ways of monitoring. This coordination problem was solved by the presence of a dense net-work linking managers and technical personnel to their counterparts in other firms. Reputation was a key factor and door opener.[137]

As a consequence, German banks had in particular a strong position in the corporate network, since they could prevent competition between companies, but the German econ-omy after 1945 was not characterised by bank hegemony as Ralf Ahrens shows in his con-tribution to this issue, analysing four case studies (Willy Schlieker, Krupp, Bilfinger-Berger, Mannesmann-Demag).[138] Banks could only obtain control in cases of serious crisis. Generally speaking, banks preferred a policy of intervention and assistance vis-à-vis their customers, rather than a short-term reduction of losses in a crisis situation. They held only a few large blocks of shares in manufacturing firms in the postwar era, but they could also exert influence by proxy voting rights and the granting of credit. In 1980, banks and insurance companies held stakes in at least 23 of the 100 major German companies, and the major German banks organised as stock corporations had most relationships within the network, because at least in critical situations, trust required a minimum of control.[139]

The corporate network in Germany was primarily an issue for large companies and it was one of the most significant institution of Rhenish Capitalism, as underlined by Ralf Ahrens, Boris Gehlen and Alfred Reckendrees in their introduction to the 'Deutschland AG'[140], even though the majority of employees and apprentices worked in small and medium-sized enterprises (SMEs) – i.e. the German *Mittelstand*. However, the share of SMEs varied widely. While more than 80 percent of sales in the hospitality and construction industry were generated by SMEs in 1997, they were only responsible for less than 15 percent in car manufacturing or in the chemical industry.[141] Gary Herrigel has already highlighted that SMEs were one of the sources of German industrial power which formed a decentralised industrial order, integrated into regional networks and producing diversified quality products.[142] The German *Mittelstand* itself was a highly politically charged concept as a counter-design to the industrial class society, its ideology promoted a more humane model of capitalism and thus became an integral, legitimating component of Rhenish Capitalism.[143] SMEs survived Germany's major political and economic crises in the first half of the 20th century, but they changed their character in the second half of the century. In its traditional form – in the 1950s and 1960s – the *Mittelstand* was characterised by family firms with long-term business strategies, by an emotional attachment of their entrepreneurs, generational continuity and a patriarchal culture as well as by a concentration of ownership and independence from external capital. In contrast to the relations between big business and large stock banks, the main banks (*Hausbanken*) of the *Mittelstand*, foremost local and regional banks, did not own substantial capital holdings of their client firms, and they were mostly not involved in alliances and networks of interlocking directorates. Thus, the whole VoC debate – in particular the dimension of corporate governance – does not take into account the vast majority of German firms.[144]

The reason for concentrating on large companies in this special issue is, firstly, the fact that they serve as an indicator for the economic development of Germany as a whole and that they were responsible for the bulk of investment.[145] Secondly, some groups of the *Mittelstand* belonged to vertically integrated production clusters dominated by large firms, for example the supplier network of the automobile industry, as the aforementioned article by Stephanie Tilly shows. A considerable ring of suppliers of electrical and mechanical engineering SMEs around Stuttgart exist which are dependent on Daimler.[146] Thirdly, the *Mittelstand* itself was subject to changes, which shifted its logic of action towards large companies, and fourthly, there is no empirically saturated historical research (not least due to the disparate archive situation). In contrast to machinery and machine tools as the third export-oriented sector in Germany, the automobile and chemical industries were less important for the German *Mittelstand*, but considering the German economy as a whole these were two of the most important industries measured by sales or employees. Hence, since general patterns of the German economy may be deduced from these two branches, they are in the focus of this special issue.[147]

We have to examine the third point more carefully. Since the 1970s, all companies – large corporations as well as SMEs – operated in a much more complex economic environment. New competitors, procedures and capital requirements and the opening of world markets often required a strategic reorientation. The goals of the predecessor generation were no longer adopted without question, in many cases the generational change proved to be a crossroad in terms of business and history – an endogenous change. From the 1980s onwards, the doctrine of shareholder value even left its mark on medium-sized family business. Consultants, bankers, and investors implemented these principles at SMEs. The rules of succession became more diverse. At the same time, the loss of importance of the owner family was accompanied by a professionalisation of management, which emphasised new economic models and contributed to the dissemination of corresponding ideas. Ultimately, opening up to external capital and the sale of whole family businesses were no longer a breach of taboo, and consequently, SMEs entered the market of corporate control as well.[148] Initially absorbed by the sociocultural and economic driving forces of the 1970s, in the end SMEs themselves contributed to the transformation of Rhenish capitalism.[149] However, German *Mittelstand* did not disappear but remained an important pillar of the German economy.

While the disintegration of the German corporate network of large companies and banks began in the 1980s, the roots of this development can be traced back to the end of the postwar boom. The end of a stable monetary system (Bretton Woods), increasing international competition, and the internationalisation of firms combined with the rise of 'neo-liberal' ideas all affected the development of enterprises profoundly as demonstrated in the aforementioned article by Christian Marx on chemical companies. In the 1970s and 1980s, German and Dutch multinationals remained part of their national networks.[150] During the 1990s at the latest, large German banks refused to continue their role as providers of patient capital since investment banking promised higher profits and leading German financial institutes – such as Deutsche Bank, Dresdner Bank, Commerzbank or Allianz – had re-orientated their strategies to global capital markets and pressed for corporate governance reforms. They wanted to become competitive players in the international financial industry – like their competitors in the Anglo-Saxon LMEs. Thus, German banks successively lost their interest in financing industry, sold industrial shares, withdrew from the supervisory boards, hereby effecting institutional change.[151] In 1993, the crisis after the boom following German reunification presented the decisive reason for questioning the corporate governance model and helped to establish principles oriented to financial markets: Instead of the network, the financial market now became a benchmark. This was also true of other CMEs such as Switzerland and the Netherlands.[152]

The strategic decisions of banks and industry to adopt the corporate objectives of their Anglo-Saxon competitors were decisive for the institutional change of the corporate network. New financial techniques allowed banks to resell their loans and to hedge against credit losses. Consequently, there were fewer reasons to control assets through the supervisory board. Furthermore, banks had a lower interest in preventing hostile takeovers (via proxy voting rights and share capital), and rather discovered takeovers as a profitable business field. Henceforth, banks barely acted as partners of industry. Many banks divested their industrial shareholdings and invested in areas which promised higher rates of profit. This brought to an end the control function of property via supervisory boards. New institutional investors – such as pension and hedge funds – had a lower need for market coordination via networks as had been typical for relations between industry and the banking sector within Germany Inc. The new owners were oriented towards the principles of the financial market and their share ownership changed frequently. By 2010, the network which had emerged at the end of the 19th century, had dissolved.[153] However, many traditional features of the corporate governance regime were preserved. According to the economic historian

Hartmut Berghoff, the trend of financialisation since the 1980s is universal, but the concept is modified across various national contexts due to divergent legal, political and cultural frameworks. He provides an explanation of Germany's delay of at least 10 years in comparison to the USA and its deviation from financialisation through various stakeholders other than shareholders and managers.[154] German capitalism changed, but German equity culture remained weak and shareholder activism continued to be less significant, while it was primarily large German companies that experienced stock market pressure.

4. The global dimension of capitalism and the prologue of the present

Some social scientists and economists have related Rhenish capitalism not only to (West) Germany, but also to continental Europe, and Japan. However, as the above text illustrates, German capitalism from the Second World War to the 1980s – with its qualification system, its financing system, its corporate network and its organization of associations – was truly an ideal type of a CME, which could be found as a carbon copy neither in France nor in Sweden, nor in Japan. Even though Japanese sets of companies with interlocking business relationships (keiretsu) were also characterised by strong inter-firm relations, these networks were based on a different logic (a community model of the firm). Thus, Germany and Japan differed in their institutions of corporate governance, finance, industrial relations, and connections between the state and the economy.[155]

It is remarkable that Hall and Soskice identified several features of German capitalism exactly at the moment when its institutions came under pressure and changed. The economic turbulences of the 1970s were an enormous challenge for companies to face which intensified structural economic change and restricted the room for manoeuvre in social policy issues in West Germany (and beyond). However, the main principles and institutions of capitalism remained intact during this decade and did not change until the 1990s – leading in particular to a higher public debt.

In the distinction between liberalism and corporatism of the postwar years, France was assigned to a third model of capitalism: statism.[156] The postwar economy in France with its elitist selection of management, its Taylorist and bureaucratic workplace organisation, the reliance on the state and its less importance of SMEs was organised in a different way than in West Germany. When the VoC-approach became prominent in the 1990s, more and more scientists tried to assign France to one of the two types of capitalism. Because of market-oriented reforms, France was seen to be on the road to Anglo-Saxon capitalism or, conversely, as a less successful CME. Nonetheless, deeper analyses of the French case demonstrated continuing differences to both LME and CME. The transformation of France was rather a move from state-led capitalism to a kind of state-enhanced capitalism organised by and around large firms.[157]

In the face of accelerated globalisation some social scientists predicted an institutional convergence between the varieties of capitalism through decentralised bargaining, deregulation, the dissolution of inter-firm relations and the withdrawal of banks from the corporate network. Germany Inc. was on the defensive.[158] Contemporary history came to the conclusion that the Fordist production regime and Rhenish capitalism as in pre-unification West Germany had become a thing of the past.[159] Still, despite the gradual liberalisation of CMEs and the dissolution of networks, national diversity persisted in the era of global financial market capitalism. CMEs such as Germany sought flexibility through a limited decentralisation.[160]

The German financial and capital market changed fundamentally in the 1990s, but differences between LMEs and CMEs remained since liberal economies pushed through extensive deregulations at the same time.[161] In Germany, new market agents – such as investment funds – put pressure on managers to restructure their firms and to turn integrated organisational subunits into independent profit centres and improve business strategy inspired by shareholder value. Corporate governance shows the clearest convergence effect.[162] Furthermore, the career patterns of top managers changed and financial specialists were more frequently selected to the executive boards to the disadvantage of production-oriented engineers.[163] At the same time, many political agents voiced doubts about the German innovation system and gave legislative support to financial liberalisation. Only large companies, however, became subject to direct stock market pressure, individual shareholding remained low on an international level, corporate law did not change and the system of co-determination was still intact.[164]

Obviously, varieties persisted at least until the 1990s. Explications on the development of German capitalism since the 1990s are hardly possible from a historical perspective due to the absence of empirical analyses. Since then, processes of change, inertia and resilience have been observed. As an ideal type of CME, Rhenish Capitalism came close to reality between the 1950s and 1980s in particular. Hence, the VoC-approach became a meaningful framework of analysis in the 1990s when competition between the capitalist and socialist economic orders had come to an end and highlighted differences between contemporary Western economies. Future historical research should however focus on the changes and interactions between these economies and examine corporations as central agents of these developments. Predictions about the future development of (German) capitalism from a historical perspective have yet to be made.[165]

Notes

1. *Hall and Soskice, Varieties; Hockerts and Schulz, 'Einleitung.'*
2. Morgan, 'Complementarities.'
3. Plumpe, 'Ende,' 6.
4. Hall and Soskice, *Varieties.*
5. Olson, *Rise.*
6. Backhouse, *Penguin History*, 173–174; Pierenkemper, *Geschichte.*
7. Leopold von Wiese, *Staatssozialismus* (1916), cited according to: Priddat, 'Vertiefung,' 391.
8. Schmoller, *Grundriss.*
9. Sombart, *Sozialismus*; ———, *Kapitalismus.*
10. They shared this attitude with important segments of the educated middle class. Cf. Doering-Manteuffel, 'Zeitbögen.'
11. Sombart, *Kapitalismus.*
12. Nützenadel, *Stunde*, 27–33; Lenger, *Sombart.*
13. Screpanti and Zamagni, *Outline.*
14. Kurz, *Geschichte*; Backhouse, *Penguin History.*
15. Pribram, *Geschichte*. Interestingly enough he spoke of the 'historical-ethical school.'
16. Söllner, *Geschichte*; Winkel, 'Schmoller.'
17. Shonfield, *Capitalism.*
18. The loci classici are Kern and Schumann, *Ende*; Piore and Sabel, *Divide.*
19. Boyer and Saillard, *Régulation*; Hollingsworth and Boyer, *Contemporary Capitalism*. Cf. for a closer analysis of the regulation theory the contribution of Morten Reitmayer in this special issue.

20. Ashford, *Policy*.
21. Schmitter, 'Corporatism.'
22. Croucher and Wood, 'Tripartism.'
23. Abelshauser, *Kulturkampf*; Streeck, 'German Capitalism.'
24. Czada, 'Konjunkturen.'
25. We use the terms 'Rhine Capitalism' and 'Rhenish Capitalism' as synonyms.
26. Albert, *Capitalism*.
27. Ibid., 240–242.
28. Esping-Andersen, *Worlds*.
29. Streeck and Yamamura, *Origins*.
30. Boyer, 'French Statism.'
31. Amable, *Diversity*, 3; Beyer, 'Deutschland AG a.D.,' 118; Kocka, 'Einleitung,' 10-11; Streeck, 'Introduction,' 2.
32. For the German discussion see especially Abelshauser, *Kulturkampf*; Berghahn and Vitols, *Kapitalismus*; Plumpe, 'Kapitalismus Ende;' Streeck, 'German Capitalism;' Streeck and Höpner, *Deutschland AG*.
33. Streeck and Yamamura, *Origins*, XIV-XV. […] added by Christian Marx and Morten Reitmayer.
34. See for example: Hall and Lamont, *Social Resilience*.
35. Hall and Soskice, 'Introduction,' 6–7.
36. Ibid., 17–19.
37. Thelen, *Varieties*. Thelen distinguishes between different dimensions and aspects of liberaliza-tion and identifies three distinct ideal-typical trajectories of liberalization under the auspices of different kinds of social coalitions. Deregulation involves the active political dismantling of coordinating capacities and is associated especially with LMEs like the USA. Dualization does not involve a direct attack on traditional institutions, but is characterized by continued strong coordination, even though the number of firms and workers covered under the arrangements declines. It takes many forms and is associated with conservative Christian Democratic coun-tries like Germany. Firms and workers outside the core have mostly an inferior status and pro-tection. Embedded flexibilization involves the introduction of new forms of flexibility within a continued strong framework that collectivizes risk; it is associated with Scandinavian Social Democratic countries.
38. Sorge and Streeck, *Diversified Quality Production Revisited*.
39. Hall and Soskice, 'Introduction,' 18–21.
40. Hall and Gingerich, *Varieties*.
41. Molina and Rhodes, 'Mixed Market Economies.'
42. Hall and Soskice, 'Introduction,' 21.
43. Dore, Lazonick, and O'Sullivan, 'Varieties;' Sluyterman, *Varieties*. Cf. for the changing nature of relations between companies, financial institutions, the labour market, the educational system and the state in Denmark, Finland, Sweden and Norway: Fellman et al., *Nordic Capitalism*.
44. Amable, *Diversity*.
45. Boyer, *Capitalisms*.
46. Hancké, Rhodes, and Thatcher, 'Introduction.'
47. Hall and Soskice, *Varieties*; Hancké, *Debating Varieties*; Hancké, Rhodes, and Thatcher, *Beyond Varieties*; Whiteley, 'Business History.' As Ferry de Goey puts it, the more criteria are included, the more models are possible. Goey, 'Varieties,' 92. Richard Whiteley stresses that the VoC approach is inadequate to describe East Asian economies and highlights differences between business systems in Europe and Asia. Cf. Whiteley, *Divergent Capitalism*.
48. Crouch, 'Typologies'; Hancké, Rhodes, and Thatcher, 'Beyond Varieties;' Herrigel and Zeitlin, 'Alternatives;' Streeck, *Re-forming Capitalism*, 16–19.
49. Pierson, 'Increasing Returns'; Mahoney, 'Path Dependence;' Martin, 'Business History Thelen, 'Historical Institutionalism;' ———, *Varieties*, 5–8.
50. Hall and Thelen, 'Institutional change.'
51. Thelen, 'Insights.'
52. North, *Institutions*.

53. Streeck, *Re-forming Capitalism*, 14-15; Thelen, 'Insights;' ———, *Political Economy of Skills*.
54. Hacker, Pierson, and Thelen, 'Drift.'
55. Mahoney and Thelen, *Explaining Institutional Change*; Streeck and Thelen, *Beyond Continuity*. Streeck points to another sort of endogenous change – dialectical change – as self-undermining of institutions and social orders in the course of their operation which is near to Thelen's ideas of institutional conversion and institutional drift. Cf. Streeck, *Re-forming Capitalism*, 2–3, 11–15.
56. Hancké, 'Introducing;' Hancké, Rhodes, and Thatcher, 'Introduction;' Whitley, 'Business History.'
57. Herrigel, *Manufacturing Possibilities*; Herrigel and Zeitlin, 'Alternatives.'
58. Streeck, *Re-forming Capitalism*, 3–4.
59. Crouch and Streeck, *Political Economy*; Streeck and Höpner, *Deutschland AG*; Streeck, 'Institutions;' Streeck and Yamamura, *Origins;* Frieden, Global Capitalism; Plumpe, Herz.
60. Hockerts and Schulz, 'Einleitung,' 12–13. Cf. for further (German) literature on Rhenish capitalism: Sattler, 'Kapitalismus.'
61. Hall and Soskice, 'Introduction,' 6–21; Streeck, *Re-forming Capitalism*.
62. Hall and Soskice, 'Introduction,' 7; Streeck and Höpner, 'Einleitung,' 11.
63. Berghoff, 'Family Business;' Hauser, *SMEs in Germany*, 5.
64. Winkler, *Organisierter Kapitalismus*.
65. Streeck, 'Conditions.'
66. Abelshauser, *Kulturkampf*, 93, 107; ———, 'Rheinische Kapitalismus;' Streeck, 'Conditions;' ———, *Re-forming Capitalism*, 57.
67. Hobsbawm, *Age of Extremes*, 403–432.
68. Hall and Soskice, 'Introduction,' 7, 28–30.
69. Streeck, 'Conditions.'
70. Thelen, 'Insights,' 222–224.
71. Kleinschmidt, *Blick*.
72. Hall and Soskice, 'Introduction,' 7.
73. Streeck, 'German Capitalism,' 33–36.
74. Hobsbawm, *Age of Extremes*, 225–400.
75. Streeck, *Re-forming Capitalism*, 57–59.
76. Ibid., 77–89.
77. ———, *Zeit*.
78. ———, *Re-forming Capitalism*, 22–23.
79. With the Netherlands, this has been made only for a relatively small country. Cf. Sluyterman, *Varieties*.
80. Morgan, 'Complementarities;' Jackson and Sorge, 'Trajectory.'
81. Hall and Soskice, 'Introduction,' 7, 24–25.
82. Müller-Jentsch, 'Chemieindustrie,' 296; Streeck, *Re-forming Capitalism*, 38-39; Thelen, *Union*.
83. Abelshauser, *Wirtschaftsgeschichte*, 342–352; Corneo, Zmerli, and Pollak, 'Germany;' Nijhof and Berg, 'Variations,' 25–31, 42–43.
84. Müller-Jentsch, 'Mitbestimmungspolitik;' Streeck, 'German Capitalism.'
85. Fourastié, *Trente Glorieuses*.
86. Windolf, 'Productivity Coalitions.'
87. Streeck, *Re-forming Capitalism*, 93.
88. Schumann et al., 'Fabrikmodell.'
89. Bridgford, 'French Trade Unions;' Nijhof and Berg, 'Variations,' 36–42; Thelen and Turner, 'Mitbestimmung,' 166–169, 178–181.
90. ———, 'Mitbestimmung,' 169–175.
91. Milert and Tschirbs, *Demokratie*; Müller, *Strukturwandel*.
92. Marx, 'Betrieb.'
93. Müller-Jentsch, *Konfliktpartnerschaft*.
94. Ellguth and Kohaut, 'Tarifbindung.'
95. Ther, *Ordnung*, 279.

96. Ibid., 277–278. Compare for the original meaning of the term 'neoliberalism;' Mirowski and Plehwe, *Road*; Slobodian, *Globalists*.
97. Hauser-Ditz et al., *Mitbestimmung*.
98. Abelshauser, *Wirtschaftsgeschichte*, 384–391; ———, 'Mitbestimmung.'
99. Lane, *Industry*, 82–100; Thelen and Turner, 'Mitbestimmung.'
100. Katzenstein, *Policy*; Manow, 'Corporatism;' Müller-Jentsch, 'Gewerkschaften.'
101. Esser, 'Funktionen;' Esser and Fach, 'Steel Industry;' Rehling, 'Spannungsfeld.'
102. Ebbinghaus, 'Mitgliederentwicklung;' Ebbinghaus and Visser, *European Labor*; Streeck, *Re-forming Capitalism*, 46–47.
103. Ebbinghaus, 'Mitgliederentwicklung; Raphael, Gesellschaftsgeschichte.'
104. Schroeder and Weßels, 'Unternehmerverbändelandschaft.'
105. Silvia, 'Mitgliederentwicklung.'
106. Müller-Jentsch, 'Chemieindustrie,' 296; Streeck, *Re-forming Capitalism*, 47–50; Streeck and Hassel, 'Social partnership.'
107. Albert, *Capitalism*, 115.
108. Hassel, 'Schwächen;' Streeck, *Re-forming Capitalism*, 52–53; Streeck and Hassel, 'Social partnership.'
109. Abelshauser, *Wirtschaftsgeschichte*, 186–199; Hentschel, *Erhard*.
110. Manow, 'Welfare State.'
111. Friedrich-Ebert-Stiftung, *Sozialstaat*; Geyer, *Sozialpolitik*; Schmidt, *Sozialpolitik*.
112. Ritter, *Sozialpolitik*.
113. Streeck, *Re-forming Capitalism*; ———, 'Nach dem Korporatismus.'
114. Ebbinghaus, *Reforming*; Streeck, *Re-forming Capitalism*, 57–59, 63–65; Streeck and Hassel, 'Social partnership,' 105; Süß, 'Flexibilisierung.'
115. Hockerts, 'Wohlfahrtsstaat.'
116. Hall and Soskice, 'Introduction,' 7
117. Thelen, *Political Economy of Skills*, 240–258.
118. Gehlen, 'Industrie- und Handelskammern;' Thelen, *Political Economy of Skills*, 259–269.
119. Albert, *Capitalism*, 114–117; Turner, *High Road*.
120. The British history shows that countries could change their economic system in the course of time. In the area of industrial training as well as in industrial relations post-war Britain developed a weak system of coordination. It was not until the beginning of the 1970s, when industrial relations and training, financing, ownership and governance of corporations developed into a market-oriented direction and the UK became a LME. Cf. Gospel and Edwards, 'Transformation.'
121. Soskice, 'Globalisierung.'
122. Abelshauser, *Wirtschaftsgeschichte*, 475–480; Finegold and Soskice, 'Failure;' Soskice, 'Production Regimes.'
123. Albert, *Capitalism*.
124. Wever, *Negotiating Competitiveness*.
125. Albert, *Capitalism*, 115–117; Hall and Soskice, 'Introduction,' 25–26.
126. Thelen, *Political Economy of Skills*, 269–277.
127. Fohlin, 'History,' 232–235.
128. Windolf, *Finanzmarkt-Kapitalismus*.
129. Abelshauser, *Wirtschaftsgeschichte*, 480–493; Hall and Soskice, 'Introduction,' 24.
130. Williamson, 'Transaction Cost Approach;' ———, *Economic Institutions*.
131. Granovetter, 'Economic Action.'
132. Hesse, 'Kartelldenken.'
133. Ahrens, Gehlen, and Reckendrees. 'Deutschland AG.'
134. Berghahn, *Americanisation*; ———,'Kapitalismus-Modell;' ———, 'Varieties of Capitalism;' Hilger, *Amerikanisierung*; Hollingsworth, 'Continuities;' Schröter, *Americanization*; Stokes, 'Technology Transfer.'
135. Bouwens and Dankers, 'Competition,' 115–120; Streeck, *Re-forming Capitalism*, 77.
136. Plumpe, 'Ende,' 7–13.

137. Hall and Soskice, 'Introduction,' 22–24; Streeck, 'German Capitalism.'
138. Cf. also: Ahrens, 'Bankenmacht;' ———, 'Kreditwirtschaft;' Ahrens and Bähr, *Ponto*, 127–204.
139. Beyer, 'Strukturen;' Fohlin, 'History,' 244–246; Sattler, 'Unternehmensfinanzierung.'
140. Ahrens, Gehlen, and Reckendrees. 'Deutschland AG.'
141. Hauser, *SMEs in Germany*, 5–8.
142. Herrigel, *Industrial constructions.*
143. Berghoff, "Mittelstand,' 93–94.
144. ———, 'Family Business,' 272–275; Lubinski, 'Familienerbe,' 210–220.
145. Berghoff, 'Relikt,' 260–261.
146. ———, 'Family Business,' 275. See for Daimler's business strategy and its changing position within the German corporate network: Freye, 'Rückzug'
147. Cf. for the development of machine construction in Germany: Ahrens, 'Industrie.'
148. Reitmayer, 'Konkurrenzkulturen.'
149. Berghoff, 'Mittelstand,' 102–109; ———, 'Family Business,' 281–285; Fear, 'Champions;' Lubinski, 'Familienerbe,' 220–228.
150. Marx, 'Internationalisierung;' Sluyterman and Wubs, 'Agents.' Cf. for the relation between multi-nationals and the VoC-approach as well: Wilkins, 'Varieties of Capitalism.'
151. Beyer, 'Deutschland AG a.D.;' Beyer and Höpner, 'Disintegration;' Streeck, *Re-forming Capitalism*, 78–87.
152. Beyer, 'Netzwerk;' David and Mach, 'Corporate Governance;' Ginalski, David, and Mach, 'Cohesion;' Westerhuis, 'Network.'
153. Beyer, 'Deutschland AG a.D.;' Windolf, 'Corporate Network,' 80–81.
154. Berghoff, 'Financialization;' Lazonick, 'Financialization.'
155. Jackson, 'Corporate Governance;' Kitschelt and Streeck, 'Stability,' 11.
156. Boyer, 'French Statism.'
157. Amable, Guillaud, and Palombarini, 'Changing French Capitalism;' Hancké, *Large Firms*; Schmidt, 'French capitalism.'
158. Abelshauser, *Kulturkampf*, 177–191; ———, *Wirtschaftsgeschichte*, 480–482.
159. Doering-Manteuffel and Raphael, *Boom*, 26–27; Plumpe, 'Ende,' 3–4; Rödder, *Gegenwart*, 47–54.
160. Lane, *Industry*; Thelen and Turner, 'Mitbestimmung,' 143–145, 196–199.
161. Berger and Dore, *National Diversity*; Deeg, 'Limits.'
162. Jackson and Sorge, 'Trajectory;' Kädtler, 'Business;' Plumpe, 'Ende,' 4; Windolf, 'Eigentümer ohne Risiko.'
163. Freye, *Führungswechsel.*
164. Berghoff, 'Financialization;' Jürgens, Naumann, and Rupp, 'Shareholder Value.'
165. Lane, 'Globalization;' ———, 'Transformation.'

References

Abelshauser, Werner. "Vom wirtschaftlichen Wert der Mitbestimmung. Neue Perspektiven ihrer Geschichte in Deutschland." In *Mitbestimmung in Deutschland. Tradition und Effizienz*, edited by Wolfgang Streeck and Norbert Kluge, 224–238. Frankfurt am Main/New York: Campus, 1999.
Abelshauser, Werner. *Kulturkampf. Der deutsche Weg in die neue Wirtschaft und die amerikanische Herausforderung*. Kulturwissenschaftliche Interventionen; 4. Berlin: Kadmos, 2003.
Abelshauser, Werner. "Der 'Rheinische Kapitalismus' im Kampf der Wirtschaftskulturen." In *Gibt es einen deutschen Kapitalismus? Tradition und globale Perspektiven der sozialen Marktwirtschaft*, edited by Volker R. Berghahn and Sigurt Vitols, 187–199. Frankfurt am Main: Campus, 2006.
Abelshauser, Werner. *Deutsche Wirtschaftsgeschichte. Von 1945 bis zur Gegenwart*. Bonn: BPB, 2011.
Ahrens, Ralf. "Bankenmacht im Aufsichtsrat? Der Bankier Jürgen Ponto und die Kontrolle deutscher Großunternehmen in den 1970er Jahren." In *Die 'Deutschland AG.' Historische Annäherungen an den bundesdeutschen Kapitalismus*, edited by Ralf Ahrens, Boris Gehlen and Alfred Reckendrees, 195–220. Essen: Klartext, 2013.

Ahrens, Ralf. "Kreditwirtschaft im »Wirtschaftswunder« – Strukturen und Verflechtungen." In *Der "Rheinische Kapitalismus" in der Ära Adenauer*, edited by Hans Günter Hockerts and Günther Schulz Rhöndorfer Gespräche; 26, 121–141. Paderborn: Ferdinand Schöningh, 2016.

Ahrens, Ralf "Eine alte Industrie vor neuen Herausforderungen. Aufbrüche und Niedergänge im ost- und westdeutschen Maschinenbau seit den 1960er Jahren." In *Der Mythos von der postindustriellen Welt. Wirtschaftlicher Strukturwandel in Deutschland 1960–1990*, edited by Werner Plumpe and André Steiner, 55–119. Göttingen: Wallstein, 2016.

Ahrens, Ralf, and Johannes Bähr. *Jürgen Ponto. Bankier und Bürger. Eine Biografie*. München: Beck, 2013.

Ahrens, Ralf, Boris Gehlen, and Alfred Reckendrees. "Die Deutschland AG als historischer Forschungsgegenstand." In *Die 'Deutschland AG'. Historische Annäherungen an den bundesdeutschen Kapitalismus*, edited by Ralf Ahrens, Boris Gehlen and Alfred Reckendrees, 7–28. Essen: Klartext, 2013.

Albert, Michel. *Capitalism against Capitalism*. New York: Wiley, 1993.

Amable, Bruno. *The Diversity of Modern Capitalism*. Oxford: Oxford University Press, 2003.

Amable, Bruno, Elvire Guillaud, and Stefano Palombarini. "Changing French Capitalism: Political and Systemic Crises in France." *Journal of European Public Policy* 19, no. 8 (2012): 1168–1187.

Ashford, Douglas E. *Policy and Politics in France. Living with Uncertainty*. Philadelphia: Temple University Press, 1982.

Backhouse, Roger E. *The Penguin History of Economics*. London: Penguin Books, 2002.

Berger, Suzanne, and Ronald Dore, eds. *National Diversity and Global Capitalism*, Conrell Studies in Political Economy. Ithaca/London: Cornell University Press, 1996.

Berghahn, Volker R. *The Americanisation of West German Industry, 1945–1973*. New York: Berg, 1986.

Berghahn, Volker R. "Das 'Deutsche Kapitalismus-Modell' in Geschichte und Geschichtswissenschaft." In *Gibt es einen deutschen Kapitalismus? Tradition und globale Perspektiven der sozialen Marktwirtschaft*, edited by Volker R. Berghahn and Sigurt Vitols, 25–43. Frankfurt am Main: Campus, 2006.

Berghahn, Volker R. "Varieties of Capitalism in the 'American Century'." *Business History Review* 84, no. 4 (2010): 661–663.

Berghahn, Volker R., and Sigurt Vitols, eds. *Gibt es einen deutschen Kapitalismus? Tradition und globale Perspektiven der sozialen Marktwirtschaft*. Frankfurt am Main: Campus, 2006.

Berghoff, Hartmut. "Historisches Relikt oder Zukunftsmodell? Kleine und mittelgroße Unternehmen in der Wirtschafts- und Sozialgeschichte der Bundesrepublik Deutschland." In *Großbürger und Unternehmer*, edited by Dieter Ziegler. Bürgertum. Beiträge zur europäischen Gesellschaftsgeschichte; 17, 249–282. Göttingen: Vandenhoeck & Ruprecht, 2000.

Berghoff, Hartmut. "Abschied vom klassischen Mittelstand. Kleine und mittlere Unternehmen in der bundesdeutschen Wirtschaft des späten 20. Jahrhunderts." In *Die deutsche Wirtschaftselite im 20. Jahrhundert. Kontinuität und Mentalität*, edited by Volker R. Berghahn, Stefan Unger and Dieter Ziegler. Bochumer Schriften zur Unternehmens- und Industriegeschichte; 11, 93–113. Essen, 2003.

Berghoff, Hartmut. "The End of Family Business? The Mittelstand and the German Capitalism in Transition, 1949–2000." *Business History Review* 80 (2006): 263–295.

Berghoff, Hartmut. "Varieties of Financialization? Evidence from German Industry in the 1990s." *Business History Review* 90, no. 1 (2016): 81–108.

Berghoff, Hartmut. "Vom Netzwerk zum Markt? Zur Kontrolle der Manager-Elite in Deutschland." In *Deutschlands Eliten im Wandel*, edited by Herfried Münkler, Grit Straßenberger and Matthias Bohlender, 177–198. Frankfurt am Main/New York: Campus, 2006.

Berghoff, Hartmut. "Die Strukturen der Deutschland AG. Ein Rückblick auf ein Modell der Unternehmenskontrolle." In *Die "Deutschland AG". Historische Annäherungen an den bundesdeutschen Kapitalismus*, edited by Ralf Ahrens, Boris Gehlen and Alfred Reckendrees, 31–56. Essen: Klartext, 2013.

Beyer, Jürgen. "Deutschland AG a.D.: Deutsche Bank, Allianz und das Verflechtungszentrum des deutschen Kapitalismus." In *Alle Macht dem Markt? Fallstudien zur Abwicklung der Deutschland AG*, edited by Wolfgang Streeck and Martin Höpner, 118–146. Frankfurt am Main/New York: Campus, 2003.

Beyer, Jürgen, and Martin Höpner. "The Disintegration of Organised Capitalism: German Corporate Governance in the 1990s." *West European Politics* 26, no. 4 (2003): 179–198. doi:10.1080/014023803 12331280738

Bouwens, Bram, and Joost Dankers. "Competition and Varieties of Coordination." In *Varieties of Capitalism and Business History. The Dutch Case*, edited by Keetie Sluyterman, 103–129. New York/ Abingdon: Routledge, 2015.

Boyer, Robert. "French Statism at the Crossroads." In *Political Economy of Modern Capitalism: Mapping Convergence and Diversity*, edited by Colin Crouch and Wolfgang Streeck, 71–101. London: Sage, 1997.

Boyer, Robert. *How and Why Capitalisms Differ. MPIfG Discussion Paper 05/04*. Köln: MPIfG, 2005.

Boyer, Robert, and Yves Saillard, eds. *Régulation Theory. The State of the Art*. London: Routledge, 2002.

Bridgford, Jeff. "French Trade Unions: Crisis in the 1980s." *Industrial Relations Journal* 21, no. 2 (1990): 126–35. doi:10.1111/j.1468-2338.1990.tb00846.x

Corneo, Giacomo, Sonja Zmerli, and Reinhard Pollak. "Germany: Rising Inequality and the Transformation of Rhine Capitalism." In *Changing Inequalities and Societal Impacts in Rich Countries. Thirty Countries' Experiences* edited by Brian Nolan, Wiemer Salverda, Daniele Checchi, Ive Marx, Abigail McKnight, István György Tóth and Herman van de Werfhorst, 271–98. Oxford: Oxford University Press, 2014.

Crouch, Colin. "Typologies of Capitalism." In *Debating Varieties of Capitalism. A Reader*, edited by Bob Hancké, 75–94. Oxford: Oxford University Press, 2009.

Crouch, Colin, and Wolfgang Streeck, eds. *Political Economy of Modern Capitalism. Mapping Convergence and Diversity*. London: Sage, 1997.

Croucher, Richard, and Geoffrey Wood. "Tripartism in Comparative and Historical Perspective." *Business History* 57, no. 3 (2015): 347–357. doi:10.1080/00076791.2014.983479

Czada, Roland. "Konjunkturen des Korporatismus. Zur Geschichte eines Paradigmenwechsels in der Verbändeforschung." In *Staat und Verbände*, edited by Wolfgang Streeck. 37–64. Opladen: Westdeutscher Verlag, 1994.

David, Thomas, and André Mach. "Corporate Governance." In *Wirtschaftsgeschichte der Schweiz im 20. Jahrhundert*, edited by Patrick Halbeisen, Margrit Müller and Béatrice Veyrassat, 831–72. Basel: Schwabe Verlag, 2012.

Deeg, Richard. "The Limits of Liberalization? American Capitalism at the Crossroads." *Journal of European Public Policy* 19, no. 8 (2012): 1249–1268. doi:10.1080/13501763.2012.709026

Doering-Manteuffel, Anselm. "Die deutsche Geschichte in den Zeitbögen des 20. Jahrhunderts." *Vierteljahrshefte für Zeitgeschichte* 62, no. 3 (2014): 321–348. doi:10.1515/vfzg-2014-0017

Doering-Manteuffel, Anselm, and Lutz Raphael, eds. *Nach dem Boom. Perspektiven auf die Zeitgeschichte seit 1970*. 3rd ed. Göttingen: Vandenhoeck & Ruprecht, 2012.

Dore, Ronald, William Lazonick, and Mary O'Sullivan. "Varieties of Capitalism in the Twentieth Century." *Oxford Review of Economic Policy* 15, no. 4 (1999): 102–120. doi:10.1093/oxrep/15.4.102

Ebbinghaus, Bernhard. "Die Mitgliederentwicklung deutscher Gewerkschaften im historischen und internationalen Vergleich." In *Die Gewerkschaften in Politik und Gesellschaft der Bundesrepublik Deutschland*, edited by Wolfgang Schroeder and Bernhard Weßels. 174–203. Wiesbaden: Westdeutscher Verlag, 2003.

Ebbinghaus, Bernhard. *Reforming Early Retirement in Europe, Japan, and the USA*. Oxford: Oxford University Press, 2006.

Ebbinghaus, Bernhard, and Jelle Visser. *European Labor and Transnational Solidarity: Challenges, Pathway and Barriers*. Mannheim: MZES, 1996.

Ellguth, Peter, and Susanne Kohaut. "Tarifbindung und betriebliche Interessenvertretung: Aktuelle Ergebnisse aus dem IAB-Betriebspanel 2007." *WSI-Mitteilungen* 9/2008 (2008): 1–5.

Esping-Andersen, Gøsta. *Three Worlds of Welfare Capitalism*. Cambridge: Polity Press, 1990.

Esser, Josef. "Funktionen und Funktionswandel der Gewerkschaften in Deutschland." In *Die Gewerkschaften in Politik und Gesellschaft der Bundesrepublik Deutschland. Ein Handbuch*, edited by Wolfgang Schroeder and Bernhard Weßels, 65–85. Wiesbaden: Westdeutscher Verlag, 2003.

Esser, Josef, and Wolfgang Fach. "Crisis Management 'Made in Germany'. The Steel Industry." In *Industry and Politics in West Germany. Toward the Third Republic*, edited by Peter J. Katzenstein, 221–48. Ithaca/London: Cornell University Press, 1989.

Fear, Jeffrey. "Straight Outta Oberberg. Transforming Mid-Sized Family Firms into Global Champions 1970–2010." *Jahrbuch für Wirtschaftsgeschichte* 1 (2012): 125–69. doi:10.1524/jbwg.2012.0007

Fellman, Susanna, Martin Jes Iversen, Hans Sjögren, and Lars Thue, eds. *Creating Nordic Capitalism: The Business History of a Competitive Periphery*. Basingstoke: Palgrave Macmillan, 2008.

Finegold, David, and David Soskice. "The Failure of Training in Britain. Analysis and Prescription." *Oxford Review of Economic Policy* 4, no. 3 (1988): 21–53. doi:10.1093/oxrep/4.3.21

Fohlin, Caroline. "The History of Corporate Ownership and Control in Germany." In *A History of Corporate Governance around the World: Family Business Groups to Professional Managers*, edited by Randall K. Morck, 223–282. Chicago: University of Chicago Press, 2005.

Fourastié, Jean. *Les Trente Glorieuses ou la Révolution Invisible de 1946 à 1975*. Paris: Fayard, 1980.

Freye, Saskia. *Führungswechsel. Die Wirtschaftselite und das Ende der Deutschland AG*. Frankfurt am Main: Campus, 2009.

Freye, Saskia. "Ein Rückzug aus der Mitte der Deutschland AG? Die strategische Neuausrichtung von Daimler-Benz in den 1980er Jahren." In *Die 'Deutschland AG'. Historische Annäherungen an den bundesdeutschen Kapitalismus*, edited by Ralf Ahrens, Boris Gehlen and Alfred Reckendrees, 323–350. Essen: Klartext, 2013.

Frieden, Jeffry A. Global Capitalism. Its Fall and Rise in the Twentieth Century. New York: Norton & Company, 2007.

Friedrich-Ebert-Stiftung, ed. *Archiv für Sozialgeschichte. Vol 47: Der Sozialstaat in der Krise. Deutschland im internationalen Vergleich*. Bonn: Dietz, 2007.

Gehlen, Boris. "Die Industrie- und Handelskammern im Netzwerk der Kooperation von Wirtschaft und Staat." In *Der 'Rheinische Kapitalismus' in der Ära Adenauer*, edited by Hans Günter Hockerts and Günther Schulz. Rhöndorfer Gespräche; 26, 51–74. Paderborn: Ferdinand Schöningh, 2016.

Geyer, Martin H., ed. *Geschichte der Sozialpolitik in Deutschland seit 1945. Bd. 6: Bundesrepublik Deutschland 1974-1982. Neue Herausforderungen, wachsende Unsicherheiten*. Baden-Baden: Nomos, 2008.

Ginalski, Stéphanie, Thomas David, and André Mach. "From National Cohesion to Transnationalization: The Changing Role of Banks in the Swiss Company Network, 1910–2010." In *The Power of Corporate Networks. A Comparative and Historical Perspective*, edited by Thomas David and Gerarda Westerhuis, 107–24. New York/Abingdon: Taylor & Francis, 2014.

Goey, Ferry de. "European Varieties of Capitalism." In *Perspectives on European Economic and Social History - Perspektiven der europäischen Wirtschafts- und Sozialgeschichte*, edited by Jan-Otmar Hesse, Christian Kleinschmidt, Alfred Reckendrees and Raymond G. Stokes, 73–100. Baden-Baden: Nomos, 2014.

Gospel, Howard, and Tony Edwards. "Strategic Transformation and Muddling Through: Industrial Relations and Industrial Training in the UK." *Journal of European Public Policy* 19, no. 8 (2012): 1229–1248. doi:10.1080/13501763.2012.709023

Granovetter, Mark S. "Economic Action and Social Structure: The Problem of Embeddedness." *American Journal of Sociology* 91, no. 3 (1985): 481–510. doi:10.1086/228311

Hacker, Jacob S., Paul Pierson, and Kathleen Thelen. "Drift and Conversion: Hidden Faces of Institutional Change." In *Advances in Comparative-Historical Analysis*, edited by James Mahoney and Kathleen Thelen, 180–208. Cambridge: Cambridge University Press, 2015.

Hall, Peter A., and Daniel W. Gingerich. *Varieties of Capitalism and Institutional Complementarities in the Macroeconomy. An Empirical Analysis. MPIfG Discussion Paper; 04,5*. Köln: MPIfG, 2004.

Hall, Peter A., and Michèle Lamont, eds. *Social Resilience in the Neoliberal Era*. Cambridge: Cambridge University Press, 2013.

Hall, Peter A., and David Soskice. "An Introduction to Varieties of Capitalism." In *Varieties of Capitalism. The Institutional Foundations of Comparative Advantage*, edited by Peter A. Hall and David Soskice, 1–68. Oxford: Oxford University Press, 2001.

Hall, Peter A., and David Soskice, eds. *Varieties of Capitalism. The Institutional Foundations of Comparative Advantage*. Oxford: Oxford University Press, 2001.

Hall, Peter A., and Kathleen Thelen. "Institutional Change in Varieties of Capitalism." *Socio-Economic Review* 7, no. 1, 2008: 7–34. doi:10.1093/ser/mwn020

Hancké, Bob. *Large Firms and Institutional Change. Industrial Renewal and Economic Restructuring in France*. Oxford: Oxford University Press, 2002.

Hancké, Bob, ed. *Debating Varieties of Capitalism. A Reader*. Oxford: Oxford University Press, 2009.

Hancké, Bob. "Introducing the Debate." In *Debating Varieties of Capitalism. A Reader*, 1–17. Oxford: Oxford University Press, 2009.

Hancké, Bob, Martin Rhodes, and Mark Thatcher. "Beyond Varieties of Capitalism." In *Beyond Varieties of Capitalism. Conflict, Contradictions, and Complementarities in the European Economy*, edited by Bob Hancké, Martin Rhodes and Mark Thatcher, 273–300. Oxford: Oxford University Press, 2007.

Hancké, Bob, Martin Rhodes, and Mark Thatcher, eds. *Beyond Varieties of Capitalism. Conflict, Contradictions, and Complementarities in the European Economy*. Oxford: Oxford University Press, 2007.

Hancké, Bob, Martin Rhodes, and Mark Thatcher. "Introduction: Beyond Varieties of Capitalism." In *Beyond Varieties of Capitalism. Conflict, Contradictions, and Complementarities in the European Economy*, edited by Bob Hancké, Martin Rhodes and Mark Thatcher, 3–38. Oxford: Oxford University Press, 2007.

Hassel, Anke. "Die Schwächen des 'deutschen Kapitalismus.'" In *Gibt es einen deutschen Kapitalismus? Tradition und globale Perspektiven der sozialen Marktwirtschaft*, edited by Volker R. Berghahn and Sigurt Vitols, 200–14. Frankfurt am Main: Campus, 2006.

Hauser-Ditz, Axel, Markus Hertwig, Pries Ludger, and Luitpold Rampeltshammer. *Transnationale Mitbestimmung? Zur Praxis europäischer Betriebsräte in der Automobilindustrie*. Frankfurt am Main: Campus, 2010.

Hauser, Hans-Eduard, ed. *SMEs in Germany. Facts and Figures 2000*. Bonn: Institut für Mittelstandsforschung, 2000.

Hentschel, Volker. *Ludwig Erhard. Ein Politikerleben*. München: Olzog, 1996.

Herrigel, Gary. *Industrial Constructions. The Sources of German Industrial Power*. Structural Analysis in the Social Sciences, 9. Cambridge: Cambridge University Press, 2000.

Herrigel, Gary. *Manufacturing Possibilities. Creative Action and Industrial Recomposition in the United States, Germany and Japan*. Oxford: Oxford University Press, 2012.

Herrigel, Gary, and Jonathan Zeitlin. "Alternatives to Varieties of Capitalism." *Business History Review* 84, no. 4 (2010): 667–74.

Hesse, Jan-Otmar. "Abkehr vom Kartelldenken? Das Gesetz gegen Wettbewerbsbeschränkungen als ordnungspolitische und wirtschaftstheoretische Zäsur der Ära Adenauer." In *Der 'Rheinische Kapitalismus' in der Ära Adenauer*, edited by Hans Günter Hockerts and Günther Schulz. Rhöndorfer Gespräche; 26, 29–49. Paderborn: Ferdinand Schöningh, 2016.

Hilger, Susanne. *'Amerikanisierung' deutscher Unternehmen. Wettbewerbsstrategien und Unternehmenspolitik bei Henkel, Siemens und Daimler-Benz (1945/49-1975)*. VSWG, Beihefte; 173. Stuttgart: Steiner, 2004.

Hobsbawm, Eric. *The Age of Extremes. The Short Twentieth Century 1914–1991*. London: Abacus, 1995.

Hockerts, Hans Günter. "Vom Wohlfahrtsstaat zum Wohlfahrtsmarkt? Privatisierungstendenzen im deutschen Sozialstaat." In *Privatisierung. Idee und Praxis seit den 1970er Jahren*, edited by Norbert Frei and Dietmar Süß, 70–87. Göttingen: Wallstein, 2012.

Hockerts, Hans Günter, and Günther Schulz. "Einleitung." In *Der 'Rheinische Kapitalismus' in der Ära Adenauer*, edited by Hans Günter Hockerts, Günther Schulz, and Rhöndorfer Gespräche, vol. 26, 9–28. Paderborn: Ferdinand Schöningh, 2016.

Hollingsworth, J. Rogers. "Continuities and Changes in Social Systems of Production: The Cases of Japan, Germany, and the United States." In *Contemporary Capitalism. The Embeddedness of Institutions*, edited by J. Rogers Hollingsworth and Robert Boyer, 265–317. Cambridge: Cambridge University Press, 1997.

Hollingsworth, J. Rogers, and Robert Boyer, eds. *Contemporary Capitalism. The Embeddedness of Institutions*. Cambridge: Cambridge University Press, 1997.

Jackson, Gregory. "The Origins of Nonliberal Corporate Governance in Germany and Japan." In *The Origins of Nonliberal Capitalism. Germany and Japan in Comparison*, edited by Wolfgang Streeck and Kozo Yamamura, 121–70. Ithaca: Cornell University Press, 2001.

Jackson, Gregory, and Arndt Sorge. "The Trajectory of Institutional Change in Germany, 1979–2009." *Journal of European Public Policy* 19, no. 8 (2012): 1146–1167. doi:10.1080/13501763.2012.709009

Jürgens, Ulrich, Katrin Naumann, and Joachim Rupp. "Shareholder Value in an Adverse Environment. The German Case." *Economy and Society* 29, no. 1 (2000): 54–79. doi:10.1080/030851400360569

Kädtler, Jürgen. "German Chemical Giants' Business and Social Models in Transition. Financialisation as a Management Strategy." *Transfer. European Review of Labour and Research* 15 (2009): 229–249. doi:10.1177/102425890901500206

Katzenstein, Peter J. *Policy and Politics in West Germany: The Growth of a Semisovereign State*. Philadelphia: Temple University Press, 1987.

Kern, Horst, and Michael Schumann. *Das Ende der Arbeitsteilung? Rationalisierung in der industriellen Produktion: Bestandsaufnahme, Trendbestimmung*. München: Beck, 1984.

Kitschelt, Herbert, and Wolfgang Streeck. "From Stability of Stagnation: Germany at the Beginning of the Twenty-First Century." *West European Politics* 26, no. 4 (2003): 1–34. doi:10.1080/0140238031233 1280668

Kleinschmidt, Christian. *Der produktive Blick. Wahrnehmung amerikanischer und japanischer Management- und Produktionsmethoden durch deutsche Unternehmer 1950–1985*. Berlin: Akademie Verlag, 2002.

Kocka, Jürgen. "Einleitung." In *Gibt es einen deutschen Kapitalismus? Tradition und globale Perspektiven der sozialen Marktwirtschaft*, edited by Volker R. Berghahn and Sigurt Vitols, 9–21. Frankfurt am Main: Campus, 2006.

Kurz, Heinz D. *Geschichte des ökonomischen Denkens*. 2nd ed. München: Beck, 2017.

Lane, Christel. *Industry and Society in Europe. Stability and Change in Britain, Germany and France*. Aldershot: Edward Elgar, 1995.

Lane, Christel. "Globalization and the German Model of Capitalism - Erosion or Survival?" *The British Journal of Sociology* 51, no. 2 (2000): 207–234.

Lane, Christel. "Institutional Transformation and System Change: Changes in the Corporate Governance of German Corporations." In *Changing Capitalism? Internationalization, Institutional Change, and Systems of Economic Organization*, edited by Glenn Morgan, Richard Whiteley and Eli Moen, 78–109. Oxford: Oxford University Press, 2006.

Lazonick, William. "The Financialization of the U.S. Corporation: What has been Lost, and How it can be Regained." *Seattle University Law Review* 36, no. 2 (2013): 857–909.

Lenger, Friedrich. *Werner Sombart 1863-1941. Eine Biographie*. München: Beck, 1994. doi:10.1086/ahr/100.3.917

Lubinski, Christina. "Zwischen Familienerbe und globalem Markt. Eigentum und Management von großen westdeutschen Familienunternehmen im Wandel (1960 bis 2008)." *Zeitschrift für Unternehmensgeschichte* 55, no. 1 (2010): 204–229. doi:10.17104/0342-2852_2010_2_204

Mahoney, James. "Path Dependence in Historical Sociology." *Theory and Society* 29 (2000): 507–548. doi:10.1023/A:1007113830879

Mahoney, James, and Kathleen Thelen, eds. *Explaining Institutional Change. Ambiguity, Agency, and Power*. Cambridge: Cambridge University Press, 2010.

Manow, Philip. "Welfare State Building and Coordinated Capitalism in Japan and Germany." In *The Origins of Nonliberal Capitalism. Germany and Japan in Comparison*, edited by Wolfgang Streeck and Kozo Yamamura, 94–120. Ithaca: Cornell University Press, 2001.

Manow, Philip. "Consociational Roots of German Corporatism. The Bismarckian Welfare State within the German Political Economy." *Acta Politica* 37 (2002): 195–212.

Martin, Cathie Jo. "Business History and the Varieties of Coordination." *Business History Review* 84, no. 4 (2010): 657–61.

Marx, Christian. "Die Internationalisierung der Chemieindustrie als Herausforderung für die Deutschland AG." In *Die 'Deutschland AG'. Historische Annäherungen an den bundesdeutschen Kapitalismus*, edited by Ralf Ahrens, Boris Gehlen and Alfred Reckendrees. Bochumer Schriften zur Unternehmens- und Industriegeschichte; 20, 247–273. Essen: Klartext, 2013.

Marx, Christian. "Der Betrieb als politischer Ort und seine legislative Verankerung. Der Einfluss der Verbände auf die Reform des Betriebsverfassungsgesetzes (BetrVG) 1972." In *Der Betrieb als sozialer und politischer Ort. Studien zu Praktiken und Diskursen in den Arbeitswelten des 20. Jahrhunderts*, edited by Knud Andresen, Michaela Kuhnhenne, Jürgen Mittag and Johannes Platz. Archiv der sozialen Demokratie der Friedrich-Ebert-Stiftung, Reihe: Politik- und Gesellschaftsgeschichte; 98, 231–58. Bonn: Dietz, 2015.

Milert, Werner, and Rudolf Tschirbs. *Die andere Demokratie. Betriebliche Interessenvertretung in Deutschland, 1848 bis 2008.* Veröffentlichungen des Instituts für soziale Bewegungen. Schriftenreihe A: Darstellungen; 52. Essen: Klartext, 2012.

Mirowski, Philip, and Dieter Plehwe, eds. The *Road from Mont Pèlerin. The Making of the Neoliberal Thought Collective.* Cambridge: Harvard University Press, 2009.

Molina, Óscar, and Martin Rhodes. "The Political Economy of Adjustment in Mixed Market Economies: A Study of Spain and Italy." In *Beyond Varieties of Capitalism: Conflict, Contradictions, and Complementarities in the European Economy*, edited by Bob Hancké, Martin Rhodes and Mark Thatcher, 223–252. Oxford: Oxford University Press, 2007.

Morgan, Glenn. "Institutional Complementarities, Path Dependency, and the Dynamics of Firms." In *Changing Capitalism? Internationalization, Institutional Change, and Systems of Economic Organization*, edited by Glenn Morgan, Richard Whiteley and Eli Moen, 415–446. Oxford: Oxford University Press, 2006.

Müller-Jentsch, Walther. "Gewerkschaften als intermediäre Organisationen." *Kölner Zeitschrift für Soziologie und Sozialpsychologie* Sonderheft 24 (1982): 408–33.

Müller-Jentsch, Walther. "Mitbestimmungspolitik." In *Die Gewerkschaften in Politik und Gesellschaft der Bundesrepublik Deutschland. Ein Handbuch*, edited by Wolfgang Schroeder and Bernhard Weßels, 451–77. Wiesbaden: Westdeutscher Verlag, 2003.

Müller-Jentsch, Walther. "Arbeitgeberverbände und Arbeitgeberpolitik in der Chemieindustrie." In *Stimmt die Chemie? Mitbestimmung und Sozialpolitik in der Geschichte des Bayer-Konzerns*, edited by Klaus Tenfelde, Karl-Otto Czikowsky, Jürgen Mittag, Stefan Moitra and Rolf Nietzard, 283–303. Essen: Klartext, 2007.

Müller, Gloria. *Strukturwandel und Arbeitnehmerrechte. Die wirtschaftliche Mitbestimmung in der Eisen- und Stahlindustrie 1945–1975. Düsseldorfer Schriften zur neueren Landesgeschichte und zur Geschichte Nordrhein-Westfalens*; 31. Essen: Klartext, 1991.

Nijhof, Erik, and Annette van den Berg. "Variations of Coordination. Labour Relations in the Netherlands." In *Varieties of Capitalism and Business History. The Dutch Case*, edited by Keetie Sluyterman, 22–49. New York/Abingdon: Routledge, 2015.

North, Douglass C. *Institutions, Institutional Change and Economic Performance*. Cambridge/New York: Cambridge University Press, 1990.

Nützenadel, Alexander. *Stunde der Ökonomen. Wissenschaft, Politik und Expertenkultur in der Bundesrepublik 1949-1974*. Göttingen: Vandenhoeck & Ruprecht, 2005.

Olson, Mancur. *The Rise and Decline of Nations. Economic Growth, Stagflation and Social Rigidities*. New Haven: Yale University Press, 1982.

Pierenkemper, Toni. *Geschichte des modernen ökonomischen Denkens. Große Ökonomen und ihre Ideen*. Göttingen: Vandenhoeck & Ruprecht, 2012.

Pierson, Paul. "Increasing Returns, Path Dependence, and the Study of Politics." *American Political Science Review* 94 (2000): 251–268. doi:10.2307/2586011

Piore, Michael J., and Charles F. Sabel. *The Second Industrial Divide. Possibilities for Prosperity*. New York: Basic Books, 1984.

Plumpe, Werner. "Das Ende des deutschen Kapitalismus." *Westend* 2, no. 2 (2005): 3–26.

Plumpe, Werner. Das kalte Herz. Kapitalismus: Die Geschichte einer andauernden Revolution. Berlin: Rowohlt, 2019.

Pribram, Karl. *Geschichte des ökonomischen Denkens. 2 Vols*. Frankfurt am Main: Suhrkamp, 1992.

Priddat, Birger P. "'Nationalökonomische Vertiefung der Rechtsphilosophie.' Adolph Wagners rechtliche Theorie der Verteilung." In *Produktive Kraft, sittliche Ordnung und geistige Macht. Denkstile der deutschen Nationalökonomie im 18. und 19. Jahrhundert*, edited by Birger P. Priddat, 391–414. Marburg: Metropolis-Verlag, 1998.

Raphael, Lutz. *Jenseits von Kohle und Stahl. Eine Gesellschaftsgeschichte Westeuropas nach dem Boom*. Berlin: Suhrkamp, 2019.

Rehling, Andrea. "Die Konzertierte Aktion im Spannungsfeld der 1970er-Jahre. Geburtsstunde des Modells Deutschland und Ende des modernen Korporatismus." In *"Nach dem Strukturbruch"? Kontinuität und Wandel von Arbeitsbeziehungen und Arbeitswelt(en) seit den 1970er-Jahren*, edited by Knud Andresen, Ursula Bitzegeio and Jürgen Mittag. Politik- und Gesellschaftsgeschichte; 89, 65–86. Bonn: Dietz, 2011.

Reitmayer, Morten. "Deutsche Konkurrenzkulturen nach dem Boom." In *Konkurrenz in der Geschichte. Praktiken - Werte - Institutionalisierungen*, edited by Ralph Jessen, 261–288. Frankfurt am Main: Campus, 2014.

Ritter, Gerhard A. *Geschichte der Sozialpolitik in Deutschland seit 1945. Bd. 11: Bundesrepublik Deutschland 1989-1994. Sozialpolitik im Zeichen der Vereinigung*. Baden-Baden: Nomos, 2007.

Rödder, Andreas. *21.0. Eine kurze Geschichte der Gegenwart*. München: Beck, 2015.

Sattler, Friederike. "Rheinischer Kapitalismus. Staat, Wirtschaft und Gesellschaft in der Bonner Republik." *Archiv für Sozialgeschichte* 52 (2012): 687–724.

Sattler, Friederike. "Unternehmensfinanzierung im »Rheinischen Kapitalismus« der Ära Adenauer." In *Der 'Rheinische Kapitalismus' in der Ära Adenauer*, edited by Hans Günter Hockerts and Günther Schulz. Rhöndorfer Gespräche; 26, 143–68. Paderborn: Ferdinand Schöningh, 2016.

Schmidt, Manfred G., ed. *Geschichte der Sozialpolitik in Deutschland seit 1945. Bd. 7: Bundesrepublik Deutschland 1982-1989. Finanzielle Konsolidierung und institutionelle Reform*. Baden-Baden: Nomos, 2005.

Schmidt, Vivien A. "French Capitalism Transformed, yet still a Third Variety of Capitalism." *Economy and Society* 32, no. 4 (2003): 526–554. doi:10.1080/0308514032000141693

Schmitter, Philippe C. "Still the Century of Corporatism?" *Review of Politics* 36 (1974): 85–131. doi:10.1017/S0034670500022178

Schmoller, Gustav von. *Grundriss der allgemeinen Volkswirtschaftslehre. 2 Vols*. Leipzig: Duncker & Humblot, 1900/1904.

Schroeder, Wolfgang, and Bernhard Weßels. "Die deutsche Unternehmerverbändelandschaft: Vom Zeitalter der Verbände zum Zeitalter der Mitglieder." In *Handbuch Arbeitgeber- und Wirtschaftsverbände in Deutschland*, edited by Wolfgang Schroeder and Bernhard Weßels, 9–24. Wiesbaden: VS, 2010.

Schröter, Harm G. *Americanization of the European Economy. A Compact Survey of American Economic Influence in Europe since the 1880s*. Dordrecht: Kluwer, 2005.

Schumann, Michael. et al. "Anti-tayloristisches Fabrikmodell – AUTO 5000 bei Volkswagen." WSI-Mitteilungen, 1 (2005): 3–10.

Screpanti, Ernesto, and Stefano Zamagni. *An Outline of the History of Economic Thought*. 2nd ed. Oxford: Oxford University Press, 2005.

Shonfield, Andrew. *Modern Capitalism. The Changing Balance of Public and Private Power*. Oxford: Oxford University Press, 1965.

Slobodian, Quinn. *Globalists. The End of Empire and the Birth of Neoliberalism*. Cambridge: Harvard University Press, 2018.

Silvia, Stephen J. "Mitgliederentwicklung und Organisationsstärke der Arbeitgeberverbände, Wirtschaftsverbände und Industrie- und Handelskammern." In *Handbuch Arbeitgeber- und Wirtschaftsverbände in Deutschland*, edited by Wolfgang Schroeder and Bernhard Weßels. 169–182. Wiesbaden: VS, 2010.

Sluyterman, Keetie, ed. *Varieties of Capitalism and Business History. The Dutch Case*, Routledge International Studies in Business History, 28. New York/Abingdon: Routledge, 2015.

Sluyterman, Keetie, and Ben Wubs. "Multinationals as Agents of Change." In *Varieties of Capitalism and Business History. The Dutch Case*, edited by Keetie Sluyterman, 156–182. New York/Abingdon: Routledge, 2015.

Söllner, Fritz. *Die Geschichte des ökonomischen Denkens*. 2nd ed. Berlin: Springer, 2001.

Sombart, Werner. *Der Moderne Kapitalismus. Historisch-systematische Darstellung des gesamteuropäischen Wirtschaftslebens von seinen Anfängen bis zur Gegenwart*. München: Duncker & Humblot, 1902/1927.

Sombart, Werner. *Deutscher Sozialismus*. Berlin: Buchholz & Weisswange, 1934.

Sorge, Arndt, and Wolfgang Streeck. *Diversified Quality Production Revisited. The Transformation of Production Systems and Regulatory Regimes in Germany. MPIfG Discussion Paper; 16/13*. Köln: MPIfG, 2016.

Soskice, David. "Divergent Production Regimes. Coordinated and Uncoordinated Market Economies in the 1980s and 1990s." In *Continuity and Change in Contemporary Capitalism*, edited by Herbert Kitschelt, Peter Lange, Gary Marks and John D. Stephens, 101–134. Cambridge: Cambridge University Press, 1999.

Soskice, David. "Globalisierung und institutionelle Divergenz. Die USA und Deutschland im Vergleich." *Geschichte und Gesellschaft* 25, no. 2 (1999): 201–225.

Stokes, Raymond G. "Technology Transfer and the Emergence of the West German Petrochemical Industry, 1945–1955." In *American Policy and the Reconstruction of West Germany*, edited by Jeffry M. Diefendorf, Axel Frohn, and Hermann-Josef Rupieper, 217–236. Cambridge: Cambridge University Press, 1993.

Streeck, Wolfgang. "On the Institutional Conditions of Diversified Quality Production." In *Beyond Keynesianism: The Socio-Economics of Production and Employment*, edited by Egon Matzner and Wolfgang Streeck, 21–61. London: Edward Elgar, 1991.

Streeck, Wolfgang. "German Capitalism. Does It Exist? Can It Survive?" In *Political Economy of Modern Capitalism: Mapping Convergence and Diversity*, edited by Colin Crouch and Wolfgang Streeck, 33–54. London: Sage, 1997.

Streeck, Wolfgang. "Introduction. Explorations into the Origins of Nonliberal Capitalism in Germany and Japan." In *The Origins of Nonliberal Capitalism. Germany and Japan in Comparison*, edited by Wolfgang Streeck and Kozo Yamamura, 1–38. Ithaca/London: Cornell University Press, 2001.

Streeck, Wolfgang. "Nach dem Korporatismus. Neue Eliten, neue Konflikte." In *Deutschlands Eliten im Wandel*, edited by Herfried Münkler, Grit Straßenberger and Matthias Bohlender, 149–75. Frankfurt am Main: Campus, 2006.

Streeck, Wolfgang. "Institutions in History: Bringing Capitalism Back in." In *The Oxford Handbook of Comparative Institutional Analysis*, edited by Glenn Morgan, John L. Campbell, Colin Crouch, Ove Kaj Pedersen and Richard Whiteley, 659–686. Oxford: Oxford University Press, 2010.

Streeck, Wolfgang. *Re-Forming Capitalism. Institutional Change in the German Political Economy*. Oxford: Oxford University Press, 2010.

Streeck, Wolfgang. *Gekaufte Zeit. Die Krise des demokratischen Kapitalismus*. 2nd ed. Berlin: Suhrkamp, 2013.

Streeck, Wolfgang, and Anke Hassel. "The Crumbling Pillars of Social Partnership." *West European Politics* 26, no. 4 (2003): 101–124. doi:10.1080/01402380312331280708

Streeck, Wolfgang, and Martin Höpner, eds. *Alle Macht dem Markt? Fallstudien zur Abwicklung der Deutschland AG*. Frankfurt am Main/New York: Campus, 2003.

Streeck, Wolfgang, and Martin Höpner. "Einleitung. Alle Macht dem Markt?" In *Alle Macht dem Markt? Fallstudien zur Abwicklung der Deutschland AG*, edited by Wolfgang Streeck and Martin Höpner, 11–59. Frankfurt am Main/New York: Campus, 2003.

Streeck, Wolfgang, and Kathleen Thelen, eds. *Beyond Continuity. Institutional Change in Advanced Political Economies*. Oxford: Oxford University Press, 2005.

Streeck, Wolfgang, and Kozo Yamamura, eds. *The Origins of Nonliberal Capitalism. Germany and Japan in Comparison*. Ithaca/London: Cornell University Press, 2001.

Süß, Dietmar. " Der Sieg der grauen Herren? Flexibilisierung und der Kampf um Zeit in den 1970er und 1980er Jahren." In *Vorgeschichte der Gegenwart. Dimensionen des Strukturbruchs nach dem Boom*, edited by Anselm Doering-Manteuffel, Lutz Raphael and Thomas Schlemmer, 109–27. Göttingen: Vandenhoeck & Ruprecht, 2016.

Thelen, Kathleen. "Historical Institutionalism in Comparative Politics." *Annual Review of Political Science* 2 (1999): 369–404. doi:10.1146/annurev.polisci.2.1.369

Thelen, Kathleen. "How Institutions Evolve: Insights from Comparative Historical Analysis." In *Comparative Historical Analysis in the Social Sciences*, edited by James Mahoney and Dietrich Rueschemeyer, 208–240. Cambridge: Cambridge University Press, 2003.

Thelen, Kathleen. *How Institutions Evolve: The Political Economy of Skills in Germany, Britain, the United States, and Japan*. Cambridge: Cambridge University Press, 2004.

Thelen, Kathleen. *Varieties of Liberalization and the New Politics of Social Solidarity*. New York: Cambridge University Press, 2014.

Thelen, Kathleen A. *Union of Parts: Labor Politics in Postwar Germany*. Ithaca: Cornell University Press, 1991.

Thelen, Kathleen A., and Lowell Turner. "Die deutsche Mitbestimmung im internationalen Vergleich." In *Mitbestimmung in Deutschland. Tradition und Effizienz*, edited by Wolfgang Streeck and Norbert Kluge, 135–223. Frankfurt am Main/New York: Campus, 1999.

Ther, Philipp. *Die neue Ordnung auf dem alten Kontinent - Eine Geschichte des neoliberalen Europa*. Berlin: Suhrkamp, 2014.

Turner, Lowell. *Defending the High Road. Labor and Politics in Unified Germany*. Ithaca: Cornell University Press, 1998.

Westerhuis, Gerarda. "The Dutch Corporate Network: Considering its Persistence." In *The Power of Corporate Networks. A Comparative and Historical Perspective*, edited by Thomas David and Gerarda Westerhuis, 89–106. New York/Abingdon: Taylor & Francis, 2014.

Wever, Kirsten. *Negotiating Competitiveness, Employment Relations and Organizational Innovation in Germany and the United States*. Boston: Harvard Business School Press, 1995.

Whitley, Richard. "Business History and the Comparative Analysis of Capitalisms." *Business History Review* 84, no. 4 (2010): 648–652.

Wilkins, Mira. "Multinational Enterprises and the Varieties of Capitalism." *Business History Review* 84, no. 4 (2010): 638–645.

Williamson, Oliver E. "The Economics of Organization. The Transaction Cost Approach." *American Journal of Sociology* 87 (1981): 548–577. doi:10.1086/227496

Williamson, Oliver E. *The Economic Institutions of Capitalism. Firms, Markets, Relational Contracting*. New York: Free Press, 1985.

Windolf, Paul. "Productivity Coalitions and the Future of European Corporatism." *Industrial Relations* 28, no. 1 (1989): 1–20. doi:10.1111/j.1468-232X.1989.tb00719.x

Windolf, Paul. ed. *Finanzmarkt-Kapitalismus. Analysen zum Wandel von Produktionsregimen, Kölner Zeitschrift für Soziologie und Sozialpsychologie. Sonderheft*; 45. Wiesbaden: VS, 2005.

Windolf, Paul. "Eigentümer ohne Risiko. Die Dienstklasse des Finanzmarkt-Kapitalismus." *Zeitschrift für Soziologie* 37, no. 6 (2008): 516–535.

Windolf, Paul. "The Corporate Network in Germany, 1896–2010." In *The Power of Corporate Networks. A Comparative and Historical Perspective*, edited by Thomas David and Gerarda Westerhuis, 66–85. New York/London: Routledge, 2014.

Winkel, Harald. "Gustav von Schmoller." In *Klassiker des ökonomischen Denkens. Vol. 2* edited by Joachim Starbatty, 97–118. München: Beck, 2009.

Winkler, Heinrich August, ed. *Organisierter Kapitalismus. Voraussetzungen und Anfänge*, Kritische Studien zur Geschichtswissenschaft; 9. Göttingen, 1974.

Whitley, Richard. *Divergent Capitalism. The Social Structuring and Change of Business Systems*. Oxford: Oxford University Press, 1999.

Whitley, Richard. "Business History and the Comparative Analysis of Capitalisms." *Business History Review*, 84, no. 4 (2010): 648–652.

The concept of social fields and the productive models: Two examples from the European automobile industry

Morten Reitmayer

ABSTRACT
The article examines the possibilities of the combination of the concept of social fields, which was developed by the French Sociologist Pierre Bourdieu, and the concept of the Productive Models, which was developed by the French Regulation School. It is the aim to give a better understanding of the activities of the different groups of agents within the capitalist enterprise, and to look for the chances and risks of single firms to change their strategy of production. A case study dealing with the two European automobile producers, VW and Renault, tests the combination of both methodological concepts on an empirical level. The question is, whether one specific economic and political context of these activities can be designated as Rhenish Capitalism.

Introduction

Explaining the strategic decisions of economic enterprises is one of the most prominent tasks of business history. Great efforts have been made in this direction and not only following Alfred Chandler's follows strategy'.[1] Yet one of the results of the debate on Chandler's predictions has been that there is not any proof for the existence of a single and universal capitalist logic that determines (successful) entrepreneurial decisions. Looking to the opposite direction, new fashions of management styles have followed each other repeatedly, each promising to have detected the 'one best way' for corporate strategy. This demonstrates the necessity to integrate cultural factors – for example the experiences and expectations of decision-makers, which have to be communicated properly – into any model of management practice. But this is not the task of this essay. Instead, I will examine some considerations from the corporate governance approach to reflect on some open questions regarding the analysis of business strategies. The concept of corporate governance originated as a means of controlling the top managers of large joint-stock companies for the benefit of shareholders by establishing a certain conduct of behaviour ('corporate governance code') and has been broadened by business historians for at least 15 years. One of the conclusions to be drawn from the current debate is the need to provide the corporate governance approach with a resilient theory of action.[2] Recent studies on the corporate governance of German corporations, such as Kim Priemel on Friedrich Flick, Bernhard Lorentz and Paul Erker on the Chemische Werke Hüls, Christian Marx on the Gutehoffnungshütte (GHH), or Johannes Bähr's summary of corporate governance structures in large German industrial corporations during the Third Reich,[3] tend either to privilege 'structure' over 'strategy' (that is, management action becomes more or less a functional result of the corporation's government structure – it is significant that these authors frequently talk about the 'corporate government *structure*' or '*system*', and not about '*exercising* corporate governance'), or to be orientated towards the dominating will of the entrepreneurial personality. Nonetheless, they are a great step forward in understanding the corporation's problem of balancing different – and often conflicting – interests within its own organisation, and integrating them into a viable corporate strategy.[4] But the epistemological problem identified by Chandler remains unsolved: the connection between structure and agency. It is not surprising that the studies named above did not bridge this gap, given that the corporate governance approach itself does not supply any means to do so. Only Marx took the next step, significantly by introducing the concept of 'network agency' (derived from sociological network analysis) to explain the specific way governance was exercised within the GHH.[5] This demonstrates the necessity to amend the corporate governance approach by adding a suitable theory of action. In my view, two key tasks must be accomplished by the new model: First, all relevant groups of agents who are able to influence the drafting of corporate strategy have to be identified and analysed regarding their agency, their interest, their power, and attitudes. Second, the model should enable business historians to embed their findings on the corporations in question into a broader context of the industrial branch, the markets concerned, and of the national economy. In this context, there is a third task to be mastered: the explanatory model should help to distinguish key features of Rhenish Capitalism within the field of corporate governance analysis. It should extend and complete the various theories and approaches or practices of research of corporate governance problems by developing a workable, resilient, and compatible concept of social action.

The first step towards a model is to conceptualise the economic enterprise as a place constituted by certain economic and social (and political) action. This means the corporation or part of a corporation are understood neither as a determined function of an economic structure nor as the institutional appendix of free entrepreneurial will and vision, but rather as a scene of confrontations. This scene is occupied by very different groups of agents: shareholders and creditors with their various different interests (such as their investment horizon), rival management factions, different groups among the workforce (highly or lesser qualified staff, experts inside and outside the production processes, immigrants and natives, men and women, office staff and manual workers, younger and older employees), suppliers and customers, but also external consultants and ultimately (since, after all, they can influence the actions of all of these groups) even competitors. This list reveals the closeness of our project to the stakeholder approach, although the last points go beyond it.[6] This approach was a great step forward as older economic and business history was unable to envisage makers of business strategies beyond the groups of owners and managers.[7] One difficulty of the stakeholder approach which was often criticized is the problem, 'who (or what) are the stakeholders of the firm?' Mitchell, Agle, and Wood have clearly described the tasks involved:

> We will see stakeholders identified as primary or secondary stakeholders; as owners and non-owners of the firm; as owners of capital or owners of less tangible assets; as actors or those

acted upon; as those existing in a voluntary or an involuntary relationship with the firm; as rights-holders, contractors, or moral claimants; as resource providers to or dependents of the firm; as risk-takers or influencers; and as legal principals to whom agent-managers bear a fiduciary duty. In the stakeholder literature there are a few broad definitions that attempt to specify the empirical reality that virtually anyone can affect or be affected by an organization's actions. What is needed is a theory of stakeholder identification that can reliably separate stakeholders from nonstakeholders. Also in the stakeholder literature are a number of narrow definitions that attempt to specify the pragmatic reality that managers simply cannot attend to all actual or potential claims, and that propose a variety of priorities for managerial attention. [...] What is needed also is a theory of stakeholder salience that can explain to whom and to what managers actually pay attention.[8]

The focal point here is that the stakeholder approach still maintains that a firm's management owns the solely legitimate authority for decision-making, and the stakeholders will only *influence* management. But this normative approach hampers the empirical analysis of key decisions: With their actions, stakeholders (or: agents and groups of agents) do not pursue an imaginary company objective, but instead conduct their decisions, alliances, and confrontations primarily with regard to the use of company resources and the distribution of profits from the utilisation of the goods produced. At the same time, these confrontations are characterised by repeated new attempts to reach a consensus on company goals and the strategy required to achieve them – irrespective of the means by which this consensus is reached. Moreover, business history has a long tradition of identifying decision-makers beyond the boards of management.

Yet adopting this perspective also demands a series of breaks with some conventional presuppositions and analytical models of economic and business history, as well as the history of (industrial) labour: a break with the market as the prerequisite and dislocated place for the exchange of goods between anonymous and fully informed utility maximisers without any social existence, with the company as a leadership-free cluster of contracts, mutual obligations, and resulting rights of disposal,[9] with an entrepreneurial figure seen either as a genius innovator (as in the Schumpeter reception) or as the utiliser of information,[10] with the 'culture' of a company as a conflict-free instrument of integration and open to manipulation,[11] but also with the idea that a commercial enterprise is completely free when it comes to selecting its business strategy or in its search for the 'one best practice' of corporate strategy, or that it does so as a result of, at most, historically sedimented path dependencies.

Admittedly, recent business history, especially with a contemporary focus, has disentangled itself from these default values, whereby in particular individual subgroups of the workforce have been examined in a much more differentiated manner than before.[12] On the other hand, in the course of this necessary correction, the context of action – that is the agents' framework of options – which determined the scope and boundaries of their actions, sometimes went missing. This framework of options is first and foremost defined by the permanent viability of the capitalist firm that employs those groups. This viability, in turn, is dependent on the company's ability to find a coherent profit strategy (more on this concept below) and to anchor it among the groups of agents involved in a consensual manner. Therefore, within the field of economic and business history it remains highly desirable to investigate the systemic connection between the profit strategies of corporations and the interests of the agents involved, and so also the strategic decisions which accomplish those strategies.

Above all, examining the firm as a social and political place therefore also means pursuing the company-related relationships of conflict, competition, and consensus between all the aforementioned groups of agents, while also keeping an eye on the social organisation of value creation in the firm. In my view, for this purpose it is appropriate to refer to some concepts from sociology and political economy. Therefore, I propose to combine the concept of Social Fields, developed by Pierre Bourdieu, with that of 'Productive Models', which was developed by members of the French Regulation School (or: Approach), and in the process to pick up on part of the critique of the Regulation Approach.

In the following I shall first briefly outline Pierre Bourdieu's concept of the social 'field' and the resulting term 'strategy', before then discussing a series of concepts and thoughts – which can be combined easily with these analytical instruments – from the field of political economy or recent economic sociology, in particular the French Regulation Approach, on questions concerning the conditions for the success of proper organisation of work within the firm. This approach does not only distinguish quite systematically different 'productive models' (for example 'standardised mass production', 'innovation and flexibility' or 'quality production'[13]); it also elaborated the idea that corporations have to establish a 'governance compromise' among all of the groups of agents involved, which is as permanent as possible, in order to be able to operate successfully. Within the horizon of this conceptual setting, I wish to introduce two case studies for what I believe to be a successful application of these concepts in the second part of this essay: strategic decisions to change the established productive model in the cases of Volkswagen and Renault will be re-examined so as to broaden our understanding of the possibilities and limits of business strategies. The aim of this undertaking, therefore, is to develop a framework that is able to solve the double problem of business history: to explain the internal processes which result in a company's business strategy (without ignoring external agents in the strict sense), and to place the company into its broader context of suppliers, available workforce, creditors, competitors, and national or international market structures.

The field analysis approach

Let us begin, therefore, with a brief sketch of Bourdieu's field analysis approach. The concept of a 'field' in the double sense – as an arena of agents who struggle for profits, as well as a structure of positions, which are located by the agents' capital – derived from Bourdieu's attempt to overcome the dichotomy between the rigidities of structuralism on the one side and the 'subjectivist' or 'spontanistic' sociology on the other. The result was his 'theory of practice', laid down in numerous books and articles and to be understood as a general theory of action in the sense mentioned above.[14] Regrettably, Bourdieu was unable to complete his 'general theory of fields' – he sometimes also refers to a 'general theory of the economy of fields' – before his death,[15] so that we must revert to compiling Bourdieu's explanations and individual studies made in various different areas (especially those on the fields of the French 'elite universities', on entrepreneurship, and on the fine arts).[16] A social field, as conceived by Bourdieu, has a double character: on the one hand, it represents a structure, i.e. a system of permanent relations, within which each relevant agent and each group of agents finds his, her, or its position. This position is defined by the possession of 'capital', i.e. of those means of power and influence that can be effective in a certain field. In a corporation these are primarily the rights of property, control, rule, participation, and disposal, the ownership of shares in company capital, relevant information about products and production processes, dependence on or towards suppliers, customers, and creditors, etc. On the other hand, such a field represents an arena of confrontations, a battlefield on which these agents wrestle in accordance with their respective interests (conceived in the manner in which they themselves perceive and define their interests, and not according to external theories, which are often economically reduced) for the field-specific profits that have been collaboratively earned. When transferred to business history, this means that an analysis of the company as a field (i.e. a place of production of economic goods and the acquisition of economic profits, as well as goods and profits which can be transferred into economic ones) examines the confrontations between all of these groups, their means of power, their interests and motives, especially to the extent that they refer to decisions on the products to be manufactured, the organisation of their production, and the structure of their working relationships, and thus the continuation of this field (i.e. the company), with the purpose of reconstructing the specific logic of the actions of its agents. The borders of a field – and the distinction between those agents belonging and those not belonging to the field (that is a reformulation of the above-mentioned question 'who is a stakeholder?') – can now be identified sufficiently: the extent of the field is identical with the extent of its effects, and its agents are all those who act within and under the influence of the field. The particular identification can only be made empirically, not a priori. After such an analysis it should hopefully be clear that, firstly, this procedure allows systematic comparisons (mainly, but not only between individual companies), and secondly, the value of universal theories of the company 'as such' is clearly relativised in favour of genuine historical findings.

Bourdieu himself described the epistemological value of this approach very vividly with reference to the workforce of a company:

> In order to truly describe this field [referring to the French watch industry, M.R.], one must include the quality of the workforce, which is very closely connected to the level of training among management, to the wage differences between management and the workforce, to the amount of capital circulating, to the degree of modernity of the machines, etc. Yesterday I conducted an interview with an engineer, who said: the Germans cannot understand – he is an engineer with Siemens –, they say that they have a highly perfected machine, and that it does not work in France. The Germans think immediately: those French, they don't understand it. In reality, the French trade union system is such that company owners cannot use certain machines because they know that the costs of using those machines would be greater than their production profits. Why? Because the workers would resist these machines, and they have the social power of resistance. Thus company owners choose less perfect machines that will save them from union battles. The yield of a machine is influenced by social features, which include the school system, etc. It would be crazy these days to run an economy without an analysis of the school system. You will be told: but we are doing an economy of the school system. In reality, the aim is to treat the school system as an economic agent, as an agent of the production of the producers.[17]

So far, so abstract. Since the field approach does indeed suggest the existence of a general economy of fields, but on the other hand assumes that each field follows its own logic,[18] because it has its own – historically changing! – structure, it is necessary for each new field analysis to compile the categories of study itself, because, for example, the intellectual field of the Federal Republic of the 1950s obviously differs from the field of the large banks in the first half of the twentieth century (not to mention the subfields of the individual credit institutions) or from that of an automobile producer before and after the first oil crisis. Thus fieldwork is very time-intensive and laborious. It therefore makes sense to fall back on previous work.[19]

Bourdieu – and his students, too, if I am right – did not apply the field approach to the investigation level of individual companies or businesses.[20] Some outstanding studies have been published in his milieu, and translated into German, about middle- and senior-level economic managers and their political/ideal needs and remarks,[21] or about workers in the Peugeot factory in Sochaux[22] But it does not seem to have been particularly attractive to Bourdieu to immerse himself in the special capitalistic logic of a commercial enterprise; quite the contrary – it was probably abhorrent to him. So we have to fill the gap by ourselves by trying to conceptualise the firm as a social field in general, and for our intention especially, the field of strategic decision-making within the firm, which is at the core of corporate governance analysis.

For this purpose, we have to distinguish at least three dimensions of power within the field[23] of strategic decision-making which shape the field: The first one is the formally secured authority to decide about the allocation of the corporation's resources. In joint-stock companies, the distribution of this authority is usually laid down in the company constitution (whether there is a Chief Executive Officer or a leading committee of 'peers'), and by company law (single-board system or double-board system), as clearly described in Boris Gehlen's article on this issue.[24] In a double-board system the supervisory board usually controls the first-rank decision-makers and can dismiss them, in other words, its members could establish a new managing committee or a new CEO to change the company's strategy.[25] As we shall see, in the case of Volkswagen, the supervisory board had to dismiss the CEO several times in order to change the company's business strategy effectively. But as the articles of this special issue demonstrate, the degree of participation by the members of the supervisory board oscillates between the control of formal standards for decisions on the one side, and more or less direct influence upon them on the other, especially on strategic decisions which tangle pretty much directly with the property rights of the shareholders. The relationship between the supervisory board's members – as representatives of the shareholders – and the executive board – the committee of the operating managers – is widely discussed from an investor's perspective in terms of the principal–agent-problem. But from a business historian's perspective, the main focus should be on all actions of these groups to define the compromise on the company's strategy, in other words on their ability to induce consensual decision-making.

Moreover, different countries provide by law different scopes and institutions for employee participation in decision-making.[26] And even in large owner-led enterprises the power to decide is commonly not concentrated solely in the hands of the property owners, but distributed in stages. In general terms, this power is spread out within German stock corporations to a higher degree among the members of top management (*Vorstandsmitglieder*) – and this makes them more responsive to consensual solutions, even with employee representatives – than in the UK or in France, where the Président-Directeur General 'once appointed, is king. Such is his autonomy that the law stipulates no criteria at all for the terms and conditions of his employment. […] In France it is the chairman who normally selects the board …, a process which has been likened to the election of the Communist Party in North Korea.'[27] Insiders describe the corporate governance of French large corporations as a 'monarchical system'.[28] CEOs and other board members in the UK seem to hold a position in between.[29]

This dimension – the distribution of formal and direct authority – has to be distinguished from the second dimension of the field, which is set up by more or less informal and indirect economic influence. This indirect influence can take place in the form of the threat to refuse the supply of credit, materials, or work – or the purchase of the company's products. But normally, cutting off the relationship with the company in question (the 'exit'-option) should only be regarded as the extreme option.[30] Convincing management to do something (the 'voice'-option) should be much more common. Business history has a long experience of analysing channels of influence, prominently the supposed power of banks to dominate industry in Central Europe.[31] However, the power of banks is only one aspect of this dimension. Strategic decisions made by a firm's management, affecting the organisation of work, labour conditions, and so on can especially cause concern on the part of employees, resulting in labour disputes, that is, the refusal to work, to induce the decision-makers to change the strategy in question. The case studies introduced in this essay demonstrate the willingness of unions to do so, but also their dependence on formal and informal rules, limits, and possibilities, shaped by the whole (legal) system of labour relations. Probably, the more unions and employees are integrated into the formal system of decision-making by rules of participation and co-determination (in the German case), the less they choose the option of strikes (though of course there are counter-examples). Nevertheless, supplier relations are also affected by any adjustments in a corporation's strategy. As can be demonstrated in the case of Renault (and as is best illustrated by Stephanie Tilly's in-depth analysis[32]), the possibilities to change (or to continue) a given strategy are limited by the supplier firms' capability to ensure quantity and quality on time, so that the demanding firm sometimes has to help its suppliers in financial or technical terms, just to pursue its own strategy.

The third dimension in question is social capital, that is, the agents' capacity to mobilise external resources, because they belong to the same social group as the holder of these resources from outside. Of course, there is an overlap with the second as well as with the first dimension. A good example for this form of capital are trade unions' leaders or shop stewards who belong to the same political party as the minister of economic affairs or labour issues, and who are able to move the minister to intervene in company affairs. Another example can be seen in family networks of entrepreneurs, where members from outside the boards (and maybe even without holding shares) try to influence the management of the firm (or other agents with formal authority) to change or maintain the strategy of the firm (for instance regarding the pay-out) in deference of family interests. A closer look at the state-owned firms in France after 1945 demonstrates the importance of an examination of this social capital. The Président-directeur général (PDGs) of these companies as well as the members of the board of directors and the state administrators who de jure elect the PDGs mostly belong to the 'grands corps' which recruit graduates from the most prestigious and exclusive universities, the 'grands écoles'. Until the 1980s, the state used these corporations for its own purpose – to enforce the economic development of France. Therefore, de facto the PDG was elected by the President of the Republic or by the Prime Minister (or by both). To share the same schools, the same 'grands corps' membership, and the same state career ensured the absence of real oversight and control of the firm, while the PDG felt loyalty only to the President or the Prime Minister.[33] Capital by formal and informal authority, as well as social capital, all in their various forms, can be regarded as the basic dimensions of the firm's field of strategic decision-making. Of course it is possible to combine them, and the model should be open for further dimensions; proof can be made only empirically.

The approach of the French Regulation School[34]

While Bourdieu's approach of field analysis provides something like a general theory of action, we now have to combine it with a concept much closer to business issues. We can borrow from authors from the social sciences, more precisely, from (political) economics, as well as from the sociology of industry, work, and organisations, which – sometimes without explicit reference to Bourdieu – share some important presuppositions (above all a relational perspective), so that the combination of both approaches should be assured. This compatibility can be assumed in the case of the French Regulation School, or better: Regulation Approach.[35]

The Regulation School emerged in the 1970s (incidentally, also under the influence of a movement in historical science, namely the French Annales School) as a Marxist, yet institutional–economic answer to the failure of the Keynesian approaches to recognising and controlling a crisis-free capitalistic economy following the end of the great postwar boom.[36] The French economist Michel Aglietta, one of the founding fathers of the Regulation Approach, wanted to analyse 'the way in which transformations of social relations create new economic and non-economic forms, organized in structures that reproduce a determining structure, the mode of production'.[37] The insistence on social relations is central to the Regulation Approach, as well as the idea that social structures shape the modus operandi for economic action. Though one point of critique has always been the supposed missing link between *structure* and *agency* in the Regulation Approach,[38] the possible convergence with Bourdieu's theory of action is clearly evident.

In the second half of the 1990s, an international research group led by Robert Boyer and Michel Freyssenet, under the banner GERPISA (*Groupe d'Etude et de Recherche Permanent sur l'Industrie et les Salariés de l'Automobile*) made a comparison between the growth strategies of large, globally operating automobile manufacturers, who at the time faced severe problems, especially in Europe and the USA. Around a dozen studies were published after 1998.[39] The starting point and intellectual challenge was the famous MIT study 'The Machine that Changed the World' by Womack and others from 1990,[40] which Boyer and Freyssenet countered with the thesis 'The World that Changed the Machine',[41] after they had emphatically rejected the idea of the 'one best way' of corporate strategy in a sector (and especially beyond that).[42] The MIT study had postulated that the entire global automobile industry would soon adopt the Japanese model of 'lean production' – or else perish. With a similar scientific and at the same time politically engaged air to that of Bourdieu, Boyer and Freyssenet also opposed such reductionist ideas that claimed universal validity. Instead, they drafted a complex but operational model of mediation between the macro level of the national *growth modus*, determined by factors such as the most important *growth source*, the *distribution modus* of the profits and *market structures*, and the micro level of the companies.

To briefly explain these terms:[43] The primary *sources of growth*, in particular for western economies after the Second World War, were and are still based on both a rapidly expanding domestic demand (especially for mass consumption goods) and on revenues that could (and can) be gained by the export of various different goods: mass industrial goods in price-sensitive markets, or specialised and high-quality goods, for which there is less marked price competition. Comprehensive raw material exports are somewhat an exception (such as in the United Kingdom, where economic growth was initially – and now again since the end of the 1970s – based on the fact that real prices sank constantly in mostly liberalised markets).

During the decades of the boom, the typical ('nationally regulated') *distribution modus* for profits thus achieved, created relatively small spreads in income in a historical comparison, not least due to the strong trade union organisations at these times. However, the extent of the coordination of income distribution at national level differed greatly, depending on tradition and the strength of the organisations involved. Here again, the United Kingdom is a special case in Western Europe (at least among democratic societies), due to the equally flexible and fragmented labour markets and the importance of the financial market during the decades of the boom. Interestingly enough, two of the most prominent economies in continental Western Europe, France and (West-)Germany, differ fundamentally in this regard. While French unions pushed strongly for higher wages in the 1960s, the 1970s and 1980s, putting workers' militancy at stake, their power eroded significantly during the 1990s. On the other hand, German unions developed a more cooperative way of interaction with highly corporatist employees, described as 'conflict-partnership'. In the long run, German unions were able to defend workers' interests much more successfully during the 1990s and after (or at least longer) than their French counterparts.

The greatest national differences existed with regard to *market structures*, despite the general spread of mass consumption. The smaller the differences in income during the decades of boom, the more continuous were the gradations of the market segments, which for example allowed the manufacturers of durable consumer goods (automobiles, kitchen devices, etc.) to diversify their product range, in other words, to be represented in every market segment with their own products. Therefore, the productive model 'volume and product differentiation' was more widespread (at least in the automobile industry) than the model of the pure 'large-scale production', which was based on the tendency to manufacture only one single model (for example: the Volkswagen 'Beetle') in large and ever-increasing quantities, to be offered at decreasing prices.

Such *economies of scale*, where fixed costs are spread across as large a production volume as possible in order to keep unit prices low, thus represent the first of the six *profit sources* as differentiated systematically by the recent Regulation Approach.[44] Company strategies are based on these profit sources; however, from a theoretical perspective, the profit sources in themselves do not represent a strategy as such, but instead must be utilised to this end. Other *profit sources* are, first, *product quality*, which allow higher prices to be attained and new markets (especially in the upper ranges) to be conquered. Secondly, *product differentiation* allows demands in different (sub-) markets to be met. Third, *product innovation* leads to profits from new products, especially when a company manages to capture as large a market share as possible in this new market for a longer period (in extreme cases: as sole provider). Fourth and fifth, profits can be gained not only based on the quantity and quality of the products, but also by adjusting the production organisation: on the one hand by means of *flexibility*, where production costs are adapted quickly to market fluctuations, on the other hand with *continuous cost reductions*, which safeguard profit margins. Of course, such pure forms are not found in capitalist practice, but rather always mixed forms, but the Regulation Approach nevertheless assumes that these different profit sources can neither be randomly combined, nor can they be equally exhausted, which is why it is necessary for companies to set priorities by developing *profit strategies*. In a sense, these *profit strategies* represent the sum of the skimming off of profit sources in certain markets (see above: *market structures*) with certain groups of employees by means of a specific *product policy*, which corresponds with a particular *production organisation*, which in turn is bound to – in each case specific – forms of *work relationships*. It is assumed that companies in a sector differ primarily with regard to their profit strategies. The 'sum' of these working units represents the so-called 'governance compromise in the company', which the relevant (aforementioned) groups of agents must negotiate, and which must be constant, in order to guarantee the profit opportunities of the company.

Incidentally, there is considerable agreement on this point with similar concepts used in the fields of political economics or economic sociology, albeit these are less systematically related to each other (since they come from different research contexts). The mediation between the macro level of an entire economy, the meso level of the industries (or regions), and the micro level of the company appears to be less stringent than in the recent Regulation Approach: they include models such as 'standardised mass production', 'diversified quality production',[45] 'flexible mass production',[46] 'flexible specialisation',[47] and so on.

In terms of embedding the *profit strategies* in each of the national growth modes[48] explained above, Boyer and Freyssenet identify six different *production models* for the automobile industry:

> Productive models can be defined as company-specific governance compromises. A productive model enables the permanent implementation of a profit strategy, if it is adapted to the growth modus of the country in which the company is active. The means used (product policy, production organization, labour relationships) must be coherent and acceptable to all agents involved.[49]

In principle, it is possible for companies to change the productive model; however, such a change involves considerable costs and risks, which is why it is generally done only during severe company crises. Examples of two such cases are presented below. What is especially important for the questions we are pursuing here is Boyer and Freyssenet's emphasis on the layout of labour relations.

It can be seen, for example from the aforementioned strategy of large-scale production, that a primarily merely semi-skilled workforce was sufficient – such as in the case of Volkswagen. Production sites were located outside of large industrial areas and, until the 1960s, the workforce was mainly composed of former refugees and labour migrants, who were attracted less by dreams of a fulfilling and varied job, but rather by the promise of higher wages.

While these workforce groups were certainly well-organised (which enabled them to enforce higher wages), they did not see any reason to fight for greater autonomy in the workplace, and no group-specific remuneration system applied to them, but rather a summary scheme related to the entire company. Incidentally, Boyer and Freyssenet call the 'large-scale production' model 'Fordism', after the production methods of the Ford Motor Company that were developed in the 1910s. However, Boyer and Freyssenet do not adopt the misleading normative meaning of the concept as a 'societal model of the short twentieth century' which became attractive to the ideologists and practitioners of authoritarian regimes, particularly during the first half of the so-called 'High Modernity'.[50]

Better qualified employees in the production process, who defended – at times militantly – their workplace autonomy and their right to have group-related wages negotiated by trusted representatives (as was the case in numerous British manufacturers), regularly rejected the specific production organisation and the labour relationships that were the prerequisites for pure large-scale production. This is why the companies in this situation did not manage to convert to the 'Fordist' productive model, even though the market structures after the Second World War would have presented the opportunity to do so due to more equal income distribution.

If, in contrast, a sufficient number of qualified workers was available, and if the employment relationships remained more stable than average, then further options arose, especially when creditors remained patient and made no short-term or exaggerated returns claims. (Remarkably, many renowned European automobile producers were and still are either controlled by owner-families or owned at least in part by the state, which mostly protected them from the pressure of the capital markets.) This means that management could guarantee job security, even in times of crisis,[51] which in turn encouraged employees to attain further qualifications, even if they were only of value to their current employer (and not transferrable to other companies). This constellation allowed companies to enter into quality production and to offer products that acted as status symbols for wealthy customers on markets that were not dominated by price competition, but rather by quality distinction and which therefore promised (and still promise) a higher or more stable profit margin.[52] Creditors expected above all a stable interest return from this productive model. Until the end of the twentieth century, however, in the case of the global automobile industry the quality strategy was limited to niche producers, due to the market structures, i.e. the relatively small market niches of the upper class. It was only at the turn of the millennium that Volkswagen managed, through aggressive branding (which also included the purchase of some niche producers) and a more quality-aware product policy, to offer high-quality models as a status symbol in every market segment. It thus successfully combined the quality strategy with the profit strategy 'volume and product differentiation', and transferred this to the broadest group of buyers (as far as I am aware, no sound research has yet been conducted on this subject). Ironically, the vulnerability of this profit strategy is demonstrated by the fact that the same corporation (Volkswagen) undermined its own branding as a quality producer by cheating on controls of exhaust emission standards.

Another possibility is to quickly occupy new market niches in order to gain high profits with innovative models, so long as there are only a few competitors in these markets. This productive model, called 'Hondaism' by Boyer and Freyssenet, is based on a very innovative product policy and requires a production organisation that is able, on the one hand, to switch models quickly, and on the other hand, to limit losses rapidly by means of production changeover. This requires a workforce that is sufficiently qualified, adaptable, and proactive (which must be encouraged by the design of labour relations), in order to guarantee this flexibility. This productive model is also dependent on patient creditors, prepared to bear the loss risk of relatively frequent production changeovers and the aggressive market strategy. So the success of profit strategies is determined not only by the question of whether the strategies of companies are adapted to the national growth modus, but whether it is possible to establish a stable reconciliation of interests within the company. This so-called 'governance compromise in the company' must coordinate product policy, production organisation and employee relations. Which brings us back to the field approach.

Even at first glance it is clear that a category such as 'profit strategy' can be very easily understood as the specific logic of a company (conceived as a 'field') that is embedded in a further field – that of the national 'growth modus'. The subfield 'company', in turn, represents a permanent balance of power between the relevant agents, which produces its own logic of action – the 'profit strategy'. This strategy, which need not be known in its entirety by all of the agents, is manifested in more or less stable patterns of action, which (must) obey the logic of the game.

The mediation between the two analytical approaches

There are obviously large similarities between the Regulation Approach and Bourdieu's categories with regard to *strategy*, the key theoretical concept of action. The greatest agreement is certainly the basic assumption on both sides that agents can by no means freely choose a random strategy, but rather that they are bound to the broader context of action. *Strategy*, therefore, is the point where Bourdieu's concepts and the Regulation School do converge. Some of the factors that determine the selection of a successful profit strategy by a company within the scope of the Regulation Approach (workforce, market structures) were described above. Bourdieu, in turn, describes the context of action in general, and calls it a 'game':

> 'Game' can also be understood to mean: that a series of people participate in a regulated activity, an activity that does not necessarily arise from the following of rules, but which obeys certain regularities. 'Game' is the place where there is an immanent necessity, which at the same time is an immanent logic. In a game, one may not simply do just anything.[53]

In this 'game', all of the agents and groups in a company are involved, but they do not all play the game equally well – otherwise there would be no insolvencies, no unsuccessful strikes, no egotistical shop stewards, and trade unions would have enormous numbers of members. For a 'game' must always involve a 'sense of the game': 'The "sense of the game", which contributes to that necessity and logic, represents the knowledge of this necessity and logic. Whoever wants to win the game, must acquire stakes, catch the ball, i.e. play a good game with all of the associate advantages, must have a "sense of the game", in other words sense of the inner necessity and logic of the game.'[54] The sense of the game is therefore not aimed at conscious or calculated actions, but rather represents a result of previous experience (and therefore ultimately the *history* of the agents): Bourdieu defines the term 'strategy' as explicitly not the 'outflow of a conscious, rational calculation'. Instead 'strategy is rather the product of a practical sense as a "sense of the game", a sense for a historically determined, particularly social game (...) The good player, in a sense the game in human form, does whatever is required and demanded by the game at all times. This demands continuous invention, in order to adapt to the endlessly variable, never quite identical situations.'[55] Thus the selection of a certain strategy by an agent (or a group) is not free, but rather socially determined, and yet at the same time open, and its success depends on the ability to anticipate the further course of the story (of the 'game').

The proximity of such a concept of strategy to Bourdieu's own category of 'habitus' (which is central to his approach) is obvious: 'the habitus as a "sense of the game" is the social game that has become incorporated, second nature. Nothing is at the same time freer *and* more compulsive than the actions of the good player.'[56] From a theoretical perspective as a model – and the empirical findings do not contradict this assumption – none of the agents in a company, therefore, can break out of the habitual limits of the possibilities for action, neither the doorman nor the personnel manager. Incidentally, the significance of habitual characterisation for the choices and actions of economic decision-makers – which naturally include not only company managers, see above! – is considered to be extremely high in recent economic-sociological and -psychological studies.[57]

Thus, the concept of 'strategy' can work as a link between the methodological approach of Bourdieu's sociology on the one side and the epistemological interests of the Regulation School on the other. This means Bourdieu's concepts can be used as tools to resolve one of the major conceptual problems of the latter, i.e. the systematic connection between the national mode of growth, or the profit strategy of a single firm (both are too often treated as if they were static), and the decisions, struggles, and alliances among different socio-economic groups (where 'class-struggle' is only one distinct form of action), or, in other words, the players' games and strategies within the economic (and political) fields of action. The openness of the Regulation Approach for such a combination can easily be demonstrated by its definition of what is called a company's profit strategy: this represents not so much a sequence of consciously calculated actions, but rather a 'mostly unintended process for the production of internal coherence of change processes and coordination with external requirements'.[58] However, at the level of the company's strategic orientation, exercised by company management, the focus is less on studying the actions of some individuals; rather, the concept of strategy represents the product of the 'collective sense of the game' of all of the agents involved. Two short examples illustrate the methodological possibilities of this 'combined field approach'.

Two case studies: VW and Renault as state-affiliated automobile producers

During the 1970s and 1980s, the two large European automobile producers Volkswagen and Renault experienced extensive changes to their productive models:[59] VW transformed from a 'Fordist'-organised one-model volume producer to the supplier of a graduated range of models, but with a continued large (indeed increasing) production volume. During nearly the same time-span, Renault changed its productive model from *volume and product differentiation* to *innovation and flexibility*. To explain these transformations, the field analysis approach enables us to compare the strategic decisions within companies systematically. Nevertheless, because we are looking for an explanation of strategic transformations, we have to adjust the setting of our inquiry – which is the field of action in both case studies. The aim is not to examine 'normal' struggles for the distribution of company returns, but strategic decisions, especially in times of crisis, when there might be no profits to be distributed. I suppose that this field of strategic action, or better: this 'field of power' within one corporation is best visible in times of crisis when problems demand a strategic transformation of the firm, including a new corporate governance compromise among all the relevant groups of agents. Needless to say, this compromise entails a new modus operandi of distributing company profits, which is why all relevant groups put all their capital into the balance in this arena (and probably only in this place).

This transformation of the productive model – from pure large-scale production to the 'volume and product differentiation' model[60] – was the result of a severe company crisis in 1974/75, when the VW Beetle (the 'one model') was obviously obsolete in terms of technology and design. The transformation was successful only because company management was able to negotiate a new governance compromise with both the workforce and the shareholders. The conversion from the 'Beetle' to the production of the Golf, Polo, and Passat (as well as the new Audi models), which drew VW back into profit in 1976, was achieved only through severe cuts in the organisation of production and in labour relations. Most of the automated processes in bodywork construction had to be reduced, and the flexibility of the machines used had to be greatly increased, in order to be able to build the Golf in different versions. This had a considerable effect on the workforce because Volkswagen was now 'overstaffed', and the remaining employees feared a reduction in their wage levels. Nevertheless, the works committee (Volkswagen did not belong to the *Gesamtmetall* employers' association so working conditions had to be negotiated with management directly) still managed to negotiate an agreement. However, this was only after the IG Metall union (prominently represented on the supervisory board) had in 1975 played a decisive role in securing the replacement of Kurt Lotz, then Chief Executive Officer, by Toni Schmücker,[61] the former labour director of a codetermined steel producer. The solution consisted on the one hand in the stopping of redundancies, and on the other in a new remuneration system (although this wasn't introduced until 1980), which minimised the income risks to employees by means of downgrading and created new wage committees with equal representation. Membership in an employers' association would have made such an agreement impossible, and indeed *Gesamtmetall* attacked the agreement immediately.[62] The 'socially acceptable' reduction in staff was carried out primarily through three measures: firstly, the non-extension of temporary contracts (those affected included 13,000 labour migrants), secondly, with severance payments for voluntary redundancies, and thirdly, by means of early retirement regulations. In addition, a recruitment freeze was announced. The special layout of labour relations and the specific governance structure of the company opened up a room for manoeuvre, which facilitated the consensual transformation of Volkswagen's profit strategy. Some of this was due to the close relationships between the CEO and the head of the works committee, which contributed greatly to the mutual trust between management and staff; trust that was anchored institutionally by the statutory rules on co-determination. Furthermore, the state influence on Volkswagen guaranteed a certain 'patience' on the part of shareholders, which gave enough time to all of the agents to deal with the change in strategy.[63] The good labour relations and the intact governance compromise therefore eased the change in profit strategy for company management, and thus also the change in the productive model. This way of solving the problem by changing the business strategy also had the by-effect of strengthening the works committee vis-à-vis management.[64]

This mutual approach to overcoming crisis, during which around 30,000 workers left the firm, marked the way forward for overcoming the next company crisis 20 years later. Once again, VW had 30,000 employees too many, and once again, mutual agreement was reached (this time with the inclusion of suppliers, i.e. groups of agents who are frequently ignored in conventional corporate history). In a number of contributions to the aforementioned GERPISA studies, Ulrich Jürgens has shown that these crisis solutions – indeed, not even the conditions of the crises themselves! – were not the result of some 'freely' made decisions by VW management, but rather that the entire field of forces within the company must be traced backed for an explanation. This force field was composed not only of company management and staff – capital and labour – who faced each other in either conflict or cooperation. Rather, the structure of the forces in the 'VW field' were determined once again and in a unique manner by the combination of German co-determination in large concerns, and the strong position – secured in the VW Act of 1960[65] – of the federal state of Lower Saxony (which was structurally weak in terms of industry and therefore very interested in the existence of the company and its jobs, and which therefore rejected Thatcherite crisis solutions). The negotiated compromises led, among other things, to a reduction in individual working hours to 28.8 h and the introduction of the '5000 for 5000' scheme in 2001 (which strengthened the VW works committee by sharing competencies in designing working conditions) with the explicit goal of limiting unemployment in the city of Wolfsburg and surrounding districts. The works committee forced through the deal that 51,000 older workers who took early retirement between 1975 and 1996 were replaced by 26,000 younger workers, following completion of their training. In addition, at the end of the 1990s, so-called 'site symposiums' were called into being, which institutionalised the exchange between the executive board and the overall works committee, and between management and the works committee at each site. None of these measures were self-evident or undisputed. They even gave Volkswagen the reputation of being a kind of 'socialist company' (as the Wall Street Journal Europe called it).[66]

Yet it could be argued, in contrast, that it was (and still is) precisely the German laws on co-determination that provided crisis solutions to managers not available to companies outside Germany. Within the horizon of the field analysis therefore, worker co-determination increases the scope for decision-making and thus the 'power' of company management (instead of restricting it, as is often claimed). For this finding alone, and of course for a more precise examination of this thesis, I believe that a comparative field analysis is worthwhile. However, VW management followed a cooperative, integrative path to reconfirm the governance compromise not only with these strong agents in the 1990s, but also with supplier companies. Admittedly these were forced by Ignacio Lopez, the board member with responsibility for purchasing and production organisation, to compromise on price, but they were also involved in the development of components required by VW by means of technology transfer.

In contrast, an otherwise increasingly stronger group of agents played hardly any role in these decisions (and this was in fact the prerequisite for the crisis solving strategy just outlined): the representatives of the financial markets. They criticised not only this strategy, but the whole corporate governance of VW per se: The Volkswagen Law, the state shares in capital and co-determination. All of this protected Volkswagen against hostile takeovers, subdued all 'share price fantasies' – and weakened the position of these confident groups of agents in the field. As long as VW remained economically successful, this relative autonomy from the financial markets obviously strengthened the productive model of the company by creating time and room for manoeuvre in which to constantly adapt its own profit strategy to the changing market conditions.

The second case study presented here is a section in the history of Renault. Following the end of the large postwar boom in the 1970s, Renault also changed its productive model. However, until that point, Renault had not practised the pure large-scale production of the Fordist productive model, but had already embarked on 'diversified mass production' in the 1960s. One of the problems for Renault was that this transition took place at a time which was characterised in France by a 'crisis of labour'.[67] In this context, however, the term 'crisis of labour' does not refer to the claimed lack of jobs, but – quite to the contrary – to a considerable increase in social conflicts regarding wages, working conditions, etc. This was fuelled not least by continued full employment, and led to a crisis in labour relations and thus, in the 1970s, to a severe crisis in the governance compromise of the company.

With regard to the product policy, the wage system and the production organisation (in which, for example, assembly line production played only a minor role) Renault, by around 1960 at the latest, followed the strategy of *volume and product differentiation*, and the dynamic of domestic mass consumption made this strategy very successful at first. One foundation of success was the 1955 agreement with many unions (including the strongest, CGT), which stabilised labour relationships for about 20 years. Among other things, this secured a renouncement of lockouts and strikes, and the linking of wages to the cost-of-living index, in effect the inflation rate. The unions at Renault were strong, although there was no solid relationship of trust between the company management and the workers.

When, at the end of the 1960s, assembly line production grew, the number of unskilled workers – including many labour migrants – increased within the constantly growing work-force (certainly a politically-driven development in the state company Renault), and in light of declining workplace autonomy, work satisfaction sank rapidly.[68] At the same time, profit-ability declined dramatically, especially due to higher wages and a high depreciation require-ment. The protesters were primarily young, unskilled workers, who had no chance of promotion within the company (an option that was available to the skilled workers only). Furthermore, monthly incomes changed constantly as a result of the continuous reorgani-sations, which increased dissatisfaction and caused a large degree of fluctuation amongst the workforce – made possible by full employment – and absenteeism. These conflicts were also aggravated by the fact that the CGT, affiliated to the Communist Party, received com-petition 'from the left', from the Maoist Gauche Prolétarienne, so that the confrontations about pay and working conditions were superimposed by attempts to carry the political class battle into the factories, with the state company Renault proving to be a particularly prominent target.

Consequently, between 1968 and 1973, there was no year without large labour conflicts in one of the Renault factories, and the initiators were always the unskilled workers. The common solution was to grant wage increases (and not to change the work organisation that was responsible for the dissatisfaction in the first place!) and a reduction in wage scales. Under the slogan 'same work, same pay' (which was also codified in the Labour Code), the unions pushed through the deal that no less than one quarter of the unskilled workers (around 15,000) were to be categorised in the highest wage category of skilled workers between 1972 and 1975.

However, the Renault management reacted only very hesitantly to these problems. It did not make any energetic efforts to render production apparatus more flexible, nor did it succeed in stabilising labour relations. In addition, Renault took over various troubled foreign companies on the orders of the state during the 1970s, which made the controllability of the corporation more difficult and pushed up debts. The first oil crisis broke the French growth trend of high domestic demand, which had been borne by the increasing purchasing power of broad sections of the population, and Renault went well into the red.[69] Company growth did continue, as Renault was not as strongly affected by the collapse in sales figures on the French and European markets as its competitors were, thanks to its attractive models (especially the R4 and the R5). In 1979 and 1980, the last year in which the firm still made profits for a long time, Renault came to be the largest car-maker in Europe, with a production volume of roughly 2 million cars per year.[70] However, costs could no longer be kept under control, and general management tried to reduce wage increases. Moreover, the unions demanded that all employees working in production should be categorised as skilled work-ers. As a result, labour conflicts escalated in 1977, when enraged strikers detained the Chief Executive Officer, Bernard Vernier-Paillez, in the factory at Billancourt and management, in turn, fired the CGT representative at the site. Renault's governance compromise lay in ruins.

Soon, increasing unemployment in France shifted the balance of power towards management. After pressure from the state, the wage development was decoupled from the development of the inflation rate, and strikes were occasionally beaten back with the help of the police. But the company's austerity programmes came too late, debts increased (to 46% of turnover), its market share in France dropped dramatically again in the early 1980s, and by 1984 Renault was facing bankruptcy. In 1984 and 1985 Renault suffered losses of more than 11 billion FFR.[71]

In this existential crisis, Renault changed its profit strategy and its productive model; establishing in the end a quite new corporate governance compromise. The volume and product differentiation strategy, with its inherently high costs and its low control capacity was abandoned in order to lower the profit threshold. In 1984, PDG Bernard Hanon had proposed the lay-off of some 15,000 workers, but widespread strikes, led by the CGT, obstructed this plan.[72] Obviously, the unions still had resources of considerable informal power to influence the company's strategy. Besides that, the then Socialist government replaced Hanon as PDG with Georges Besse early in 1985. It is nonetheless very questionable whether the union leaders' social capital prompted the French government to do so, because Besse was even tougher in changing Renault's strategy against the unions than Hanon. The most massive lay-offs to be suffered by the Renault workforce occurred around 1985 under Besse's directorate, when nearly 12,000 workers lost their jobs (though most of them were received by state-funded early retirement schemes).[73] Though labour disputes escalated – workers occupied buildings of the Renault plants, managers were sequestrated, armed police troops secured free access to the plants, and finally terrorists assassinated Besse in 1986 –, all these attempts to influence management failed. This pressure from the workers was resisted by the decision-makers with formal authority, first and foremost the PDG, as well as by those with informal authority, namely the French government, and both were backed by high unemployment. But in spite of these 'victories', Renault's governance compromise lay in ruins and had to be replaced by a new one.

The first step in this direction was the withdrawal of the state, which renounced a lot of its indirect influence on the corporation. This was due to different reasons. On the one hand, the Renault management called for more room to manoeuvre, in order to restructure the whole strategy and organisation of the firm. On the other, the European Commission demanded the privatisation of Renault, because the firm had received massive subsidies up to 1986.[74] So the liberal-conservative Chirac government planned to privatise Renault. The withdrawal of the state was only one side of the new corporate governance compromise, freeing management (especially the PDG) from strong governmental influence and control. The other involved management getting rid of the influence exercised up to that point by the unions. The largest Renault plant, Billancourt, a stronghold of the CGT, was closed in 1992, after a massive reduction of the workforce during the 1980s. The second largest plant, Flins, was also downsized. Both plants employed most of the low-skilled workers – the prime cause for the troubles during the recent decades.[75] The domestic workforce in the automobile branch fell from more than 100,000 in 1980 to less than 80,000 in 1986, but the process of downsizing continued; after 1994 the number dropped under 60,000, falling to little more than 40,000 in 2007. With the exception of the year of 1996, income at Renault was more or less stable, but the numbers of workers had fallen dramatically.[76] Renault had been a symbol for the French growth model since 1945; assuming this was still true after the 1970s, the economic problem of France was not the competitiveness of its industry, but the fact that by then French industry needed fewer workers to make profits.

Back at Renault, no more discussions were held with the CGT with a view to weakening the union; company shares and subsidiaries were sold and the company organisation was centralised in order to increase the internal control capability. Above all, however, there were dramatic job cuts; while Renault now built 'cars for living' (as stated in an official advertising slogan in the 1990s), it no longer created jobs for a whole lifetime career. Within only three years, from 1984 to 1987, the number of workers in car construction declined by more than one quarter, whereby older workers were given early retirement. There were no negotiations with the unions on this point: while there were some factory sit-ins by the workers after the announcement of the job-cutting programmes, the police quickly put an end to them, and the CGT representatives were fired. The socialist government placed itself firmly on the side of the company management.

The turnaround was achieved in 1987; Renault returned to the profit zone. In the previous year, however, the CEO of the company had been shot dead by radical left-wing terrorists. By 1990 the new Renault productive model had taken clear shape. With new and innovative models such as the Clio, the Espace, and the R19, as well as a quality offensive, Renault successfully occupied or created different market areas. In the factories, not only was production organised more flexibly: more flexible working hours, more challenging jobs, and internal qualification programmes and promotion opportunities (which had opened up not least because of the exit of the much older colleagues) laid the foundation for improved work relations. In 1989 the company management concluded an agreement with various trade unions (significantly not with the CGT!), establishing the new governance compromise. The 'innovation and flexibility' productive model brought Renault continuously increasing profits, even if conflicts over pay remained on the agenda. The firm was privatised in 1995 – the state was no longer needed as owner.

Conclusion

The different paths taken by Volkswagen and Renault since the 1960s demonstrate both strong similarities and clear differences. In addition, both were symbols of the German and the French national productive model respectively. On the one hand, both were state-owned or state-affiliated companies with a strong trade union presence, which were forced to change their previously successful productive model during a severe company crisis. On the other hand, Renault – in contrast to Volkswagen – changed its profit strategy without any consideration of the unions, indeed it even tried (successfully) to break their power. These differences speak against summarising both cases under the same concept of 'Rhenish Capitalism'. Indeed, further research might suggest that Albert's phrase was primarily political, coined to convince the French people (especially the political and economic elites) to adopt elements of the German productive model into the French one.

A comparison of these two cases not only shows how different company strategies can be used within the same sector: it also demonstrates the dependence of a firm's successful strategy on the social, political, and economic context, i.e. on the dominant rational productive model. Obviously, these models differed to such a scale that one can hardly speak of one 'Rhenish' model. Beyond this, our brief examination illustrates that a systematic comparison as such is only possible with uniform categories of inquiry, such as those provided by the recent Regulation Approach and the field analysis. At the same time, it is clear that the strategies of the economic agents involved in these confrontations were by no means ever only aimed at immediate profit or wage maximisation. Categories such as 'trust' – and its institutional guarantee – played a large role, which in turn highlights the importance of explanatory approaches and methods that are enriched by cultural history.

A combination of the concept of social fields with that of the productive models can help, therefore, to explain why productive models do change, or, are transformed. Different groups of agents with different (not necessarily solely economic) aims struggle for the product of their work by sheer economic power, information, militancy, or in coalitions. The strength of their economic, social and political asserts determines the result of these struggles, i.e. the continuation of or the change of the existing productive model. Here we have tried to examine such a process on the level of the firm. In this sense, economic and corporate history, as well as the history of industrial labour, still have a wide field ahead; it is only through this perspective that the firm as a social and political place becomes visible at all.

Notes

1. Chandler, *Strategy and Structure*.
2. Pierenkemper, *Unternehmensgeschichte*; Berghoff, *Moderne Unternehmensgeschichte*; Plumpe, 'Unternehmen'; Plumpe, 'Wie entscheiden Unternehmen?'; Erker, 'Aufbruch'; Erker, 'New Business History'; Erker, 'Externalisierungsmaschine'; Casson, *Unternehmer*.
3. Priemel, *Flick*; Lorentz, *Chemie und Politik*; Erker 'Corporate Governance'; Marx, *Paul Reusch*; Bähr, 'Corporate Governance'.
4. For the German debate on the corporate governance approach see Erker, 'Corporate Governance'.
5. Marx, *Paul Reusch*.
6. Freeman, *Strategic Management*.
7. See for example Chandler and Daems, 'Rise' (Introduction).
8. Mitchell, Agle, and Wood, 'Theory of Stakeholder Identification', 853–886.
9. Borchardt, 'Property Rights-Ansatz', 140–156.
10. Casson, *Unternehmer*, 524–544; Casson, *Entrepreneur*. A brief overview can be found in Berghoff, *Unternehmensgeschichte*, 39–41.
11. Cf. for example Wischermann, Borscheid, and Ellerbrock (eds.), *Unternehmenskommunikation*; Wischermann et al. (eds.), *Unternehmenskommunikation* (cf. on this point the review by Schug in: H-Soz-u-Kult, 16.08.2004, https://hsozkult.geschichte.hu-berlin.de/rezensionen/2004-3-100 (retrieved on 26.09.2013). On other criticism, cf. Welskopp, *Unternehmenskulturen*, 265–272.
12. Some examples that can be named here include Lauschke, *Hoesch-Arbeiter*; Süß, *Kumpel*; Rosenberger, *Experten*; cf. also the contribution by Mark Spoerer to the discussion on the status of corporate historical research, Spoerer, *Mikroökonomie*. Recent anthologies, which provide introductions and overviews, at least document a careful opening of the *mainstream* of economic and corporate history to action- and agent-related approaches. Cf. Pierenkemper, *Unternehmensgeschichte*; Berghoff, *Unternehmensgeschichte*; Plumpe, 'Unternehmen'.
13. The concept 'diversified quality production' was developed more or less independently from the Regulation Approach by the German political economists Wolfgang Streeck and Arndt Sorge. Cf. Sorge and Streeck, 'Industrial Relations'; Streeck, 'Institutional Conditions'; Sorge and Streeck, 'Diversified quality production'.
14. Bourdieu, *Entwurf*; Bourdieu, *Sozialer Sinn*; Bourdieu, *Praktische Vernunft*.
15. Bourdieu, 'Genese', 71, 73; Bourdieu, *Anthropologie*, 124–147.
16. Bourdieu, *Staatsadel*; Bourdieu, *Homo Academicus*; Bourdieu., *Regeln der Kunst*; Bourdieu et al., 'Kapital und Bildungskapital'.
17. Bourdieu, 'Ökonomie', 85–86.
18. Boltanski, *Führungskräfte*.

19. Sociological attempts: Dörre and Brinkmann, 'Finanzmarkt-Kapitalismus'.
20. However, Bourdieu himself presented a critical analysis of some fundamental economic categories and the social conditions of their practical application. Cf. Bourdieu, 'Das Ökonomische Feld'.
21. Boltanski and Chiapello, *Geist*.
22. Beaud and Pialoux, *Zukunft*.
23. This is related to Bourdieus concept of 'capital' that structures a social field. Cf. Bourdieu, 'Ökonomisches Kapital'.
24. Gehlen, 'Corporate Law'.
25. For case-studies in banking history see Reitmayer, *Bankiers*. For general and international trends, though primarily concerned with managerial capitalism and the growth of corporations see Daems and Van der Wee (eds.), *Rise*; Chandler and Daems (eds.), *Hierarchies*; see also the vast literature on corporate governance problems in footnotes 3 and 4.
26. For an overview see Ferner and Hyman (eds.), *Relations*.
27. Maclean, 'Corporate Governance', 102, 104.
28. Schmidt, *From State*, 389.
29. Maclean, 'Corporate Governance', 103.
30. Hirschman, *Exit*.
31. Winkler (ed.), *Kapitalismus*; Wellhöner, *Großbanken*; Tanner, 'Bankenmacht', 19–34.
32. Tilly, 'Supplier relations'.
33. Schmidt, *From State*, 386–392.
34. Boyer and Saillard (eds), Regulation Theory; Hollingsworth and Boyer (eds), Contemporary Capitalism For a criticism and discussion of the Regulation approach, see Jessop, 'Review'; Atzmüller, 'Fit mach mit?'; Röttger, 'Glanz und Elend'.
35. Though Jessop insists on speaking of the *Parisian* Regulation Approach, since different French 'schools' did exist, for example one closer to orthodox Marxism and another established at the University of Grenoble, both with little connection to Paris. Very obviously, Jessop himself does not belong to any of them. Jessop, 'Review'.
36. Numerous 'canonical' texts of the Regulation approach are compiled in Bob Jessop five volumes of edition *Regulation Theory and the Crisis of Capitalism*.
37. Aglietta, cited in Boyer and Saillard (eds.), *Regulation Theory*, 1.
38. *Ibid.*, 2.
39. Cf. Boyer and Freyssenet, *Produktionsmodelle*, 153–154.
40. Womack, Jones, and Roos, *Machine*.
41. Boyer and Freyssenet, *World*.
42. Freyssenet et al. (eds.), *One Best Way?*
43. Cf. for the following Boyer and Freyssenet, *Produktionsmodelle*.
44. Boyer and Freyssenet, *Produktionsmodelle*, 36–37.
45. Streeck, 'Institutional Conditions'.
46. Boyer, *The Eighties*.
47. Piore and Sabel, *Massenproduktion*, 286–307.
48. The Regulation approach dedicates a separate research field to the problem that arises when a productive model is 'transplanted' by developing production facilities in countries with a different growth modus – in other words, the 'hybridisation' of productive models. Cf. Boyer et al., *Imitation*.
49. Boyer and Freyssenet, *Produktionsmodelle*, 43.
50. Hachtmann, 'Fordismus', in: Docupedia-Zeitgeschichte 27.10.2011, URL: https://docupedia.de/zg/Fordismus?oldid=84605 (retrieved on 23.09.2013); Boyer and Freyssenet, *Produktionsmodelle*, 73–85. A flexible and undogmatic definition of Fordism can be found in: Boyer, 'French Statism'; Herbert, 'Europe'.
51. For example, this constellation took the following form at Daimler-Benz in the 1970s: normally, customers had to wait many months before receiving a new Mercedes, i.e. a high-quality status symbol. If received orders declined, the company could use this waiting period as a 'buffer' and shorten it without having to lay off a single employee. The market structure, labour relationships

and profit strategy were therefore mostly coherent, and acted as a model for VW. Cf. Jürgens, *Development*, 289.

52. This was described emphatically, taking the company BASF as an example. Cf. Abelshauser, *BASF*; Abelshauser, *Kulturkampf*; Abelshauser, *Deutsche Wirtschaftsgeschichte*.
53. Bourdieu, *Regel*, 85.
54. Bourdieu, *Regel*, 85.
55. Bourdieu, *Regel*, 83.
56. Bourdieu, *Regel*, 84.
57. Cf. Koller, 'Psychologie und Produktion'.
58. Boyer and Freyssenet, *Produktionsmodelle*, 25.
59. The following examination is based on: Jürgens, *Development*; Jürgens, 'Final Chapter', in: Freyssenet (ed.), *Second Automobile Revolution*, 225–245; Freyssenet, *Renault*, 371–377; Freyssenet, 'Renault, 1992–2007'; Hancké, *Large Firms*.
60. Tolliday, 'Enterprise', 273–350; Wellhöner, *Wirtschaftswunder*. Interestingly enough, Wellhöner uses the Regulation Approach for his analysis, but his study investigated only the 1950s and early 60s.
61. Koch, *Arbeitnehmer*, 149–54; Grieger, *Geist*.
62. Jürgens, *Development*, 290.
63. Doleschal and Dombois (eds.), *Wohin läuft VW?*
64. Haipeter, *Mitbestimmung*, 149–155.
65. Gesetz über die Überführung der Anteilsrechte an der Volkswagenwerk Gesellschaft mit beschränkter Haftung in private Hand (*VWGmbHÜG*) of 9 May 1960, in: Bundesgesetzblatt.
66. Cited from Jürgens, *Development*, 238.
67. Freyssenet, *Mass Production*, 365.
68. In 1965 Renault employed almost 63,000 workers, in 1973 there were more than 100,000; the proportion of labour migrants grew in the same period from 13.2 % to 21.5 %. Cf. Freyssenet, *Mass Production*, 373.
69. Cf. the figures in the annex in Freyssenet, *Mass Production*, 391–392.
70. Hancké, *Firms*, 92.
71. Hancké, *Firms*, 94.
72. Hancké, *Firms*, 93.
73. Hancké, *Firms*, 99.
74. Hancké, *Firms*, 94.
75. Hancké, *Firms*, 101–103.
76. Data from Freyssenet, 'Renault 1992–2007', 284–285.

Disclosure statement

No potential conflict of interest was reported by the author.

References

Abelshauser, Werner. *Die BASF. Eine Unternehmensgeschichte*. München: C.H. Beck, 2002.
Abelshauser, Werner. *Kulturkampf. Der deutsche Weg in die Neue Wirtschaft und die amerikanische Herausforderung*. Berlin: Kadmos Kulturverlag, 2003.
Abelshauser, Werner. *Deutsche Wirtschaftsgeschichte von 1945 bis zur Gegenwart*. München: C.H. Beck, 2011.

Ambrosius, Gerold, Dietmar Petzina, and Werner Plumpe, eds. *Moderne Wirtschaftsgeschichte. Eine Einführung für Historiker und Ökonomen*. München: Oldenbourg, 1996.

Atzmüller, Roland. "Fit mach mit? Theoretisch-politische Perspektiven des Regulationssatzes – ein Rezensionsessay." In *Grundrisse, Zeitschrift für linke Theorie & Debatte*. Accessed September 23, 2013. https://www.grundrisse.net/grundrisse10/10regulationsansatz.htm

Bähr, Johannes. "'Corporate Governance' im Dritten Reich. Leistungs- und Kontrollstrukturen deutscher Großunternehmen während der nationalsozialistischen Diktatur." In *Wirtschaftsordnung, Staat und Unternehmen*, edited by Werner Abelshauser, Jan-Otmar Hesse, and Werner Plumpe, 61–80. Essen: Klartext, 2003.

Beaud, Stéphane, and Michel Pialoux. *Die verlorene Zukunft der Arbeiter. Die Peugeot-Werke von Souchaux-Montbéliard*. Konstanz: UVK, 2004.

Berghoff, Hartmut. *Moderne Unternehmensgeschichte*. Paderborn: UTB, 2004.

Berghoff, Hartmut, and Jakob Vogel, eds. *Wirtschaftsgeschichte als Kulturgeschichte*. Frankfurt am Main: Campus Verlag, 2004.

Boltanski, Luc. *Die Führungskräfte. Die Entstehung einer sozialen Gruppe*. Frankfurt am Main: Campus Verlag, 1990.

Boltanski, Luc, and Chiapello Ève. *Der neue Geist des Kapitalismus*. Konstanz: UVK, 2003.

Borchardt, Knut. "Der ‚Property Rights-Ansatz' in der Wirtschaftsgeschichte – Zeichen für eine systematische Neuorientierung des Faches?" In *Theorien in der Praxis des Historikers. Forschungsbeispiele und ihre Diskussion*, edited by Jürgen Kocka, 140–156. Göttingen: Vandenhoeck & Ruprecht, 1977.

Bourdieu, Pierre. *Entwurf einer Theorie der Praxis auf der ethnologischen Grundlage der kabylischen Gesellschaft*. Frankfurt am Main: Suhrkamp, 1976.

Bourdieu, Pierre. *Sozialer Sinn. Kritik der theoretischen Vernunft*. Frankfurt am Main: Suhrkamp, 1987.

Bourdieu, Pierre. *Homo Academicus*. Frankfurt am Main: Suhrkamp, 1988.

Bourdieu, Pierre. *Reflexive Anthropologie*. Frankfurt am Main: Suhrkamp, 1996.

Bourdieu, Pierre. *Praktische Vernunft. Zur Theorie des Handelns*. Frankfurt am Main: Suhrkamp, 1998.

Bourdieu, Pierre. *Die Regeln der Kunst. Genese und Struktur des literarischen Feldes*. Frankfurt am Main: Suhrkamp, 1999.

Bourdieu, Pierre. *Der Staatsadel*. Konstanz: UVK, 2004.

Bourdieu, Pierre. "Von der Regel zu den Strategien." In *Rede und Antwort*, edited by Pierre Bourdieu, 79–98. Frankfurt am Main: Suhrkamp, 1992.

Bourdieu, Pierre. "Für einen anderen Begriff der Ökonomie." In *Der Tote packt den Lebenden*, edited by Pierre Bourdieu, 79–100. Hamburg: VSA Verlag, 1997.

Bourdieu, Pierre. "Zur Genese der Begriffe Habitus und Feld." In *Der Tote packt den Lebenden*, edited by Pierre Bourdieu, 59–78. Hamburg: VSA Verlag, 1997.

Bourdieu, Pierre. "Das Ökonomische Feld." In *Der Einzige und sein Eigenheim*, edited by Pierre Bourdieu, 162–204. Hamburg: VSA Verlag, 1998.

Bourdieu, Pierre. "Ökonomisches Kapital – Kulturelles Kapital – Soziales Kapital." In *Die verborgenen Mechanismen der Macht*, edited by Pierre Bourdieu, 162–204. Hamburg: VSA Verlag, 1998.

Bourdieu, Pierre, Luc Boltanski, Minique de Staint Martin, and Pascale Maldidier "Kapital und Bildungskapital. Reproduktionsstrategien im sozialen Wandel." In *Titel und Stelle. Über die Reproduktion sozialer Macht*, edited by Pierre Bourdieu, Luc Boltanski, Minique de Staint Martin, and Pascale Maldidie, 23–87. München: Europäische Verlagsanstalt, 1978.

Boyer, Robert. *The Eighties. The Search for Alternatives to Fordism*. CEPREMAP Working Papers, 1989. Accessed September 23, 2013. https://econpapers.repec.org/scripts/redir.pf?u=http%3A%2F%2Fwww.cepremap.fr%2Fdepot%2Fcouv_orange%2Fco8909.pdf;h=repec:cpm:cepmap:8909

Boyer, Robert, and Michel Freyssenet. *Produktionsmodelle. Eine Typologie am Beispiel der Automobilindustrie*. Berlin: Edition Sigma, 2003.

Boyer, Robert, and Michel Freyssenet. *The World that Changed the Machine*. Synthesis of GERPISA Research Programs 1993-1996. Accessed September 23, 2013. https://gerpisa.org/ancien-gerpisa/actes/31/31-3.pdf

Boyer, Robert, and Yves Saillard, eds. *Regulation Theory. The State of the Art*. London: Routledge, 2002.

Boyer, Robert. "French Statism at the Crossroads." In *Political Economy of Modern Capitalism. Mapping Convergence and Diversity*, edited by Colin Crouch and Wolfgang Streeck, 71–101. London: Sage, 1997.

Boyer, Robert, Elsie Charron, Ulrich Jürgens, and Steven Tolliday. *Between Imitation and Innovation. The Transfer and Hybridization of Productive Models in the International Automobile Industry.* Oxford: Oxford University Press, 1998.

Casson, Mark. *The Entrepreneur. An Economic Theory.* Oxford: Martin Robertson, 1982.

Casson, Mark. "Der Unternehmer. Versuch einer historisch-theoretischen Deutung." *Geschichte und Gesellschaft* 27 (2001): 524–544.

Chandler, Alfred. *Strategy and Structure. Chapters in the History of the Industrial Enterprise.* Cambridge: M.I.T. Press, 1962.

Chandler, Alfred D., and Herman Daems. "Introduction. The Rise of Managerial Capitalism and its Impact on Investment Strategy in the Western World and Japan." In *The Rise of Managerial Capitalism*, edited by Herman Daems and Herman van der Wee, 1–34. Leuven: University Press, 1974.

Doleschal, Reinhard, and Rainer Dombois, eds. *Wohin läuft VW? Die Automobilproduktion in der Wirtschaftskrise.* Reinbek: Rowohlt, 1982.

Dörre, Klaus, and Ulrich Brinkmann. "Finanzmarkt-Kapitalismus. Triebkraft eines flexiblen Produktionsregimes?" In *Finanzmarktkapitalismus. Analysen zum Wandel von Produktionsregimen*, edited by Paul Windolf, 85–116. Wiesbaden: Verlag für Sozialwissenschaften, 2005.

Erker, Paul. "Aufbruch zu neuen Paradigmen. Unternehmensgeschichte zwischen sozialgeschichtlicher und betriebswirtschaftlicher Erweiterung." *Archiv für Sozialgeschichte* 37 (1997): 321–365.

Erker, Paul. "'A New Business History'? Neuere Ansätze und Entwicklungen in der Unternehmensgeschichte." *Archiv für Sozialgeschichte* 42 (2002): 557–604.

Erker, Paul. "'Externalisierungsmaschine' oder, Lizenznehmer' der Gesellschaft? Trends, Themen und Theorien in der jüngsten Unternehmensgeschichtsschreibung." *Archiv für Sozialgeschichte* 46 (2006): 605–658.

Erker, Paul. "Corporate Governance – ein neuer Untersuchungsansatz der historischen Unternehmensforschung?" In *Unternehmensgeschichte heute. Theorieangebote, Quellen, Forschungstrends*, edited by Rudolf Boch, Petra Listewnik, Eva Pietsch, and Michael Schäfer (Hg.), 29–46. Leipzig: Universitätsverlag, 2005. (Veröffentlichungen des Sächsischen Wirtschaftsarchivs; 6).

Ferner, Anthony, and Richard Hyman, eds. *Industrial Relations in the New Europe.* Oxford: Blackwell, 1992.

Freeman, R. Edward *Strategic management. A stakeholder approach.* Boston: Pitman Publishing, 1984.

Freyssenet, Michel. "Renault. From Diversified Mass Production to Innovative Flexible Production." In *One Best Way? Trajectories and Industrial Models of the World's Automobile Producers*, edited by Michel Freyssenet, Andrew Mair, Koichi Shimizu, and Giuseppe Volpato, 365–394. New York: Oxford University Press, 1998.

Freyssenet, Michel. "Renault. 1992-2007. Globalization and Strategic Uncertainties." In *The Second Automobile Revolution. Trajectories of the World Carmakers in the 21st Century*, edited by Michel Freyssenet, 267–286. Basingstoke: Palgrave Macmillan, 2009.

Freyssenet, Michel, Andrew Mair, Koichi Shimizu, and Giuseppe Volpato, eds. *One Best Way? Trajectories and Industrial Models of the World's Automobile Producers.* New York: Oxford University Press, 1998.

Gehlen, Boris. "Corporate Law and Corporate Control in West Germany after 1945." *Business History* (Forthcoming).

Grieger, Manfred. "Der neue Geist im Volkswagenwerk. Produktinnovation, Kapazitätsabbau und Mitbestimmungsmodernisierung." In *Unternehmen am Ende des „goldenen Zeitalters. Die 1970er Jahre in unternehmens- und wirtschaftshistorischer Perspektive*, edited by Morten Reitmayer and Ruth Rosenberger, 31–66. Essen: Klartext, 2008.

Hachtmann, Rüdiger. "Fordismus, Version: 1.0." In *Docupedia-Zeitgeschichte*, October 27, 2011. Accessed September 23, 2013. https://docupedia.de/zg/Fordismus?oldid=84605

Haipeter, Thomas. *Mitbestimmung bei Volkswagen. Neue Chancen für die betriebliche Interessenvertretung?* Münster: Verlag Westfälisches Dampfboot, 2000.

Hancké, Bob. *Large Firms and Institutional Change. Industrial Renewal and Economic Restructuring in France.* Oxford: Oxford University Press, 2002.

Herbert, Ulrich. "Europe in High Modernity. Reflections on a Theory of the 20th Century." *Journal of Modern European History* 5 (2007): 5–21.

Hesse, Jan-Otmar, Christian Kleinschmidt, and Karl Lauschke, eds. *Kulturalismus. Neue Institutionenökonomik oder Theorievielfalt. Eine Zwischenbilanz der Unternehmensgeschichte.* Essen: Klartext, 2002.

Hirschman, Albert O. *Exit, Voice and Loyalty. Responses to Decline in Firms, Organizations and States.* Cambridge, MA: Harvard University Press, 1970.

Hollingsworth, J. Rogers, and Robert Boyer, eds. *Contemporary Capitalism. The Embeddedness of Institutions.* Cambridge: Cambridge University Press, 1998.

Jessop, Bob, ed. *Regulation Theory and the Crisis of Capitalism.* 5 vols. Cheltenham: Edward Elgar, 2001.

Jessop, Bob. "Review of 'Boyer, Robert/Saillard, Yves (eds.). Regulation Theory: The State of the Art.'" *New Political Economy* 7, no. 3 (2002): 463–472.

Jürgens, Ulrich. "The Final Chapter of the 'VW Model'? The VW Trajectory 1995-2005." In *The Second Automobile Revolution. Trajectories of the World Carmakers in the 21st Century*, edited by Michel Freyssenet, 225–245. Basingstoke: Palgrave Macmillan, 2009.

Jürgens, Ulrich. "The Development of Volkswagen's Industrial Model." In *One Best Way? Trajectories and Industrial Models of the World's Automobile Producers*, edited by Michel Freyssenet, Andrew Mair, Koichi Shimizu, and Giuseppe Volpato, 273–310. Oxford: Oxford University Press, 1998.

Koch, Günther. *Arbeitnehmer steuern mit. Belegschaftsvertretung bei VW ab 1945.* Köln: Bund Verlag, 1987.

Koller, Barbara. "Psychologie und Produktion. Die Entwicklung der persönlichkeitsbezogenen Anforderungsprofile an die Wirtschaftselite seit den sechziger Jahren." In *Die deutsche Wirtschaftselite im 20. Jahrhundert. Kontinuität und Mentalität.*, edited by Volker R. Berghahn, Stefan Unger, and Dieter Ziegler, 337–351. Essen: Klartext, 2003.

Lauschke, Karl. *Die Hoesch-Arbeiter und ihr Werk. Sozialgeschichte der Dortmunder Westfalenhütte während der Jahre des Wiederaufbaus 1945-1966.* Essen: Klartext, 2000.

Lauschke, Karl, and Thomas Welskopp, eds. *Mikropolitik im Unternehmen. Arbeitsbeziehungen und Machtstrukturen in industriellen Großbetrieben.* Essen: Klartext, 1994.

Lorentz, Bernhard, and Paul Erker. *Chemie und Politik. Die Geschichte der Chemischen Werke Hüls 1938 bis 1979. Eine Studie zum Problem der Corporate Governance.* München: C.H. Beck, 1979.

Maclean, Mairi. "Corporate Governance in France and the UK: Long-Term Perspectives on Contemporary Institutional Arrangements." *Business History* 41 (1999): 88–116.

Marx, Christian. *Paul Reusch und die Gutehoffnungshütte. Leitung eines deutschen Großunternehmens.* Göttingen: Wallstein, 2013.

Mitchell, Ronald K., Bradley R. Agle, and Donna J. Wood. "Toward a Theory of Stakeholder Identification and Salience. Defining the Principle of Who and What Really Counts." *The Academy of Management Review* 22, no. 4 (1997): 853–886.

Pierenkemper, Toni. *Unternehmensgeschichte. Eine Einführung in ihre Methoden und Ergebnisse.* Stuttgart: Franz Steiner Verlag, 2000.

Piore, Michael J., and Charles Sabel. *Das Ende der Massenproduktion.* Fischer: Frankfurt am Main, 1989. (original 1984).

Plumpe, Werner. "Wie entscheiden Unternehmen?" *Zeitschrift für Unternehmensgeschichte* 61, no. 2 (2012): 141–159.

Plumpe, Werner. "Unternehmen." In *Moderne Wirtschaftsgeschichte. Eine Einführung für Historiker und Ökonomen*, edited by Gerold Ambrosius, Dietmar Petzina, and Werner Plumpe, 47–66. München: Oldenbourg, 1996.

Priemel, Kim Christian. *Flick. Eine Konzerngeschichte vom Kaiserreich bis zur Bundesrepublik.* Göttingen: Wallstein, 2007.

Reitmayer, Morten, and Ruth Rosenberger, eds. *Unternehmen am Ende des "goldenen Zeitalters". Die 1970er Jahre in unternehmens- und wirtschaftshistorischer Perspektive.* Essen: Klartext, 2008.

Rosenberger, Ruth. *Experten für Humankapital. Die Entdeckung des Personalmanagements in der Bundesrepublik Deutschland.* München: Oldenbourg, 2008.

Röttger, Bernd. "Glanz und Elend der Regulationstheorie. Einige Reflexionen zum Begriff der Regulation." *Sozialistische Politik und Wirtschaft (SWP)* 135 (2004). Accessed September 23, 2013. https://www.spw.de/data/rttger_spw135.pdf

Schmidt, Vivien A. *From State to Market? The Transformation of State and Business in France*. Cambridge: Cambridge University Press, 1996.

Sorge, Arndt, and Wolfgang Streeck. *Diversified quality production revisited the transformation of production systems and regulatory regimes in Germany* (MPIfG Discussion Paper, no. 16/13). Cologne: MPIfG, 2016.

Sorge, Arndt, and Wolfgang Streeck. "Industrial Relations and Technical Change: The Case for an Extended Perspective." In *New Technology and Industrial Relations*, edited by Richard Hyman and Wolfgang Streeck, 19–44. Oxford: Blackwell, 1988.

Spoerer, Mark. "Mikroökonomie in der Unternehmensgeschichte? Eine Mikroökonomik der Unternehmensgeschichte." In *Kulturalismus, Neue Institutionenökonomik oder Theorievielfalt. Eine Zwischenbilanz der Unternehmensgeschichte*, edited by Jan-Otmar Hesse, Christian Kleinschmidt, and Karl Lauschke, 175–195. Essen: Klartext 2002.

Streeck, Wolfgang. "On the Institutional Conditions of Diversified Quality Production." In *Beyond Keynesianism. The Socio-Economics of Production and Full Employment*, edited by Egon Matzner and Wolfgang Streeck, 21–61. Aldershot: Edward Elgar, 1991.

Süß, Dietmar. *Kumpel und Genossen. Arbeiterschaft und Sozialdemokratie in der bayerischen Montanindustrie*. München: Oldenbourg, 2003.

Tanner, Jakob. "'Bankenmacht'. Politischer Popanz, antisemitischer Stereotyp oder analytische Kategorie?" *Zeitschrift für Unternehmensgeschichte* 43, no. 1 (1998): 19–34.

Tilly, Stephanie. "Supplier relations within the German automobile industry. The case of Daimler-Benz, 1950-1980." *Business History*. doi:10.1080/00076791.2016.1267143.

Tolliday, Steven. "Enterprise and the State in the West German Wirtschaftswunder. Volkswagen and the Automobile Industry 1939-1962." *Business History Review* 69, no. 3 (1995): 273–350.

Wellhöner, Volker. *Großbanken und Großindustrie im Kaiserreich*. Göttingen: Vandenhoeck & Ruprecht, 1989.

Wellhöner, Volker. *Wirtschaftswunder" – Weltmarkt – westdeutscher Fordismus. Der Fall Volkswagen*. Münster: Verlag Westfälisches Dampfboot, 1996.

Welskopp, Thomas. "Unternehmenskulturen im internationalen Vergleich – oder eine integrale Unternehmensgeschichte in typisierender Absicht." In *Wirtschaftsgeschichte als Kulturgeschichte*, edited by Hartmut Berghoff and Jakob Vogel, 265–294. Frankfurt am Main: Campus-Verlag, 2004.

Winkler, Heinrich August, ed. *Organisierter Kapitalismus*. Göttingen: Vandenhoeck & Ruprecht, 1974.

Wischermann, Clemens, Peter Borscheid, and Karl-Peter Ellerbrock, eds. *Unternehmenskommunikation im 19. und 20. Jahrhundert. Neue Wege der Unternehmensgeschichte*. Dortmund: Ardey-Verlag, 2000.

Wischermann, Clemens, Anne Nieberding, and Britta Stücker, eds. *Unternehmenskommunikation deutscher Mittel- und Großunternehmen. Theorie und Praxis in historischer Perspektive*. Münster: Ardey-Verlag, 2003. (cf. on this point the review by Alexander Schug in: H-Soz-u-Kult, 16.08.2004. Accessed September 26, 2013. https://hsozkult.geschichte.hu-berlin.de/rezensionen/2004-3-100

Womack, James P., Daniel T. Jones, and Daniel Roos. *The Machine that Changed the World. The Story of Lean Production*. New York: Rawson Associates, 1990.

Corporate law and corporate control in West Germany after 1945

Boris Gehlen

ABSTRACT

According to the 'Varieties of Capitalism' and 'Law and Finance' approaches, legal institutions regulating corporate finance and governance shape specific national varieties of capitalism. This article analyses legal debates and practices of corporate control in post-war Germany from the perspective of business history. It argues that the stock corporation law did not have a significant impact on control practices. The law only roughly outlined rights of the supervisory boards and defined minimum standards. There was considerable room for manoeuvre within the corporations, and various effective and some ineffective control arrangements were possible. The article indicates that not only legal institutions but external political and economic factors were important for Germany's coordinated market economy and for the development of greater capital market control.

Introduction

Over the last decade, the Varieties of Capitalism (VOC) approach has stimulated a fruitful interdisciplinary discussion between economists, social scientists and (business) historians. Yet the approach is a genuinely ahistorical one in that it refers to historical developments mostly in order to construct different types of capitalism. Most articles about the German case – as the paragon of a coordinated market economy in the sense of Hall and Soskice[1] – analysed varieties (or similarities) of pre-World War I capitalism and tended to adopt a macro-perspective. For example, scholars discussed the effects of corporate governance on capital market efficiency or the presence of banks on boards in general.[2] But there is still a lack of historical literature on those structures and periods that the VOC-approach initially referred to, namely the post-war 'economic miracle' and its aftermath until the 1980s.[3]

Whenever Germany's specific path of capitalism is discussed its structures are considered from an institutional perspective. The Law and Finance literature, first and foremost La Porta et al., pointed out that civil law played a crucial role for the comparably poor capital market development in continental Europe because institutions designed to protect minority shareholders were underdeveloped.[4] In contrast, business historians were mostly sceptical on this count and doubted that such a formal perspective could properly explain capitalism and its varieties. Instead, they maintained that politico-economic factors were far more important where corporate governance and performance were concerned.[5]

However, others – especially some political scientists – frequently argued that Germany's coordinated market economy was a deliberate political creation whose structure was actively defended by a large coalition including corporations and business associations.[6] According to this point of view, corporate control – which mostly was said to have been de facto executed by large banks – was part of a political consensus to tame and to govern markets in order to achieve a politically desirable outcome. The numerous labels for Germany's Coordinated Market Economy tend to consistently emphasise the prominent role of stock corporations and provisions for cooperative arrangements within the entire national economy. First and foremost this holds true for the model 'Deutschland AG' (Germany Inc.) that has been developed and interpreted by social scientists since the 1990s. It describes structures and dimensions of financial and personal interlocking in post-war West Germany,[7] and beyond this it tries to explain the specifics of German market economy and its implications for society.[8] Moreover it explicitly refers to the 'AG' (short for 'Aktiengesellschaft'), the German stock corporation. In this regard it identifies four main instruments of corporate governance that – at least for some authors – had a stabilising impact on economy and society: the bipartite governance system with an executive (Vorstand) and a supervisory board (Aufsichtsrat), (banks') proxy voting rights, interlocking directorates and – since the 1950s – codetermination, which mutually fostered a bank-based, stakeholder-oriented insider system and protected the insiders from hostile takeovers.[9]

According to the 'classical' juxtaposition of the Law and Finance literature, Germany's corporate governance system seemed to be voice-based because large shareholders influenced business strategies via the supervisory board. In contrast, Anglo-American systems especially were exit-based and controlled by capital markets because shareholders sold their stock if they were dissatisfied with a corporation's performance.[10] The main narrative about German capitalism thus describes a system with stable investor and customer relationships, irenic effects on social conflicts, patient capital (and shareholding) and long-time investment strategies; this, it is suggested, explains why Germany's economy focuses more on quality production than on innovation. The way large corporations were controlled thus was not only a question of governance but had – or seemed to have – an impact on Germany's economy and society as a whole. In a macro-perspective this governance system enabled cooperative arrangements and communication between stakeholders. Especially bankers, employees and trade union' officials, but also politicians and scientists could, by joining a supervisory board promote social goals, shape business strategies in significant ways.[11]

However, most of the abstract views on Germany's capitalism are somewhat unsatisfactory from a historical perspective. The practical level of corporate control and in particular corporate governance still deserve closer attention.[12] In a broader perspective, such an analysis should, of course, include a closer look at industrial relations, tax policy (and evasion), as well as at accounting standards etc. This article concentrates chiefly on the relevance and the effects of corporate law as the main legal basis for strategic action. It argues – partially in contrast to the Law and Finance approach – that the stock corporation act merely supported, but did not in any essential way cause, the emergence of a Coordinated Market Economy in West Germany. Its persistence was much more a result of path dependency than of political goals, economic considerations or a social consensus. The act provided a flexible,

self-regulated governance system which devolved comprehensive responsibility for corporate control to managers and business leaders and otherwise functioned as a permanent
implicit threat that encouraged compliance with 'super-ordinated' values and informal norms
such as social and political responsibility.

This governance system only functioned within the specific historical framework of an
economic nationalism, broadly understood: as long as national perceptions dominated politics and business, and as long as stock capital was primarily owned by Germans, it did not
appear desirable to alter the legal framework and control practices. As long as these arrangements worked, criticism remained muted. The impact of globalisation and 'financialisation'
since the 1970s then gradually changed the perception within companies, business associations, and political parties.[13]

However, these general observations are not only true for Germany but also for many
developed countries. For example, even in the Netherlands – a rather liberal market
economy – corporate control post-1945 (and until the 1980s) relied on a stakeholder model,
and minority shareholder's rights were even curtailed during the post-war period.[14] Although
it is obvious that those substantial changes from the 1970s onward affected more or less all
Western economies and their institutions, such a perspective cannot be fully developed in
this article. It instead focuses on a 'negative reasoning' for the German case: an analysis of
patterns of corporate control should cast doubt on the often alleged essential (direct) role
of the stock corporation act within and for Germany's Coordinated Market Economy, and
present some evidence for the way the law contributed indirectly to Germany's (corporate)
governance: by putting forward a code of conduct for businesses that conformed to the
demands of the German public. Therefore the article refers to what is in German called
'Aktienrechtswirklichkeit' (reality of company law). On the one hand this term simply describes
the discrepancy between the law as written – typical of a country with a civil and public law
tradition – and its actual effects on businessmen's behaviour. On the other hand, the term
casts doubt on the idea that there can be a single, unique legal effect: if such a discrepancy
exists, several modes of corporate control may coexist, and the law will be a much more
subordinated factor than the law and finance literature indicates. The article will present, in
the next section, some arguments why capital market control could not have been an option
in post-war Germany. It will then, in the third section, outline legal structures and contemporary debates and discuss in the fourth section, to what extent German companies were
affected by the stock corporation act, how control (and decision-making) was restrained by
law (or not) and which general types of corporate control existed. The latter question implies
that a general pattern of corporate control did not exist. The fifth section will therefore
present some qualitative (but not representative) evidence from case studies to underline
the great variety of control arrangements in German companies; it will also implicitly present
evidence that the change of markets, stock composition and opportunity costs gradually
altered corporate control from 'self-regulation' to 'capital market control' – even under the
auspices of the 'cooperative' stock corporation act.

The lack of capital market control in post-war-Germany: some historical explanations

For capital market control to be effective, capital cannot be concentrated in the hands of a
few; rather, shares must be owned by a large number of investors. For a variety of reasons

this necessary precondition did not exist in post war-Germany – at least until the (late) 1970s. First, from 1914 onwards, the German capital market had been a national one. Foreign direct investments remained negligible until the 1970s,[15] and, with some specific exceptions, for-eigners were prohibited – by instruments such as multiple vote-, preferred-, and depot-shares – from purchasing significant amounts of shares during the Weimar and the Nazi period. As a result, German stocks were concentrated and mostly owned by Germans, especially family groups and banks.[16]

The capital concentration was not so much an effect of weak minority investors' protection but the result of capital scarcity after two inflations within 25 years (1923 and 1948). The loss of savings reduced the amount of potential minority investors while tangible assets like stocks had not been devalued. Moreover, unlike in the US (retail) investments in stocks never had been a prominent factor in private capital formation – not least because of a rarely considered provision: from 1884 to 1965, the minimum nominal amount of one share was generally laid down at 1000 M (respectively RM/DM), which policymakers explicitly devised as a prohibitive sum even for the upper middle classes. In the aftermath of the financial crisis of 1873 and in later decades, the 'retail investor' was to be protected from 'insecure' shares and instead buy assets such as mortgages, mortgage bonds (Pfandbriefe), industrial, state and communal obligations or turn to savings banks.[17] Arguably, this regulation had a some-what delayed effect. As recent studies have shown, structures of stockholding in Germany did not differ significantly from other developed countries prior to 1913 but did afterwards.[18] One consequence was that financial and business experts as late as the 1950s and 1960s regarded the minimal nominal amount of 1000 DM as one major obstacle for retail investors, and argued in favour of a notably reduced amount as in the US.[19]

Institutional investors (especially life insurances and savings banks) also traditionally invested most of their capital in such other assets and securities.[20] Pension funds – due to the existence of a public pension insurance – as well as investment trusts – which in Germany only emerged from the mid-1950s onwards[21] – were for a long time relatively absent from the German capital market; as a result, (institutional) investments into stocks remained at a comparably low level.[22] Tellingly, from the mid-1920s to the 1980s, initial public offerings were extremely rare occasions on German stock exchanges. Moreover, only roughly 10% of stock corporations were listed on stock exchanges and thus provided fungible shares.[23]

Certainly, government policies encouraged this development during post-war recon-struction. Investments in public infrastructure and housing were needed to overcome the severe war damages and to integrate millions of displaced persons. These priorities were hard to achieve considering that capital was scarce following the currency reform of 1948, and that a viable capital market did not exist. Any unnecessary reliance on the capital market had therefore to be avoided. Auto-financing of corporations was therefore promoted through fiscal means, thus further enhancing a concentration of capital.[24]

The rapid concentration of capital only a few years after decartelisation soon became a political issue and influenced debates about a reform of the stock corporation act. Already, in 1954, the Association of German Chambers of Commerce demanded a revision, and aimed, among other things, to strengthen the position of retail shareholders in order to bring about a viable stock market.[25] But these discussions were only a subordinated part of a broader debate on asset policy in West-Germany, especially on asset de-concentration. Legislators made several provisions to counteract capital concentration: The Law against Restrictions of Competition (Gesetz gegen Wettbewerbsbeschränkungen 1957) became the German anti-trust-law, a so-called Minor Stock Law Reform (kleine Aktienrechtsreform 1959) improved balance sheet transparency, acts to foster the capital market (Kapitalmarktförderungsgesetz 1952) and private asset accumulation (Vermögensbildungsgesetz 1961) as well as the (part-) privatisation of state-owned stock corporations such as Preussag (1959), Volkswagen (1960), and Veba (1965), whose shares – the so-called 'Volksaktien' – were sold to private households at preferable terms. In terms of stock market vitalisation these measures were more or less ineffective. Germans still preferred life insurances, bank deposits, and building savings agreements, of which the latter were state-sponsored. While public grants for bank deposits were abolished for fiscal reasons in 1980, building savings agreements to this day are subsidised for low-income earners.[26]

Arguably, German asset policy at least had a side-effect regarding corporate control: As long as Germans benefited from the economic upswing public discourses about corporate governance and related issues did not take place. Tellingly, the debates about corporate governance became more vigorous in the 1970s and then again in the 1990s when the zeitgeist challenged the welfare state, instead championing individualism, privatisation, and shareholder-value. [27] In this perspective, the revision of the stock corporation act in 1998 could[28]– along with the Mannesmann-Vodafone takeover in 1999 and the decision of Deutsche Bank in 2001 not to delegate their managers in supervisory boards anymore – be interpreted as 'milestones' of the 'Americanisation' of the German economy – including, more or less, greater (wealth) inequality.[29] Such a 'Piketty-style argument would probably be somewhat simplistic and evidence for a comprehensive 'Americanisation' of German corporate governance is still poor anyway,[30] but it is obvious that issues of corporate control must be integrated into a larger framework if they should explain social change more generally (which is not the purpose of this article).

However, the overarching goal of the asset and competition policy of the 1950s and 1960s was not to improve the stock market as such but to abolish the exceptional restraints of competition and to return to a 'normal' market order. The effects of this – not yet comprehensive – liberalisation policy were long in coming. Thus, there is no evidence that political and economic elites in the 1950s and 1960s generally wanted to preserve those structures, which made capital market control impossible and somewhat superfluous. However, the modes of corporate control defined by the stock corporation law were maintained anyway in the revision of the stock corporation act of 1965.

Law and corporate control

The 1965 reform was one of only four major revisions (1884, 1931/37, 1965, 1998) of the Germany stock corporation act whose origins date back to 1870. Despite those revisions, the legal instruments of corporate control remained largely unchanged throughout the twentieth century: from a formal point of view, the intention of the legislator was (and still is) fairly clear: § 111 of the German stock corporation act stipulates in plain terms that the supervisory board has to supervise the management, a provision that can be traced to the very beginning of the modern stock corporation in 1870.[31]

Of course, some rules gradually became more sophisticated over time. For example, the 1884 reform contained a strict separation of membership in supervisory and executive boards, and in 1931 the external revision of annual accounts became mandatory. The 1937 law recalibrated the balance of power between the three major organs, weakening the shareholders meeting and strengthening – in accordance with the 'Führerprinzip' – the executive board. But such genuine Nazi elements remained the exception rather than the rule. In general, the 1937 revision was a response to the economic circumstances of the 1920s when reform discussions began. The weakening of the shareholders meeting did not in any case change the practice of corporate control because major shareholders planted representatives in the supervisory board, and there were simply too few minority shareholders for their inclusion to become an issue.[32]

Until 1937 the supervisory board's duties had not been restricted to supervision. They could explicitly be extended and genuine obligations of the management could, for example, be devolved to the supervisory board. This option was finally and formally permitted in the 1937 revision of the act. But its existence indicates that in German stock corporations there never had been a strict division of duties between executive and supervisory boards. Moreover, there is some evidence that supervisory board members, mostly of course its heads, were de facto responsible for determining business strategies they formally should only have supervised.[33] This kind of co-executive entrepreneurship was prohibited de jure in 1937 but – as we will see below – it persisted nevertheless in practice.

Because the 1937 law was – with the exception of some scattered Nazi elements – an extension of its predecessors, and because the structures of corporate finance and capital markets were what they were, a revision of the law was not needed immediately after 1945. Nevertheless, already in the early 1950s, interested agents prepared themselves for the upcoming debates. Four issues were the main subjects of discussion.

(1) There was a broad consensus that the existing division of competencies between executive and supervisory board should be maintained in its traditional form – including interlocking directorates. Moreover, business associations rejected suggestions that the supervisory board henceforth should comment on the executive board's statements, considering it a first step towards an Anglo-American board system.[34]

But it is clear that the business community aimed to fend off restrictions of self-governing. Therefore, they argued frequently – and over time – that a comprehensive statutory regulation was evidently impossible, or at least not viable. Instead they favoured a comprehensive self-regulation which, in their perspective, would guarantee sufficient freedom of manoeuvre and flexibility. The other side of the coin, it was admitted, was an implicit necessity to properly incorporate political, social, and environmental issues. Otherwise, it was believed, the legislator would force the companies' hands by amending the relevant statutes.[35]

This however, is not only typical of corporate control but of the German model of capitalism in general.[36] Legislation was, more or less, a solution of last resort. Although relevant historical studies remain a desideratum, it appears that moral suasion or an informal adjustment of business strategies on the one hand, and political and social goals on the other, played an essential role in Germany's capitalism. In this perspective, legislation can be seen as a permanent public threat in order to guarantee (big) business' compliance with (national) society.

Tellingly, business associations greeted the 1965 revision with approval – at least regarding its essentials.[37] Only one important provision regarding the supervisory board had been controversial and was nevertheless tightened: henceforth, each supervisor only could hold up to 10 board seats in total – as opposed to 20 before. Moreover, cross-company interlocking was restricted: if an executive board member of company A was a member of company B's supervisory board, an executive board member of company B could not be a member of company A's supervisory board anymore. Both regulations relied on the same reasoning as the corresponding ones from 1931: too many supervisory board mandates were believed to make a person's control less possible and less effective. Naturally, this new rule limited the scope of 'big linkers' and thus further reduced the density of the 'Germany Inc.' network – as the 1931 regulation and the forced disappearance of the German-Jewish economy elite since 1933 had done earlier. But control practices themselves were not affected for a long time; only the pool of supervisors (and probably that of individual control priorities) had been extended.[38]

(2) Proxy voting – and implicitly the voting power of banks – was always an issue in public debates about stock corporation law because it seemed to be an instrument that undermined minority shareholders' interests. But the 1965 act did not change this instrument as such. It only determined that henceforth the shareholder had explicitly to provide the bank managing their portfolio with a mandate. Proxy voting persisted mainly because of juridical concerns within the German Ministry of Justice. It is often claimed that business and banking associations argued in favour of it but the available evidence does not support this argument (although it is true they generally agreed with maintaining proxy voting). Interested business associations feared, for instance, that an abolishment of proxy voting could benefit small but well-organised groups that could use their voting power in the shareholder meeting to further their own interests at the expense of the company's and other shareholders' interests. This was, however, the traditional patriarchal perspective of the German legislator on stock corporations; ironically, it was inspired by the aim to protect minority investors' interests.

(3) Issues of capital concentration and trust-building shaped the reform; thus, not only the single stock corporation but affiliated companies too were taken into account. The so-called 'Konzernrecht' was meant to protect an affiliated company from possibly disadvantageous decisions on the holding-level. Therefore, from 1965, any equity investment larger than 25% had to be disclosed to both the respective company and the public in general.

(4) It was uncontroversial that transparency standards should be increased in order to alter corporate finance and to revive the stock market. The minor reform of 1959 had already anticipated this goal to some extent. Furthermore, courts had expanded the information rights of 'retail investors'.[39] The stock corporation act of 1965 did not go far beyond these previous achievements. On the one hand, following an intense discussion about their suitability, provisions were included designed to hamper the concealing of inner reserves in the balance sheets. On the other hand the act reduced the minimum nominal value of one share from 1000 to 50 DM. Arguably, only the persistence of fairly management-friendly accounting standards that still allowed inner reserves indicates an aversion towards an overly extensive capital market control. Only with regard to corporate control in general can we describe the 1965 revision of the stock corporation as a moderate modernisation that abolished the specific Nazi elements, and improved transparency gradually; apart from that, it also adjusted regulations. All in all, even in the heyday of what Andrew Shonfield called in the same year 'organized private enterprise' and Michel Albert would later on call 'Rhenish Capitalism',[40] corporation law and corporate control were in principle the same as in the 1880s. In this decade, of course, neither Germany's corporate governance nor the output and efficiency of the German stock market differed significantly from national economies later on described as contrasting types of capitalism.[41]

But how specifically did the stock corporation act affect corporate control? A very brief answer would be: not at all. A more elaborated one therefore should start exactly with this observation: the stock corporation act is only a rough outline of the definition of property rights within companies. There were general rules for each body – the shareholder meeting (Hauptversammlung), the executive board and the supervisory board. The company's statutes then defined further rights for each of them. Taken together, they provided the framework for corporate control but did not regulate it in detail.

Although the supervisory board is the main control body within German companies, from a juridical perspective the corporations are not organised in a hierarchical but in a collegial way. The competencies of shareholder meetings and especially of the supervisory board thus limited the executive board's scope in two ways. (1) companies' statutes usually stipulated that strategic decisions had to be explicitly approved by the control body. In the 1960s, nearly 50% of stock corporations even allowed the supervisory board to extend its competencies unilaterally. Based on voluntary agreements, in the late 1970s supervisory boards explicitly had to approve managers' strategic decisions.[42]

The most important and far-reaching obligation of the supervisory board members was to hire and fire the executives. This, of course, implies a cooperative business conduct: any executive who permanently acted against the supervisory board's interests certainly would not have maintained his position for a long time. At the same time, the formal division of management and supervision was watered down to some degree. The executive board had to convince the supervisory board that its intended strategy was the right one. Therefore, the management had to inform its supervisors about its plans before it could implement them. Thus, the supervisory board was involved in strategic decision-making even though the stock corporation act made this mandatory only in 1998. A side-effect of this 'compulsory cooperation' between the supervisors and executives had been a continuity of conduct and (mutual) strategies – most prominently epitomised by the practice of appointing former CEOs as heads of the supervisory board to govern their successors. All in all, supervisory boards had to fulfil a dual role – de facto, not de jure: on the one hand they were control bodies, which had to ensure that the business policy was *legitimate*, and on the other hand they were as advisory bodies involved in strategic management and therefore had to ensure that business policy was *appropriate*.[43]

Only the first role was regulated by law. The second role was not pre-determined but negotiated by individuals within the company. Accordingly, there was a wide range of internal control arrangements that could differ from company to company. Moreover, for the supervisory board generally acting as a trustee of the shareholders, principal-agent conflicts – e.g. regarding strategies or dividend payments – were inevitable.

Varieties of corporate control: dimensions and typology

Formal corporate control as required by law was more or less a routine matter. Supervisory boards roughly held four meetings a year that lasted up to four hours each. Legally relevant decisions were usually unanimous.[44] But, of course, corporate control went far beyond the legally necessary. In the 1960s, less than 10% of German stock corporations made use only of the control rights provided by law. 60% had established informal and cooperative forms of control, and another 30% had even formalised additional reporting standards for the executive boards. The 1965 law did not change this general system of corporate control as Table 1 indicates.

Obviously, voluntary and cooperative instruments were very important for German corporate governance. For example, in 1979, 13% of the supervisory boards did not use the legally mandatory auditor's report to control the management as the report only had to attest whether the business policy was legitimate but not whether it was appropriate. However, 87% used these reports for control purposes, which indicates that they generally contained more than only legally relevant information. [45]

All in all, the stock corporation act encouraged collegial arrangements and therefore conceived potential sanctions as instruments of last resort. It enabled the supervisory board to audit account books autonomously, to query the executive board's business policy in the shareholder meeting, to convoke an extraordinary shareholder meeting, to sue the executive board, and to recall executive board members for cause. In theory, these rights enabled the supervisory to intervene in significant ways; in practice the rights more or less implied compliance, and were rarely used. Only special audits (with about 10%) and the right to recall executives (with about 5%) were relevant in the samples of 1960 and 1979. However, only business groups with a dominant shareholder recalled executives. This probably indicates that this right was used to implement new strategic focuses rather than being a mere control instrument.

To a certain extent, the degree of stock concentration was important for internal control arrangements. Depending on the companies' power relations the supervisory board could permanently overrule the executive board – at least in some cases. This was, of course, not the law's intention but it was legal. According to contemporary studies (mentioned above; see also Table 2) there was a correlation between stock concentration and the authority to decide within corporations. High capital concentration tended to foster a strong position of the supervisory board not intended by the stock corporation act. This could be detrimental

Table 1. Use of various control instruments in German supervisory boards 1960 (*n*=132) and 1979 (*n*=295)

	Use in …% of stock corporations	
Instrument	1979	1960
Executive board's reporting (turnover, state of business)	98	92
Auditor's report	87	
Additional reports requested by the supervisory board	42	25
Additional autonomous audit by the supervisory board	8	12
Additional constant consulting	66	75
Reports on prospective strategies/business plans	72	
Additional constant reports on relevant issues	87	

Sources: Vogel, *Aktienrecht*, 162; Werth, *Vorstand*, 47–49. Not all data are available for 1960.

Table 2. Power relations and authority to decide on German stock corporations depending on structure of stock (in %) (1960)

Decisive body	Dominated corporations	Powerful owners	Widespread stock	Total
Executive board only	44.0	50.0	73.3	48.5
Executive and supervisory board	49.5	50.0	26.7	47.0
Supervisory board only	6.5	0.0	0.0	4.5

Sources: Werth, *Vorstand*, 98. Dominated corporations = 50% of stock and more in one hand; Powerful owners = less than 50, but more than 25% in the hand of major shareholders.

to the depending affiliates' strategy: for example, Agfa, an affiliate of the Bayer AG, failed to properly react to the challenges of photography's digitalisation and instead maintained a photo-chemistry-based strategy – not least because this was what the chemical parent company wanted.[46]

Otherwise, a widespread structure of shareholders made a – legally intended – control system with a deciding executive board and a controlling (and advising) supervisory board more likely. But widespread share ownership did not necessarily improve control. As in US corporations, the problem and control powers only shifted: the supervisory board was more powerful in corporations with concentrated ownership than in those with widespread stock, and the more ownership and control fell apart, the more the management extended its competencies.[47]

Where dominant families or the state as the main share owner were concerned, control arrangements were influenced by an additional logic. Frequently, family companies established bodies beside the firm in order to coordinate family interests before discussing them in the corporation's bodies where a significant share of family members had mandates anyway. But de facto the family bodies that obviously were not captured by the stock corporation law were more important for business politics than the corporation itself. Public authorities harmonised their interests using similar means. According to contemporary surveys those types of corporations seemed to come closer to that intended by the law than many other companies because the management had a comparably strong position (see Table 3). But if we take the parallel control bodies into account the picture appears slightly different as they de facto substituted the supervisory boards. For this reason, the executives formally obtained more power.

The shareholders' composition clearly had an abstract impact on control arrangements but informal structures were arguably even more important. As the statutory provisions merely defined minimal standards, formal sanctions were mostly instruments of last resort. More relevant as far as business policy and its control were concerned were the internal arrangements and especially the relationship between executive and supervisory board. The supervisory board was designed by law as a mere control body but, as described, its function within the companies went far beyond its legally defined duties. It was an advisory board rather than a control board – not by law but in practice. In the 1970s, for example, nearly every other strategic decision – such as equity or facility investments and mergers – had its *origin* in the supervisory board.[48]

The chairman or – where established – a collegial head of the supervisory board (Aufsichtsratspräsidium) usually acted as the 'communicative centre' of the control body (see

Table 3. Power relations and business-policy-making power in German stock corporations depending on company type (1970s)

Actors	Total	Type			
		Independent*	Dependent*	Family company	Public (influenced)
Executive and supervisory Board	75%	73%	84%	64%	76%
Executive board only	17%	24%	7%	30%	22%
Supervisory board only	1%	0%	1%	0%	0%
Dominant shareholder(s)	7%	3%	8%	6%	2%
N	290	173	115	76	46

Source: Vogel, *Aktienrecht*, 232.
*In (German) legal terms, company A is regarded as being dependent ('beherrschtes Unternehmen'), if company B influences – in a mediate or an immediate way – company A's business policy. Usually, a stockholding of 50% indicates dominance, although other indicators may apply.

Table 4. Specific informal contacts of executive and supervisory board (ca. 1979, N=295); in %.

Frequency of contacts	Head of supervisory board	Shareholder's delegates	Employee's delegates
Weekly	15	13	15
Monthly	25	25	31
Several times a year	16	32	28
No contacts, no accessible information, no formal head of the supervisory board	34	30	26

Sources: Vogel, *Aktienrecht*, 181. According to data presented by Werth, *Vorstand*, 48 contacts increased over time. In 1960, only 44% of the executives contacted members of the supervisory board informally, but 56% did not.

The comparable higher proportion of informal contacts to employee's delegates from the industrial councils or trade unions resulted from their legal competencies in all social questions, e.g. employment law, social compatibility, or downsizing. This made an early approach reasonable, allowing the management to identify potential conflicts and resistance at an early stage.

Table 4). They either informally pre-discussed decisions with the executive board or initiated a decision-making process because of information advantages they derived from a central position in business elite networks. This is especially true for 'big linkers' such as Hermann Josef Abs (Deutsche Bank) or Jürgen Ponto (Dresdner Bank).[49]

The existence of big linkers and personal interlocking in general is often described as an essential feature of German (or Rhenish) Capitalism. A special emphasis is placed on the coordinative function and the influence on the distribution of (informational) resources. Some authors even detected a predominant position of a small number of bank directors – who, it is alleged, thereby distort competition. The supervisory board's chairman had as a rule a discrete scope of action, which certainly could be a power resource. But it is rather doubtful, whether the informal communication *as such* was an instrument of exerting influence on business policies. But in certain constellations, especially during crises, it *could* become a resource: there is some implicit evidence that corporations which were linked to the financial and personal business networks had more options to overcome a crisis than companies from the outside.[50] But being part of the 'Germany Inc.' was no guarantee of better managing business difficulties. The network (as any network) only provided additional opportunities.

For the 1960s and 1970s we may distinguish three types of corporate governance arrangements. (1) The supervisory board as the de facto executive body with a weak and uninfluential (but legally responsible) executive board. (2) The supervisory board as a control body with advisory functions as intended by legislators. (3) The supervisory board as a body of representation, which only exercised the legal minimum control. Roughly 60% of the sample conforms to the second type, which fully matched the legal norm. The other 40% of companies either had a superior supervisory or a superior executive board. However, those 40% still acted on a legal basis even though they did not meet the law's expectations.[51]

Varieties of corporate control: qualitative evidence

This classification, deduced from contemporary surveys, can clarify some dimensions of different governance regimes within Germany but it does not show whether belonging to one of the three categories made corporate control more or less effective. Several case studies indicate that an effective corporate control did *not* depend on an ideal adaptation of rules laid down by law. Instead, the law left enough room to implement (or even to test) control arrangements that were regarded as favourable for the company's performance.

Especially in family-dominated companies, even the three categories mentioned above cannot adequately describe the 'real' control structures because parallel 'control bodies' had been established over time. However, these structures – on which the law had nothing to say – were clearly only changed when companies' financial development or a(n) (in)ability to manage large investments or capital increases made change necessary; legal requirements by contrast did not play a role.[52]

The Metallgesellschaft, a metal trading company, shows the almost 'chaotic' shape corporate control could take. The traditional family firm had pursued a specific control arrangement since the 1920s, which was built on personal relationships and personal trust. Only businessmen who were also close associates were chosen as supervisors and delegates from banks remained a rare exception. As a result of decartelisation, in the 1950s members of the Merton family only held a minority of stock, and for the first time a large bank, the Rhein-Main-Bank, a successor of the unbundled Dresdner Bank, became a relevant shareholder. But even then a group of family members and companions in practice controlled the company's property rights – regardless of whether they were a member of the executive or the supervisory board. The primus inter pares within these fluid management and supervisory structures, Richard Merton, was for instance the head of the supervisory board and determined the business policy. The formal position in Metallgesellschaft's bodies had a legal significance but did not say anything about internal power relations. The effect of this insider structure was that the Metallgesellschaft lacked consistent reporting and accounting standards. Managers or supervisors responsible for a subsidiary usually had a vast experience in the related business and thus reported more or less impressionistically about current developments. However, these thoroughly confusing reporting and control structures at the Metallgesellschaft had no significant negative impact on business policy during the tenure of those businessmen who were used to these control arrangements; conversely, external shareholders did not have an impact on business policies or on significant control rights. Although the Rhein-Main-Bank, in particular, was convinced that the way in which Merton and his companions managed the company violated the stock company law it was reluctant to enforce its own property rights. This incidentally serves as a good example of how limited the power of a bank could be in practice. In the end, the scepticism of the Rhein-Main-Bank turned out to be valid. After all executives and supervisors who had been in charge since the 1920s and 1930s had left the firm it gradually slid into a first severe crisis in the early 1970s even though accounting and reporting standards had been modernised from the 1960s onwards.[53] However, in 1993/94 the Metallgesellschaft finally went bankrupt. Again, deficits in corporate control came to light: the head of the supervisory board, Ronaldo Schmitz (Deutsche Bank) was blamed for having backed the executive board's speculative dealings for too long.[54]

To some extent, outdated reporting forms and control structures had accelerated the development from a family-dominated to a more public company. This was true as well for the attempts of the Daimler-Benz' executives in the mid-1960s who finally evaded the far-reaching control that its major shareholder, Friedrich Flick, demanded. Flick was used to an authoritarian management style which over time came to conflict with the interests of self-confidant executives who led one of Germany's most successful companies.[55] In a similar manner Heinrich Schlieker had refused to restructure his companies. His group of companies

was not organised as a stock corporation, and – among others – it was engaged in shipbuilding. When the industry's global decline and its negative impact on the Schlieker group
became clear in the early 1960s, Heinrich Schlieker refused to yield to his creditors' conditions,
which included a conversion into a stock corporation. Schlieker simply did not want to cede
control and influence to outsiders but to maintain his far-reaching property rights. As a
consequence, Schlieker's former business partners denied further credits and the group
went bankrupt.[56]

These cases sounded the death knell for control arrangements with concentrated property rights and/or person-centred managements (at least in capital intensive industries).
While in individual cases even such 'outdated' control arrangements still worked in the 1950s
and 1960s, there is some evidence – detailed studies are still a desideratum – that management styles and corporate control substantially changed from the 1970s and 1980s onwards
when – beyond 'macro-processes' such as globalisation, the paradigm-shift to 'neo-liberalism',
and financialisation – not only the composition of stockholders changed but a new generation of managers was put in charge; they were better educated, more sophisticated, and
less authoritarian.[57]

It is not a coincidence that the role of personality and personal skills began to enter the
limelight in the early 1970s. Managers' and supervisors used the concept of 'personal skills'
as the predominant argument in the – short but intense – discussion about corporate control
(and bank power) only some years after the stock corporation act reform in 1965; a debate
that now included public enterprises as well.[58] From a contemporary point of view established control arrangements seemed to have triggered the visible increase of corporate
crises and failures at that time. Nowadays, these developments instead appear as symptoms
of global structural changes after the end of Bretton Woods and the 1970s' oil crises when
(global) competitiveness suddenly became an issue for German companies. Not by chance,
recent studies emphasise the long-term effects of the radical changes since 1973 for
Germany's capitalism, the beginning of the 'Germany Inc.'-network's dissolution and the
gradual adaption of Anglo-American business practices and concepts of market organisation.[59] Obviously, these 'market developments' affected Germany's economy more than the
alleged failures of corporate control and the debate about yet another reform ended quickly.
This assumption corroborates, as it were, the argument that personality and/or proper
self-regulation were crucial factors for an effective corporate control. Of course, such more
or less individual factors presented the legislator with severe imponderables, which legal
regulations could not adequately address. This, however, is a time-invariant issue that businessmen and their associations frequently underlined in debates about (German) corporate
governance throughout history: in their perspective, workable and functional corporate
control depended only marginally on laws and statutes but all the more on personality and
self-regulation. Therefore, in the supervisors' collective self-image, the development of the
managerial staff's human resources gradually became their most relevant duty. This 'personality argument' was widely accepted. But, of course, it had a strongly exclusionary character, because only businessmen should (and could) decide which kind of corporate
governance was appropriate; the general public, which theoretically was represented by
the public law, could make no such decisions. One effect was to encourage cooperative
behaviour such that only a comparably small group made decisions about values, norms,
formal and informal institutions in Germany's Big Business. On the one hand, the stock
corporation act and related laws enabled behavioural certainty but, on the other and by

doing so, this created a cooperative, networked-based, protected, patriarchal, co-opting and self-recruiting governance system that perpetuated an elitist businessmen's self-image by de facto precluding an effective public control.[60]

As the cases of Metallgesellschaft, Flick and Schlieker have already shown, individual factors could be very relevant where matters of control arrangements and efficiency were concerned. The case of Stollwerck AG, a chocolate producer, fits this pattern as well. Its corporate control changed substantially after Alfred Herrhausen had followed Hans Janberg as head of Stollwerck's supervisory board in 1970. Both supervisors had been delegated by Deutsche Bank. Stollwerck's major shareholder held more than 25% of the stock. During his mandate, Janberg was content with sparse personal information and corporate control became more or less a 'tiresome' business routine. Not least this lack of control rigidity encouraged the management to defraud the supervisory board. It engaged in creative accounting and withheld essential information about the company's imbalance from the late 1960s onwards. Although it served an expanding market, Stollwerck had failed to adjust its strategy properly, not least because of debatable personnel decisions on the part of the supervisors; their decision to appoint a stubborn industry outsider, Eberhard Weissenfeld, as CEO who more or less co-opted Alfred Geimer into the executive board, proved particularly misguided. Although already in the 1960s there had been signs of weakness, both the executive and the supervisory board had ignored them as Stollwerck continued to pay dividends of up to 16%. When Herrhausen succeeded Janberg he demanded comprehensive information, business plans and further details which the managers were unable to provide. Weissenfeld meanwhile had – for reasons of age – been delegated into the supervisory board but Geimer was still in charge. He then was immediately fired by Herrhausen who then, for a brief period, made all strategic decisions. He finally found an investor who took over most of Stollwerck's stock including the shares of Deutsche Bank.[61]

Clearly, then, personnel changes influenced control arrangements. But beyond that, the Stollwerck story tells us something about the so-called 'bank power'. Deutsche Bank never had been interested in the company itself. Its equity stake resulted from the Stollwerck crisis of 1931 when Deutsche Bank had restructured the company and had restored its profitability. It then took over the shares from the Stollwerck family and retained them in its portfolio by default. At first it proved to be a stable financial asset; there had been no demand in the stock markets anyway during the Nazi and the reconstruction period. In Stollwerck's 1971 crisis, Deutsche Bank lost interest in the stock for it was no longer a valuable asset. This is why it (successfully) tried to sell it. But during the 40 years between the company's crises and being the major stockholder, Deutsche Bank never tried to influence Stollwerck's business strategies – although it would have had the power to do so. Instead, the bank more or less confined itself to a minimum of control as stipulated by the stock corporation act. From a formal juridical point of view, the control arrangements at Stollwerck were almost ideal. With regard to business policy, however, they were definitely dysfunctional: Stollwerck's business policy was both legitimate and correct but not appropriate.

Deutsche Bank was also involved in what was arguably the most important 'triumph' of minority investors at that time. Since the mid-1950s, the bank had, as primus inter pares in the supervisory board, tried to implement a new sustainable business strategy for the beleaguered BMW-company. It therefore established a CEO, Heinrich Richter-Brohm, who supported the bank's business policy to enter the booming market for mid-range cars. This strategy afforded a significant capital increase and Deutsche Bank engineered negotiations about a jumbo merger with Daimler-Benz. Richter-Brohm favoured this solution and for this reason failed to consistently inform the supervisory board about possible alternatives. Consequently, executive and supervisory board presented the plan to merge as a mutual programme which, however, in the end had to be approved by BMW's shareholder meeting. But the minority shareholders defeated that motion because they were taken by surprise, felt misinformed and were indignant that they had not been involved in the considerations at an earlier stage. However, due to the banks' proxy votes they did not have sufficient voting power, and thus resorted to playing politics and prolonging the meeting with discussions and applications until the next day when Daimler's takeover bid became void.[62]

Certainly, the BMW case is a rare exception in German business history. But it indicates, on the one hand, that minor investors were not generally 'unprotected' and powerless. In most cases, they were clearly satisfied with the advocacy displayed by agents of 'Germany Inc.' on their behalf. On the other hand, there is of course some evidence that the control structure *could* be used to implement social or political goals, especially when it came to matters of national security – as in the case of Daimler-Benz in the 1980s – or when it became necessary to address structural crises (e.g. in coal mining and steel production).[63] However, as a result of the partial privatisation and other historical factors, public authorities could influence business policies of formally private stock corporations directly and indirectly via their property rights – especially in the energy and banking sectors. At the same time, these 'public' control structures were criticised in the same way as 'private' ones. Only the targets of criticism differed: bankers on the one hand and politicians on the other were blamed for control failures.[64]

Conclusion

The German Stock Corporation act had an intensifying effect on the interlocking of 'Germany Inc.' but it did not necessarily guarantee an effective control of legitimate *and* appropriate business politics. Corporate laws could neither prevent deficits of business control nor business failures. They provided a structure for managers and supervisors – which led to both effective and ineffective control arrangements in West German corporations.

Certainly, business history presents some evidence of 'bank power' (but mostly in company crises), a negligible role of retail investors (but in the BMW case the opposite), of the exclusion of outsiders (Schlieker), of legally correct but not appropriate control (Stollwerck) as well as of legally questionable but workable arrangements (Metallgesellschaft). All in all, such special forms of corporate control were transitory rather than enduring – and they were more or less exceptions. As a rule, de facto corporate control first and foremost was geared towards appropriate business strategies and thus economic success. However, the few examples presented here indicate that control arrangements and economic success did not necessarily depend on each other and that, moreover, the framework of corporate control was nothing without the 'right' personnel – which by no means implies that law was useless. But it was liberal rather than restrictive and thus encouraged personal responsibility on the part of businessmen – including the freedom to make bad decisions and to solve problems within their own peer-group. The legal framework, then, allowed for comprehensive self-regulation and flexible control arrangements. On the one hand, this structure ensured expertise and business-adequate forms of corporate control in general. But on the other hand, it caused lock-in-effects, co-optation including patronage, and in particular non-transparency. But as long as those negative effects remained more or less isolated cases, no further legal action was required. This informal consensus between business and state kept statutory corporate control arrangements quite stable from the late nineteenth century onwards. Supervisors by law only had to ensure minimum standards, which was a matter of business routine. Conflicts usually arose from the malleable relationship of the executive and the supervisory board, which made an effective corporate control in Germany a task for insiders and businessmen rather than for the legislator. This also explains why the 'Germany Inc.'-network could emerge and dissolve without substantial changes of the stock corporation act. Companies were flexible enough to 'shift' from a 'German' type of cooperative control to a more 'Anglo-American' type of market control. This legal flexibility is, however, not a specifically German issue but can be observed in several developed countries as Hannah and Kasuya have recently shown.[65]

In a broader (VOC-)perspective, these findings indicate that the stock corporation act itself played only a minor role in terms of corporate governance. Its most essential contribution to Germany's Coordinated Market Economy had been – by regulating self-regulation – to provide executives and supervisors with considerable leeway. As a quid pro quo, they entered into a tacit agreement to incorporate non-business issues into their business strategies. However, the stock corporation act – especially with its bipartite governance system – and related laws provided a stable infrastructure for cooperation, and playing the game was usually rewarded while infringements of informal rules often had negative consequences. While in this way the laws shaped a fairly cooperative type of capitalism they were not at all sacrosanct. They were changed without much ado when the composition of stock capital changed – at first only in practice, then (in the late 1990s) also in the statute books. This became more and more significant in the context of national capital formation, business internationalisation and globalisation–processes, which for several reasons had a negligible impact on Germany's economy from 1914 to the (late) 1970s. Before and after that, cross-country varieties in stock market capitalism were small rather than relevant.

Notes

1. Hall/Soskice, 'Introduction', 8–9.
2. For example, Fohlin, *Finance Capitalism*; Gelman and Burhop, Taxation; Fear and Kobrak, 'Banks on Board'.
3. Exceptions are Fohlin, 'Corporate Ownership and Control'; Ahrens, Gehlen, and Reckendrees, 'Deutschland AG'.
4. La Porta, Lopez-de-Silanes, Shleifer. 'Corporate Ownership'; La Porta, Lopez-de-Silanes, Shleifer, and Vishny. 'Law and Finance'.
5. Morck and Steier, Corporate Governance, 57–58; Fohlin, 'Corporate Ownership and Control', 224, 268–269; for a more general analysis see Musacchio and Turner, 'Law and Finance'.
6. Streeck and Höpner, 'Alle Macht dem Markt?', 11; with a broader perspective Streeck, *Re-Forming Capitalism*.
7. Among others: Beyer, 'Strukturen der Deutschland AG'.
8. For examples of the broader interdisciplinary discourse between sociology and history see Berghahn and Vitols (eds), *Gibt es einen deutschen Kapitalismus*; Windolf (ed.), *Finanzmarkt-Kapitalismus*; Dyson (ed.), *Politics of Regulation*.
9. Among many others, Dutzi, Aufsichtsrat, 15–25.
10. Noteboom, 'Voice and Exit-based forms', 846.
11. For example, Streeck and Höpner, 'Alle Macht dem Markt', 11; Hall and Soskice, 'Introduction', 22–27; Abelshauser, *Dynamics of German Industry*, 18–19.

12. Gehlen, 'Aktienrecht und Unternehmenskontrolle', 166; Bähr, 'Corporate Governance'; however, the legal history is comprehensively analysed in Bayer and Habersack (eds), *Aktienrecht im Wandel*.
13. Ahrens, Gehlen, and Reckendrees, 'Deutschland AG', 16–24.
14. De Jong et al., 'Evolving Role of Shareholders', 64–66, for similar developments in Switzerland David et al., *De la 'Forteresse des Alpes'*.
15. Cf. Deutsche Bundesbank (ed), *50 Jahre Deutsche Mark*.
16. Fohlin, 'Corporate ownership and Corporate Control', 233–237.
17. Hofer, 'Aktiengesetz von 1884', 406–408; Hannah, '"Divorce" of Ownership', 407.
18. Hannah, '"Divorce" of Ownership', Burhop, Chambers, and Cheffins, 'Regulation'.
19. Deutscher Industrie- und Handelstag, *Reform*, 27–28.
20. With a comparative view see: Michie, 'Different in Name only?', 52–55.
21. Bähr, 'Errichtung von Investmentgesellschaften', 363–367.
22. A good indicator is the data presented by Rajan and Zingales 'Great reversals', 15 (Table 3). Compared with 23 countries, the ratio of German stock corporations' market value to GDP remained at a low level throughout the twentieth century (especially after 1918).
23. Rudolph, 'Effekten- und Wertpapierbörsen', 322–325; Fohlin 'Corporate Ownership and Corporate Control', 230–234.
24. Spindler, 'Satzungsfreiheit', 521–542; Kropff, Reformbestrebungen, 684–687.
25. Deutscher Industrie- und Handelstag, *Reform*, 17.
26. See Dietrich, *Eigentum für jeden*; Schulz, 'Sparkassen', 348–350.
27. See Köhler, 'Havarie'.
28. Cioffi, 'Restructuring "Germany Inc"'.
29. Streeck and Höpner, 'Alle Macht dem Markt?'; Streeck, *Re-Forming Capitalism*; for a 'long duree' see Schröter, *Americanization*.
30. Although increasing numbers of mergers and acquisitions or less influence of banks indicate undisputed changes in German capital markets, empirical studies still underline the persistence of 'traditional elements' with regard to corporate governance. For example, Weber, 'Empirical Analysis'; Fliaster, Marr, 'Change of the insider-oriented corporate governance'; Jackson, Miyajima, 'Varieties of Capitalism'; Goergen, Manjon, Rennebog, 'Recent Developments'.
31. For a comprehensive overview see Lutter, 'Aufsichtsrat'.
32. Bähr, 'Corporate Governance', 72–73.
33. For example, Gehlen, *Paul Silverberg*, 156–157.
34. *Gemeinsame Denkschrift*, 59–63.
35. Plenty of evidence is, for example, presented by Jungkind, *Risikokultur*.
36. Abelshauser, *Dynamics of German Industry*, 114–115.
37. For details see Kropff, 'Reformbestrebungen'; Fohlin, 'Corporate Ownership and Control', 266–68.
38. For a recent summary of the rise and decline of the 'Germany Inc.' network see Windolf, 'Corporate Network', especially chapter 4.
39. The small but rather influential 'minority investor's movement' is illustrated by Anzinger et al., 'Aktive Minderheiten'; Schanetzky, 'Charme'; Sattler, 'Napoleon'.
40. Shonfield, *Modern Capitalism*; Albert, *Captialism against Capitalism*.
41. For example, Fohlin, *Finance Capitalism*; Fear and Kobrak, 'Banks on Board'; Burhop, Chambers, and Cheffins, 'Regulation'.
42. Werth, *Vorstand*, 69; Vogel, *Aktienrecht*, 158, 234–235.
43. Werth, *Vorstand*, 15–17.
44. Vogel, *Aktienrecht*, 260f. Bleicher, *Aufsichtsrat*, 48.
45. Vogel, *Aktienrecht*, 163f.
46. Fengler, *Entwickelt*, 134–142, 259.
47. Wiethölter, *Interessen und Organisation*, 302–303; Pross, *Manager und Aktionäre*, 102–120.
48. Vogel, *Aktienrecht*, 234–235.
49. For details see Gall, *Hermann-Josef Abs*; Ahrens and Bähr, *Jürgen Ponto*.
50. Tilly, 'Trust and Mistrust'.
51. Vogel, *Aktienrecht*, 217–274.

52. For example, Bähr and Erker, *Bosch*, 301–311.
53. Reichel, *Metallgesellschaft*, 112–113, 154–164, 211–285; Ahrens and Bähr, *Jürgen Ponto*, 141–149; for a less abrupt transition from a family dominated firm to a rather public one see Flemming, 'MAN Gruppe', 375, 404–408, 429, 445–449.
54. Tilly, 'Trust and Mistrust', 128–131.
55. Frei et al., *Flick*, 651–653.
56. Tilly, *Schlieker*, 143–161.
57. Freye, *Führungswechsel*, 169–176; Hartmann, 'Kontinuität oder Wandel', 74–75.
58. For example, Sattler, 'Bewusste Stabilisierung', 227–234; see also Köhler, 'Havarie'.
59. Raphael and Doering-Manteuffel, *Nach dem Boom*; Ahrens, Reckendrees, and Gehlen (eds.), *Deutschland AG*; Kopper 'Abschied'.
60. Bleicher, *Aufsichtsrat*, 19, 31; Gall, *Hermann-Josef Abs*, 335; Börsig, 'Role', 110; Hartmann, 'Homogenität', 45–49.
61. Kronenberg and Gehlen, 'Versager des Jahres', 332–339.
62. Triebel and Grunert, 'Krisenerfahrung', 24–27; Seidl, *Motorenwerke* (2002), 149–51, 200–230, 244, 250–2; Knoll, 'BMW Hauptversammlung' (1995).
63. For Daimler, see Freye, *Führungswechsel*, 129–166; for the Iron and Steel industry, Lauschke, *Halbe Macht*, 231–330.
64. Typical conflicts within (semi-public) enterprises are discussed by Stier, 'Wiederaufbau', 461–466, 514–516; for the perspective of public banks see Seikel, *Kampf um öffentlich-rechtliche Banken*, 103–129.
65. Hannah and Kasuya, 'Twentieth Century Enterprise Forms', 106–107.

Disclosure statement

No potential conflict of interest was reported by the author.

Bibliography

Abelshauser, Werner. *The Dynamics of German Industry: Germany's Path toward the New Economy and the American Challenge*. New York: Berghahn Books, 2005.
Ahrens, Ralf, and Johannes Bähr. *Jürgen Ponto. Bankier und Bürger. Eine Biografie* [Jürgen Ponto. Banker and Bourgeois. A Biography]. Munich: C.H. Beck Verlag, 2013.
Ahrens, Ralf, Boris Gehlen, and Alfred Reckendrees. "Die Deutschland AG als historischer Forschungsgegenstand" [Historizing Germany Inc.] In *Die „Deutschland AG": Historische Annäherungen an den bundesdeutschen Kapitalismus* ["Germany Inc.": Historical Approaches to West-Germany's Capitalism.], edited by Ralf Ahrens, Boris Gehlen, and Alfred Reckendress, 7–28. Essen, Klartext Verlag, 2013.
Albert, Michel. *Capitalism against Capitalism*. London: Murr, 1993.
Anzinger, Heribert. "Sebastian Karach, Steffen Meinshausen, and Dirk Schiereck. „Aktive Minderheiten und die Rechte des Kleinaktionärs. Die Entwicklung des Aktionärsaktivismus am Beispiel Erich Nold"

[Active Minorities and Minority Shareholder's Rights: Shareholder-Activism and the Example of Erich Nold]. *Bankhistorisches Archiv: Banking and Finance in Historical Perspective* 38, no. 1 (2012): 1–34.

Bähr, Johannes, and Paul Erker. *Bosch. Geschichte eines Weltunternehmens* [Bosch. History of a Global Player]. Munich: C. H. Beck Verlag, 2013.

Bähr, Johannes. "'Corporate Governance' im Dritten Reich: Leitungs- und Kontrollstrukturen deutscher Großunternehmen während der nationalsozialistischen Diktatur" ['Corporate Governance' during the Third Reich: Corporate Control in German Big Business during Nazi Dictatorship]. In *Wirtschaftsordnung, Staat und Unternehmen: Neue Forschungen zur Wirtschaftsgeschichte des Nationalsozialismus. Festschrift für Dietmar Petzina zum 65. Geburtstag* [Economic Order, State, and Companies: New Research on the Economic History of the Nazi period. Essays in Honor of Dietmar Petzina], edited by Werner Abelshauser, Jan-Ottmar Hesse, and Werner Plumpe, 61–80. Essen: Klartext Verlag, 2003.

Bähr, Johannes. "Die Errichtung von Investmentgesellschaft und die Einführung des persönlichen Kleinkredits 1956/59: Beginnender Massenwohlstand und der Wettbewerb um den Privatkunden" [The Invention of Investment Trusts and Retail Credits 1956/59: Growing Affluence and Competition for the Retail Customer]. In *Schlüsselereignisse der deutschen Bankengeschichte* [Key events in German Banking History], edited by Dieter Lindenlaub, Carsten Burhop, and Joachim Scholtyseck, 362–374. Stuttgart: Steiner Verlag: 2013.

Bayer, Walter, and Mathias Habersack, eds. *Aktienrecht im Wandel, 2 volumes* [Law in Stock Companies in Transition, 2 volumes]. Tübingen: Mohr Siebeck, 2007.

Berghahn, Volker R., and Sigurt Vitols, eds. *Gibt es einen deutschen Kapitalismus? Tradition und globale Perspektiven der sozialen Marktwirtschaft* [Is there a German Capitalism? Tradition and Global Perspectives of the Social Market Economy]. Frankfurt a.M.: Campus, 2006.

Beyer, Jürgen. "Die Strukturen der Deutschland AG: Ein Rückblick auf ein Modell der Unternehmenskontrolle" [Structures of Germany Inc.: A Model of Corporate Control in Retroperspective]. In *Die „Deutschland AG": Historische Annäherungen an den bundesdeutschen Kapitalismus"* ["Germany Inc.": Historical Approaches to West-Germany's Capitalism], edited by Ralf Ahrens, Boris Gehlen, and Alfred Reckendress, 31–56. Essen: Klartext Verlag, 2013.

Bleicher, Knut. *Der Aufsichtsrat im Wandel: Eine repräsentative Studie über Aufsichtsräte in bundesdeutschen Aktiengesellschaften im Auftrag der Bertelsmann Stiftung* [The Supervisory Board in Transition. A Representative Survey about Supervisory Boards in West-German Corporations Initiated by the Bertelsmann Stiftung]. Gütersloh: Verlag Bertelsmann Stiftung, 1987.

Börsig, Clemens. "The Role of the Supervisory Board in Respect of the Management Board." In *Corporate Governance Report 2006*, edited by Gerhard Cromme, 103–112. Stuttgart: Schaeffer-Poeschel Verlag, 2006.

Deutsche Bundesbank, ed. *50 Jahre Deutsche Mark: Monetäre Statistiken 1948-1997 auf CD-ROM* [50 years Deutsche Mark: Monetary Statistics 1948-1997, CD-ROM]. Munich: C.H. Beck, 1998.

Burhop, Carsten, David Chambers, and Brian Cheffins. "Is Regulation Essential to Stock Market Development? Going Public in London and Berlin, 1900-1913." Preprints of the Max Planck Institute for Research on Collective Goods Bonn 15, 2011.

Cioffi, John W. "Restructuring 'Germany Inc.': The Politics of Company and Takeover Law Reform in Germany and the European Union." *Law & Policy* 24, no. 4 (2002): 355–402. doi:10.1111/j.0265-8240.2002.00161.x.

David, Thomas, André Mach, Martin Lüpold, and Gerhard Schnyder. *De la «Forteresse des Alpes» à la valeur actionnariale. Histoire de la gouvernance d'entreprise suisse (1880–2010)* [From the 'Alpine Fortress' to Shareholder Value. History of Swiss Corporate Governance]. Zürich: Seismo, 2015.

De Jong, Abe, Ailsa Röell, and Gerarda Westerhuis. "The Evolving Role of Shareholders in Dutch Corporate Governance 1900–2010. In *Varieties of Capitalism and Business History. The Dutch Case*, edited by Keetie Sluyterman, 50–77. New York and London: Routledge 2015.

Deutscher Industrie- und Handelstag. *Zur Reform des Aktienrechts* [About Reforming the Stock Corporation Act]. Bonn: Deutscher Industrie- und Handelstag, 1954.

Deyson, Kenneth, ed. *The Politics of German Regulation*. Aldershot: Dartmouth Publishers, 1992.

Dietrich, Yorck. *Eigentum für jeden: Die vermögenspolitischen Initiativen der CDU und die Gesetzgebung 1950-1961* [Property for Everyone. German Asset Policy, 1950-1961]. Düsseldorf: Droste Verlag, 1996.

Dutzi, Andreas. *Der Aufsichtsrat als Instrument der Corporate Governance. Ökonomische Analyse der Veränderungen im Corporate-Governance-System börsennotierter Aktiengesellschaften* [The Supervisory Board as an Instrument of Corporate Covernance. An Economic Analysis of the Changes in Corporations Listed at the Stock Markets]. Wiesbaden: Gabler, 2005.

Fear, Jeffrey, and Christopher Kobrak. "Banks on Board: German and American Corporate Governance, 1870–1914." *Business History Review* 84, no. 4 (2010): 703–736. doi:10.1017/S0007680500001999.

Fengler, Silke. *Entwickelt und fixiert. Zur Unternehmens- und Technikgeschichte der deutschen Fotoindustrie, dargestellt am Beispiel der Agfa AG Leverkusen und des VEB Filmfabrik Wolfen (1945-1995)* [Developed and Grounded: A Business and Technological History of the German Photo-Industry]. Essen: Klartext-Verlag, 2009.

Flemming, Thomas. "Der Weg zur heutigen MAN-Gruppe (1960-2008)" [The Road to the Current MAN-group (1960-2008)]. In *Die MAN: Eine deutsche Industriegeschichte* [MAN. A German Business History], edited by Johannes Bähr, Ralf Banken, and Thomas Flemming, 365-474. Munich: C. H. Beck Verlag, 2008.

Fliaster, Alexander, and Rainer Marr. "Change of the Insider-oriented Corporate Governance in Japan and Germany: Between Americanisation and Tradition." *Journal of Change Management* 1, no. 3 (2007): 242–256. doi:10.1080/714042470.

Fohlin, Caroline. *Finance Capitalism and Germany's Rise to Industrial Power*. Cambridge: Cambridge University Press, 2007.

Fohlin, Caroline. "Does Civil Law Tradition and Universal Banking Crowd out Securities Markets? Pre-World War I Germany as Counter-Example." *Enterprise & Society* 8, no. 3 (2007): 602–641. doi:10.1093/es/khm068.

Fohlin, Caroline. "The History of Corporate Ownership and Control in Germany." In *A History of Corporate Governance Around the World: Family Business Groups to Professional Managers*, edited by Randall K. Morck, 223–277. Chicago, IL: The University of Chicago Press, 2007.

Frei, Norbert, Ralf Ahrens, Jörg Osterloh, and Tim Schanetzky. *Flick: Der Konzern. Die Familie. Die Macht* [Flick: The Concern, the Family, the Power]. Munich: Karl Blessing Verlag, 2009.

Freye, Saskia. *Führungswechsel: Die Wirtschaftselite und das Ende der Deutschland AG* [Change of Management and the End for Gemany Inc.] Frankfurt a. M.: Campus, 2009.

Gall, Lothar. *Der Bankier Hermann Josef Abs. Ein Biographie* [The Banker Hermann Josef Abs. A Biography]. Munic: Beck, 2004.

Gehlen, Boris. *Paul Silverberg (1876 bis 1959). Ein Unternehmer* [Paul Silverberg (1876-1959). An Entrepreneur]. Stuttgart: Steiner-Verlag, 2007.

Gehlen, Boris. "Aktienrecht und Unternehmenskontrolle: Normative Vorgabe und unternehmerische Praxis in der Hochphase der Deutschland AG" [Coporate Law and Corporate Control: Norms and Business Practices during the heyday of Germany Inc]. In *Die „Deutschland AG": Historische Annäherungen an den bundesdeutschen Kapitalismus* ["Germany Inc.": Historical Approaches to West-Germany's Capitalism], edited by Ralf Ahrens, Boris Gehlen, and Alfred Reckendress, 165-193. Essen: Klartext Verlag, 2013.

Gelman, Sergey, and Carsten Burhop. "Taxation, Regulation and the Information Efficiency of the Berlin Stock Exchange, 1892-1913." *European Review of Economic History* 12, no. 1 (2008): 39–66. doi:10.1017/S1361491608002104.

Gemeinsame Denkschrift zum Referentenentwurf eines Aktiengesetzes [Joint Memorandum Regarding the Refent's Exposé of a Stock Corporation Act]. Köln/Bonn: Selbstverlag, 1959.

Goergen, Marc, Miguel C. Manjon, and Luc Renneboog. "Recent Developments in German Corporate Governance." *International Review of Law and Economics* 28, no. 3 (2008): 175–193. doi:10.1016/j.irle.2008.06.003.

Habersack, Mathias, and Jan Schürnbrand. "Modernisierung des Aktiengesetzes von 1965" [Modernization of the Stock Corporation Act]. In *Aktienrecht im Wandel, vol. 1: Entwicklung des Aktienrechts* [Law in Stock Companies in Transition, vol. 1: Development of Stock Companies' Law], edited by Walter Bayer and Mathias Habersack, 889-943. Tübingen: Mohr Siebeck, 2007.

Hall, Peter A., and David Soskice. "An Introduction to the Varieties of Capitalism." In *Varieties of Capitalism*, edited by Peter A Hall and David Soskice, 1–68. Oxford: Oxford University Press, 2001.

Hannah, Leslie. "The 'Divorce' of Ownership from Control from 1900 Onwards: Re-calibrating Imagined Global Trends." Business History 49, no. 4 (2007), 404–438. http://doi.org/10.1080/00076790701295821

Hannah, Leslie, and Makoto Kasuya. "Twentieth-Century Enterprise Forms: Japan in Comparative Perspective." *Enterprise & Society* 17 (2016): 80–115. doi:10.1017/eso.2015.51.

Hartmann, Michael. "Kontinuität oder Wandel? Die deutsche Wirtschaftselite zwischen 1970 und 1995" [Continuity or Change? The German Business Elite between 1970 and 1995]. In *Großbürger und Unternehmer. Die deutsche Wirtschaftselite im 20. Jahrhundert* [Bourgeoisie and Businessmen. The German Business Elite during the 20th Century], edited by Dieter Ziegler, 73-92. Göttingen: Vandenhoeck & Ruprecht, 2000.

Hartmann, Michael. "Soziale Homogenität und generationelle Muster der deutschen Wirtschaftselite seit 1945" [Social Homogeneity and Generational Patterns within the German Business Elite since 1945]. In *Die deutsche Wirtschaftselite im 20. Jahrhundert. Kontinuität und Mentalität* [The German Business Elite during the 20th Century. Continuity and Mentality], edited by Volker Berghahn, Stefan Unger, and Dieter Ziegler, 31-50. Essen: Klartext-Verlag, 2003.

Herrigel, Gary. "Coporate Governance." In *The Oxford Handbook of Business History*, edited by Geoffrey Jones, and Jonathan Zeitlin, 470-497. Oxford: Oxford University Press, 2007, 2010.

Hofer, Sibylle. "Das Aktiengesetz von 1884 – ein Lehrstück für prinzipielle Schutzkonzeptionen" [The Stock Corporation Act of 1884 – A Lesson for a General Legal Protection]. In *Aktienrecht im Wandel, vol. 1: Entwicklung des Aktienrechts* [Law in Stock Companies in Transition, vol. 1: Development of Stock Companies' Law], edited by Walter Bayer and Mathias Habersack, 388–414. Tübingen: Mohr Siebeck, 2007.

Jackson, Gregory, and Hideaki Miyajima. "Varieties of Capitalism, Varieties of Markets: Mergers and Acquisitions in Japan, Germany, France, the UK and USA." RIETI Discussion Paper Series 07-E-054, 2007.

Jungkind, Thilo. *Risikokultur und Störfallverhalten der chemischen Industrie: Gesellschaftliche Einflüsse auf das unternehmerische Handeln von Bayer und Henkel seit der zweiten Hälfte des 20. Jahrhunderts* [Culture of Risk and Conduct in Case of Incidents: Public Influence on Strategic Behaviour at Bayer and Henkel since the Second Half of the 20th Century]. Stuttgart: Steiner Verlag, 2013.

Knoll, Leonhard. "Die BMW Hauptversammlung vom 9.12.1959 – eine historische Fallstudie zu der (Ohn-)Macht des Kleinaktionärs und der Rolle der Depotbanken" [BMW's Shareholders Meeting, December, 9th, 1959 – A Historical Case Studie about Minor Investor's (lack of) Power and the Role of Depositary Banks]. *VSWG: Vierteljahrschrift für Sozial- und Wirtschaftsgeschichte* 82 (1995): 478-495. http://www.jstor.org/stable/20738411.

Köhler, Ingo. "Havarie der 'Schönwetterkapitäne'? Die Wirtschaftswunder-Unternehmer in den 1970er Jahren" [Fair-weather Captains' Average? The Businessmen of the Economic Miracle in the 1970s]. In *Pleitiers und Bankrotteure. Geschichte des ökonomischen Scheiterns vom 18. bis zum 20. Jahrhundert* [Bankrupts. A History of Economic Failure from 18th to 20th Century], edited by Ingo Köhler and Roman Rossfeld, 251-283. Frankfurt a.M.: Campus, 2012.

Kopper, Christopher. "Der langsame Abschied von der Deutschland AG? Die deutschen Banken und die Europäisierung des Kapitalmarkts in den 1980er Jahren" [The Decline of Germany Inc. German Banks and the Europeanisation of capital markets]. *Archiv für Sozialgeschichte* 52 (2012): 91–110.

Kronenberg, Cathrin, and Boris Gehlen. "Der „Versager des Jahres". Die Krise der Gebrüder Stollwerck AG, Köln 1970/71" ['Failure of the year'. The Crisis of Gebr. Stollwerck AG, Cologne, 1970/71]. In *Pleitiers und Bankrotteure. Geschichte des ökonomischen Scheiterns vom 18. bis zum 20. Jahrhundert* [Bankrupts. A History of Economic Failure from 18th to 20th Century], edited by Ingo Köhler and Roman Rossfeld, 317-340. Frankfurt a.M.: Campus, 2012.

Kropff, Bruno. "Reformbestrebungen im Nachkriegsdeutschland und die Aktienrechtsreform von 1965" [Reform Efforts and the reform of the stock corporation act in 1965]. In *Aktienrecht im Wandel, vol. 1: Entwicklung des Aktienrechts* [Law in Stock Companies in Transition, vol. 1: Development of Stock Companies' Law], edited by Walter Bayer and Mathias Habersack, 670-997. Tübingen: Mohr Siebeck, 2007.

La Porta, Rafael, Florencio, Lopez-de-Silanes, Andrei, Shleifer, and Robert W., Vishny. "Law and Finance." *Journal of Political Economy* 106, no. 6 (1998): 1113–1155. doi:10.1086/250042.

La Porta, Rafael, Florenco, Lopez-De-Silanes, and Andrei, Shleifer. "Corporate Ownership Around the World." *The Journal of Finance* 54, no. 2 (1999): 471–517. doi:10.1111/0022-1082.00115.

Lauschke, Karl. *Die halbe Macht: Mitbestimmung in der Eisen- und Stahlindustrie 1945 bis 1989* [Half the Power: Co-Determination in the Iron and Steel Industry 1945 to 1989]. Essen: Klartext-Verlag, 2007.

Lutter, Marcus. "Der Aufsichtsrat im Wandel der Zeit – von seinen Anfängen bis heute" [The Supervisory Board in transition – from the beginnings until today]. In *Aktienrecht im Wandel, vol. 2: Grundsatzfragen des Aktienrechts* [Law in Stock Companies in Transition, vol. 2: Basic Issues of Stock Companies' Law], edited by Walter Bayer and Mathias Habersack, 389-429. Tübingen: Mohr Siebeck, 2007.

Michie, Ranald. "Different in Name Only? The London Stock Exchange and Foreign Bourses, c.1850–1914." *Business History* 30, no. 1 (1988): 46-68.

Morck, Randall K., and Lloyd Steier. "The Global History of Corporate Governance: An Introduction." In *A History of Corporate Governance Around the World: Family Business Groups to Professional Managers*, edited by Randall K. Morck, 1–64. Chicago, IL: The University of Chicago Press, 2007.

Mussachio, Aldo, and John D. Turner. "Does the Law and Finance Hypothesis Pass the Test of History?" *Business History* 55, no. 4 (2013): 524–542.

Nooteboom, Bart. "Voice- and Exit-Based Forms of Corporate Control: Anglo-American, European, and Japanese". *Journal of Economic Issues* 33, no. 4 (1999): 845–860. http://www.jstor.org/stable/4227503.

Pross, Helge. *Manager und Aktionäre in Deutschland: Untersuchungen zum Verhältnis von Eigentum und Verfügungsmacht* [Managers and Shareholders in Germany. A Survey about Property Rights]. Frankfurt a. M.: Europäische Verlagsanstalt, 1965.

Rajan, Raghuram G., and Luigi Zingales. "The Great Reversals: The Politics of Financial Development in the Twentieth Century." *Journal of Financial Economics* 69 (2003): 5–50. doi:10.1016/S0304-405X(03)00125-9.

Raphael, Lutz, and Anselm Doering-Manteuffel. *Nach dem Boom. Perspektiven auf die Zeitgeschichte seit 1970* [After the Boom. Perspectives on Contemporary History since 1970]. 3rd ed. Göttingen: Vandenhoeck & Ruprecht, 2012.

Reichel, Clemens. *Vom Verbund zum Konzern: Die Metallgesellschaft AG 1945–1975* [From Combination to Concern: Metallgesellschaft AG, 1945-1975]. Darmstadt: Hessisches Wirtschaftsarchiv, 2008.

Rudolph, Bernd. "Effekten- und Wertpapierbörsen, Finanztermin- und Devisenbörsen seit 1945" [Stock, Securities, Futures, and Forex Exchanges since 1945]. In *Deutsche Börsengeschichte* [History of German Exchanges], edited by Hans Pohl, 293-375. Frankfurt a.M.: Fritz Knapp Verlag, 1992.

Sattler, Friederike. "Der ,Napoleon des deutschen Aktienmarktes': Hermann D. Krages und die Netzwerke des ,rheinischen Kapitalismus': Die Geschichte einer scheiternden Karriere." [Napoleon of the German Stock Market: Hermann D. Krages and the Networks of Rhenish Capitalism: The Story of a Declining Career]. *Jahrbuch für Wirtschaftsgeschichte/ Economic History Yearbook* 51, no. 2 (2010): 165–198. doi: 10.1524/jbwg.2010.51.2.165.

Schanetzky, Tim. "Wider den diskreten Charme des ,rheinischen Kapitalismus': Anfänge der Berufsopposition in den westdeutschen Hauptversammlungen" [Against the Discretion of Rhenish Capitalism. The Beginnings of Professional Opposition in West-German Shareholder's Meetings]. *Akkumulation. Informationen des Arbeitskreises für kritische Unternehmens- und Industriegeschichte* 26 (2008): 1–7.

Schröter, Harm G. *Americanization of the European Economy. A Compact Survey of American Economic Influence in Europe since the 1880s.* Dordrecht: Springer, 2005.

Schulz, Günther. "Die Sparkassen vom Ende des Zweiten Weltkriegs bis zur Wiedervereinigung" [Savings banks form the end of World War II until Re-Unification]. In *Wirtschafts- und Sozialgeschichte der deutschen Sparkassen im 20. Jahrhundert* [Social and economic history of German savings banks in the 20th Century], edited by Hans Pohl, Bernd Rudolph and Günther Schulz, 249–428. Stuttgart: Deutscher Sparkassenverlage 2005.

Seidl, Jürgen. *Die Bayerischen Motorenwerke (BMW) 1945–1969. Staatlicher Rahmen und unternehmerisches Handeln* [BMW 1945-1969. Public Framework and Strategic Action]. Munich: C. H. Beck Verlag 2002.

Seikel, Daniel. *Der Kampf um öffentlich-rechtliche Banken: Wie die Europäische Kommission Liberalisierung durchsetzt* [The Struggle for Public Banks: How the European Commission enforces Liberalization]. Frankfurt a.M.: Campus Verlag, 2013.

Shonfield, Andrew. *Modern Capitalism: The Changing Balance of Public and Private Power*. London: Oxford University Press, 1965.

Spindler, Gerald. "Die Entwicklung der Satzungsfreiheit und Satzungsstrenge im deutschen Aktienrecht" [Statutes' freedom and rigidity in German stock corporation law]. In *Aktienrecht im Wandel, vol. 2: Grundsatzfragen des Aktienrechts* [Law in Stock Companies in Transition, vol. 2: Basic Issues of Stock Companies' Law], edited by Walter Bayer and Mathias Habersack, 995–1026. Tübingen: Mohr Siebeck, 2007.

Stier, Bernhard. "Zwischen Wiederaufbau, Strukturveränderung und strategischer Neuausrichtung: Die Preussag von 1945 bis zum Beginn der 1980er Jahre" [Between Reconstruction, Structural Change, and Realignment: Preussag from 1945 to the Early 1980s]. In *Von der Preussag zur TUI: Wege und Wandlungen eines Unternehmens 1923-2003* [From Preussag to Tui: A Company's Transitions 1923-2003], edited by Bernhard Stier and Johannes Laufer, 387–561. Essen: Klartext-Verlag 2005.

Streeck, Wolfgang. *Re-Forming Capitalism: Institutional Change in the German Political Economy*. Oxford: Oxford University Press, 2009.

Streeck, Wolfgang, and Martin Höpner. "Einleitung: Alle Macht dem Markt?" [Introduction: All Power to the Market?]. In *Alle Macht dem Markt? Studien zur Abwicklung der Deutschland AG* [All Power to the Market? Essays about Winding-Up Germany Inc.], edited by Wolfgang Streeck and Martin Höpner, 11–59. Frankfurt a. M.: Campus, 2001.

Tilly, Richard. "Trust and Mistrust: Banks, Giant Debtors, and Enterprise Crises in Germany, 1960–2002." In *Jahrbuch für Wirtschaftsgeschichte/Economic History Yearbook* 46, no. 1 (2005): 107–135. doi:10.1524/jbwg.2005.46.1.107.

Tilly, Richard. *Willy H. Schlieker: Aufstieg und Fall eines Unternehmers (1914–1980)* [Willy H. Schlieker. A Businessman's Rise and Decline, 1914-1980]. Berlin: Akademie-Verlag, 2008.

Triebel, Florian, and Manfred Grunert. "Krisenerfahrung bei der BMW AG: Zur Typologie des Phänomens Unternehmenskrise" [Crises experience at BMW. A Typology of the phenomenon Company Crisis]. *Jahrbuch für Wirtschaftsgeschichte/Economic History Yearbook* 47, no. 2 (2006): 19–30. doi:10.1524/jbwg.2006.47.2.19.

Vogel, Wolfgang C. *Aktienrecht und Aktienwirklichkeit: Organisation und Aufgabenteilung von Vorstand und Aufsichtsrat. Eine empirische Untersuchung deutscher Aktiengesellschaften* [Company Law and its Reality: Organization and Division of Labour between Executive and Supervisory Board. An Empirical Survey of German Corporations]. Baden-Baden: Nomos, 1980.

Weber, Anke. "An Empirical Analysis of the 2000 Corporate Tax Reform in Germany: Effects on Ownership and Control in Listed Companies." *International Review of Law and Economics* 29, no. 1 (2009): 57–66. doi:10.1016/j.irle.2008.07.011.

Werth, Heinz-Jürgen. *Vorstand und Aufsichtsrat in der Aktiengesellschaft* [Executive and Supervisory Boards within the Corporation]. Düsseldorf: Verlagsbuchhandlung des Instituts der Wirtschaftsprüfer, 1960.

Wiethölter, Rudolf. *Interessen und Organisation der Aktiengesellschaft im amerikanischen und deutschen Recht*. [Interests and Organization of the Corporation in German and American Law]. Karlsruhe: C.F. Müller, 1961.

Windolf, Paul, ed. *Finanzmarkt-Kapitalismus: Analysen zum Wandel von Produktionsregimen* [Financial Capitalism. Analyzing Production Regimes' Transitions]. Wiesbaden: VS Verlag für Sozialwissenschaften, 2005.

Windolf, Paul. "The Corporate Network in Germany 1986–2010." In The Power of Corporate Networks: A Comparative and Historical Perspective, edited by Gerarda Westhuis and Thomas David, 66–88. London: Routledge, 2014.

Zapf, Wolfgang. *Wandlungen der deutschen Elite. Ein Zirkulationsmodell deutscher Führungsgruppen 1919–1961* [Transitions of the German Elite. A Circulation Model of German leader's groups, 1919-1961]. München: Piper, 1965.

Between national governance and the internationalisation of business. The case of four major West German producers of chemicals, pharmaceuticals and fibres, 1945–2000

Christian Marx

ABSTRACT
Although German companies lost their foreign assets after World War II, they returned quickly to the world market after 1945. While internationalisation during the post-war boom was mainly based on exports, foreign direct investment (FDI) increased enormously since the late 1960s. Simultaneously, the companies remained part of the German corporate network as a typical characteristic of Rhenish capitalism. Unlike many Varieties-of-Capitalism (VoC) studies dealing with the macro-level picture of whole economies, the article reconsiders the idea that firms should be at the centre of analysis and examines the responses of four major West German producers of chemicals, pharmaceuticals and fibres to the tension between national corporate governance and increasing internationalisation.

Introduction

The organisational structures and business strategies of companies are not only a product of managerial decisions, but also dependent on the political, legal, and cultural contexts of business.[1] Many strategic decisions can only be explained in the light of the company's specific environment and its political economy. Conversely, owners and managers of firms could make choices based on dominant national rules – particularly in the context of the growing openness of the international economy. According to Peter A. Hall and David Soskice the institutional structure conditions corporate strategies, but it does not fully determine it.[2] Thus, the Variety-of-Capitalism (VoC) approach is a meaningful conceptual consideration to explain different ways of company development and locates the firm at the centre of the analysis. The idea, that solving coordination problems differed in national political economies – reflected in corporate governance, in inter-firm relations, in laws and in the practices of economic agents – is the starting point of the following reflections. As described by Michel Albert in heuristic form and more analytically in the VoC literature, Rhenish capitalism is characterised by a close relationship between companies and banks.[3] Even if the question as to how much one type of capitalism needs to change before it constitutes a new model has not yet been fully answered, changes in one sphere of the economy do indicate a change of the whole economy due to institutional complementarities. Where dense corporate networks prevented hostile takeovers, for instance, those same networks supported collaborative systems of vocational training and collective standard-setting. Hence, there is justification for taking a closer look at one principal sphere of capitalism.[4] However, not every change could be equated with convergence to another model. Institutional arrangements frequently change over periods of time without breaking down. Institutions can be held in place while their context shifts in ways that alter their effects or agents can redirect institutions toward purposes beyond their original intent. Institutional survival in the face of shifts in the social, political or economic environment is often connected to elements of institutional transformation and involves a renegotiation of the coalition base. At the same time, institutions show a high degree of resilience because of specific mechanisms of reproduction, and as a consequence, they do not always break down in the face of exogenous shocks or endogenous challenges.[5]

Using the example of four major West German producers of chemicals, pharmaceuticals and fibres (BASF, Bayer, Hoechst, Glanzstoff) in the second half of the twentieth century, this article focuses on the institutional arena of the corporate network and analyses non-market modes of coordination. According to the literature about VoC and Rhenish capitalism, Germany was characterised by interlocking directorates and financial links between joint-stock companies. These dense networks linked managers of one company to their counterparts in others and provided a place for the exchange of information and confidential agreements.[6] The article analyses these networks on the level of the firm and examines – as otherwise often omitted in research about corporate networks on the macro-level[7] – the functionality and content of relations in the light of increasing internationalisation. While the distinction between different types of capitalisms predominantly refers to national differences, increasing international integration – especially in Western Europe – after World War II was a challenge for all national models. Consequently, this article asks whether the close inter-firm relationships remained permanently or disintegrated as a result of increasing internationalisation and if the Rhenish model changed in the logic of institutional evolution or approached other types of capitalism.

The position of West German industry in 1945 differed fundamentally to that of other European countries or the US. With the victory over Nazi Germany, German companies lost both their foreign assets as well as their trademark and patent rights abroad. Many business relations were discontinued in the 1930s as part of the Nazi policy of autarchy and with the expropriation in 1945 foreign relations reached their nadir. At the same time, the chemical industry had become a precondition for the minimum supply of goods from the food, health and clothing sector by the mid-twentieth century. Hence, the restrictions imposed by the Allies were soon eased and as a result West German chemical and pharmaceutical companies regained their pre-war economic success in the 1950s, even though they had missed technological developments in petrochemicals and antibiotics research as a result of World War II. In addition to German reconstruction, export was the engine of expansion. After the post-war boom had peaked in the 1960s, many traditional industries faced huge challenges. Enormous growth and sales rates had covered low profitability during the boom, but in times of economic downturn these problems came to light and led to a broad economic change in the last third of the twentieth century.[8] The chemical industry was traditionally a capital-intensive industry because of its high costs for research and development, and the spread of mass production during the twentieth century meant its need for capital even increased. This situation intensified the sector's interest in long-term relations between banks and industry and the problem of access to finance in general, even though the big German chemical companies could finance a lot of their investments through internal resources. In comparison to their US competitors, German companies relied to a much greater extent on debt. This access to 'patient capital' was central for the long-term predictability of business as a valuable asset of the German system. German banks took on part of the risks caused by the companies' strategies directly, becoming co-entrepreneurs, and as a consequence had an interest in controlling the development of companies through representatives on the supervisory boards, whereas in the USA banks often acted as financial intermediaries offering share issues and bonds.[9] For this reason, the relationship between industrial companies and banks will be given special attention in the following.

The article is structured in four parts. The first chapter analyses the return of the German chemical industry to the world market after World War II. Then, the main characteristics of internationalisation since the end of the 'economic miracle' in the 1960s are illustrated. According to the economic historian Ulrich Wengenroth, a major change took place in the strategies of the German chemical industry in the 1960s: 'a shift to internationalization of production instead of forced exports from the well-protected home-base.'[10] For this reason, in a further step, the article explores the consequences of different forms of internationalisation on the German corporate governance system across the whole period. Did the Coordinated Market Economy (CME) in Germany remain stable because of increasing returns effects, was it characterised by a kind of institutional evolution or did it break down?[11] Was there a convergence towards other forms of capitalism? And to what extent did national networks become inefficient in the context of global flows of commodities, global labour division, and global capital flows? These questions are answered in the case of four major West German producers of chemicals, pharmaceuticals and fibres with a focus on Farbwerke Hoechst AG (Hoechst) and Vereinigte Glanzstoff-Fabriken AG (VGF). The erosion of some parts of the German model in the 1990s – the fourth part – shows that there were alternative forms of corporate control. The article then suggests reasons for the dissolution of the network and examines the influence of internationalisation on this process.

The return to the world market after 1945

Until World War I, the German chemical industry had had a dominant worldwide position in several fields of production, but was cut off from many foreign markets after 1914/18. Although it recovered in the interwar period and the sector became more important for the German economy during the Nazi era, the Second World War terminated its rise, and after 1945, the Allies again put the industry under restrictive controls.[12] But reconstruction without the chemical industry would have been difficult; hence, the lack of chemical products induced the Allies to allow the resumption of work quickly. As the pharmaceutical industry was less resource-dependent, this part of the chemical industry reached the pre-war level in 1948. In the field of synthetic fibre, the industry had to build new capacities in West Germany after 1945 to secure the supply of the population with clothes. Rubber for tyres as well as soap and other chemical products were needed urgently. The plastics industry was not only able to satisfy the German market, but already exported significant quantities in 1949. All in all German chemical companies experienced a fast rise after the war and formed a dominant cluster of internationally competitive enterprises in the 1970s and 1980s.[13] This reconstruction on international markets suggests – as Christopher Kobrak has argued for the German pharmaceutical company Schering in the first half of the twentieth century – that companies competing in industries in which Germany had a competitive advantage required a high level of internationalisation to generate full economic potential.[14]

Although IG Farben lost two thirds of its assets in East Germany and abroad, its three West German successors (BASF, Bayer, Hoechst) reached 90% of total sales of IG Farben (1943) in 1953. Export was the engine of growth. Due to the Korea boom, the German chemical industry recovered and was responsible for about 15% of all German exports. Chandler notes that the German and Swiss chemical and pharmaceutical companies remained the main competitors of US firms in the long run. He argues that market entry barriers in the chemical industry were so large after the 1920s that it was nearly impossible for newcomers to gain market shares, albeit that German companies did lose markets shares temporarily as a result of the Second World War. In fact, established German, Swiss and American companies diversified successfully in the following decades.[15] German chemists had favoured coal chemistry for a long time and argued that the best sources of raw materials were at home until the 1950s, whereas internationally the rise of the petrochemical industry loomed since World War II. West German chemical companies followed this trend with some years of delay, but soon they were able to catch up with their international competitors. German companies did not see petrochemical technology as fundamentally new. In the early 1960s, half of West German organic chemicals was produced from crude oil.[16] Bayer relied on special plastics, chemical fibres and dyes, as well as crop protection and pharmaceuticals, whereas BASF had a different product portfolio with basic chemicals, fertilisers and industrial products. Hoechst had its main focus in the production of pharmaceuticals, synthetic fibres and plastics. Until the early 1980s benchmarking among the big three remained an integral part of their business policy.[17]

At BASF, Bayer and Hoechst the re-conquest of foreign markets was a central goal after 1945. After losing their foreign assets, all three companies strove particularly to establish joint ventures with foreign companies in the 1950s and 1960s in order not to lose touch with technological developments and foreign markets. BASF formed a joint venture with Royal Dutch Shell and Dow Chemical, Bayer with British Petroleum and Monsanto, and Hoechst with Hercules Powder Company. Bayer restarted its internationalisation via export business and sales agencies, then built up production capacities in the US and Brazil in the 1950s, and in the following decade, it invested more and more in Europe. Hoechst also returned to the world market through sales and trade agencies and relied on its experience from the first half of the twentieth century.[18] After the end of Allied restrictions in 1952 its rate of foreign activities increased for the first time. Hoechst drew up an agency agreement with Pontosan SA in Brazil in 1949 which became Hoechst do Brazil in 1957. In France and Great Britain, the return began with the opening of sales offices, such as the Société Peralta or Lawfer Chemical Company, which evolved into the typical national companies (Société Française Hoechst and Hoechst UK Ltd.) in the following years. Hoechst often used personal contacts to re-establish its business abroad. In the case of Peralta for example, Hoechst had a good mediator in France, as Paul Neumann, a former member of the executive board of Schering who had emigrated to Paris during the Nazi period, founded this French company in 1950 which became the centre of Hoechst's activities in France for many years.[19] In the USA, Hoechst founded Intercontinental Chemical Corporation (ICC) in 1953. Again, the expansion was accompanied by investments in several sales companies, such as

Progressive Color & Chemicals Co. Inc. (1953), the Carbic Color & Chemical Company, Inc. (1957) or the Lloyd Bros., Inc. (1960); in 1961 ICC was renamed in American Hoechst Corporation (AHC).[20] While Hoechst generated only about one million DM in foreign production and the export of domestic production amounted to DM 169 million in 1952, the share of foreign production increased continuously from the late 1950s and reached DM 582 million in 1965 – at least 25% of foreign turnover (DM 2,241 million). Here the gradual transition of foreign activities from sales organisations to production plants becomes apparent.[21] In addition to market intimacy, lower production and transport costs played an important role for internationalisation – even before the two oil crises –, and the positive development of the common market within the EEC drew the attention of West German managers to places beyond the West German frontier. Thus BASF, Bayer and Hoechst opened works at the infrastructure nodes of Antwerp and Vlissingen in the 1960s. Not least, the rise of the petrochemical industry caused a location change within the chemical industry, in which chemical plants often moved towards oil refining centres and maritime ports.[22]

Hoechst passed through the different phases of internationalisation – as described in the Uppsala model – in a tour de force.[23] Market-specific knowledge explains only one part of this expansion. It was mainly driven by contemporary expectations of future foreign markets – with regard to the single European market or South American growth markets – and by the experience of the pre-1945 period. In 1967, Hoechst's foreign sales (including its majority shareholdings) became equal to the domestic sales. This value rose to two-thirds of world turnover in 1975 and demonstrates the rapidly growing importance of foreign markets at the end of the boom. In this period, the rate of foreign activities increased for a second time.[24] The shift to foreign markets was not least a reaction to the expansion of American companies to Europe and increasing competition at home and abroad. When the French journalist Jean-Jacques Servan-Schreiber warned about the American challenge – Le Défi américain – he meant the conquest of central European industrial structures by US corporations.[25] While Canada and Latin America were the major investment regions of US chemical companies in 1964/65, the EEC took on this position in 1966. West Germany was especially attractive for US investments due to the underestimation of its currency (DM) and its position within the EEC market.[26] It was in this context that in 1965 the US chemical giant DuPont acquired a large site to construct a synthetic fibre factory at Uentrop, and Dow Chemical Company established a chemicals centre at Rheinmünster in West Germany.[27]

The export orientation was not specific to Hoechst, but was typical for West German industry in general and was based – in addition to its technological innovativeness – on the constraints of a small market compared to the US. Other German companies such as Henkel or Glanzstoff also turned to the world market after 1945. As a result, Henkel dominated almost 50% of the European detergent market in 1968.[28] In the process, the export quota of the West German chemical industry rose steadily from 23% in 1960 to 36% in 1974. In the following years, the importance of exports still increased – in 1984 the export quota crossed the 40% mark – but above all foreign direct investment (FDI) had become more important since the 1960s. From the mid-1980s to the mid-1990s the export quota did not significantly increase, only later rising and reaching 50% in 2000 (cf. Table 1).

Table 1. Export quota of the West German chemical industry (1953–2000).

Year	Export quota	Year	Export quota	Year	Export quota	Year	Export quota
1953	17.7	1965	25.0	1977	32.8	1989	43.7
1954	20.0	1966	27.3	1978	33.9	1990	41.9
1955	20.5	1967	29.0	1979	35.1	1991	39.9
1956	21.4	1968	30.8	1980	37.3	1992	38.9
1957	22.9	1969	31.1	1981	39.7	1993	39.5
1958	22.5	1970	31.1	1982	39.6	1994	40.9
1959	23.4	1971	30.8	1983	39.9	1995	41.6
1960	23.3	1972	32.1	1984	42.1	1996	43.3
1961	22.9	1973	33.9	1985	43.1	1997	45.8
1962	22.9	1974	36.0	1986	42.1	1998	46.2
1963	24.8	1975	33.0	1987	42.2	1999	47.2
1964	25.2	1976	33.2	1988	43.6	2000	50.2

Note: Statistical Yearbook of West Germany (Statistisches Bundesamt, ed. Statistisches Jahrbuch für die Bundesrepublik Deutschland / Produzierendes Gewerbe / Umsatz (1953–2001))

Internationalisation after the boom

The global economic slump of the 1970s intensified the expansion into foreign markets. German companies were forced to rationalise production and reduce costs to compensate for higher raw material and energy prices. They tried to respond to the global shocks of the 1970s – such as the disintegration of the monetary system and the oil crises – by entering new markets. Especially the producers of chemicals, plastics and fibres got into trouble.[29] The crisis of the chemical industry began in the late 1960s and was characterised by increasing global competition, declining growth and significant overcapacities in some chemical fields, and it lasted until the early 1980s.[30]

Hoechst CEO Rolf Sammet (1969–1985) identified the foreign markets as an engine of growth. In the light of rising costs for labour, energy and raw materials, the domestic economy appeared less promising to the chemical managers. Their appeals for moderate wage agreements received scant regard at the end of the 1960s. Indeed, large parts of the population supported the concept of 'social symmetry' with high wage demands accepted by the Minister for Economic Affairs Karl Schiller. Wildcat strikes were considered as a legitimate form of a 'second wage round'.[31] Sammet therefore underlined that the focus of investments in West Germany would be on rationalisation and that new plants would only be built for newly developed products; domestic investments aimed at exports lost importance. In the mid-1970s Sammet declared that 'growth will not take place at home but abroad'.[32] He argued that foreign production was a decision due to structural constraints. In fact, it was rather a strategic option within the entrepreneurial scope of action.[33]

Hopes placed in the future markets of the 1960s in South America were fulfilled only partially, and, as a result, Hoechst's expansion efforts turned to the US and Europe. With the end of polyester patents in 1966, ICI and US corporations entered the continental European market; conversely foreign markets were opened to Hoechst's Trevira products. In the same year, Hoechst and the US company Hercules Powder founded a joint venture, Hystron Fibers Inc., to be well set for the US market. After Hoechst had taken over the Hercules shares of Hystron, the company was renamed Hoechst Fibers Industries and integrated in AHC in 1972.[34] According to the new AHC president Dieter zur Loye, it had sufficed to be present on the US market up to the mid-1970s, while in a subsequent phase up to the mid-1980s management had tried to make production profitable, and it was only since the mid-1980s that AHC had aimed at generating profits as high as US chemical companies.[35] Since the mid-1980s the – traditionally export-orientated – West German chemical companies had become convinced that they had to have production sites throughout all high-selling regions of the world, and with the acquisition of Celanese Corporation for almost six billion DM in 1986, Hoechst demonstrated its determination to become an inherent part of the US market.[36]

In the late 1960s and early 1970s the Hoechst Group expanded more in Europe than in the US. As growth had been primarily based on acquisitions since the end of the boom, the specific abilities of merger partners became a decisive motive. While the areas of fibres, high-performance substances and organic chemistry were strengthened by the Celanese deal in the 1980s, the reasons for cooperation with the French pharmaceutical company Roussel Uclaf were based on its research knowledge and its position on the French market. In 1974, Hoechst bought the majority of Roussel Uclaf shares. With this acquisition – the largest single investment of Hoechst in the pharmaceutical area – Hoechst became the world's largest pharmaceutical manufacturer.[37] In addition to its expanding activities abroad in fibres (Trevira) and the pharmaceutical business (Roussel Uclaf), Hoechst also expanded in the field of paint production, and in 1970, Hoechst UK took over the British paint producer Berger, Jenson & Nicholson (BJN). Due to another prospective buyer this project proved to be much more difficult and showed the increasing competition on the market for corporate control. While Bayer was eliminated early from the race at Roussel Uclaf, Hoechst had already to fight against an American consortium during the acquisition of Reichhold Chemie AG. In the case of BJN, an US competitor only pulled out after Hoechst had significantly increased its offer on the UK stock market. In January 1970, Hoechst UK owned 56% of the BJN's share capital, and Hoechst contracted a cooperation with the British Reed Group (formerly Albert E. Reed) according to which Reed took over the remaining shares of BJN. Overall, Hoechst had to spend DM 243 million for the acquisition of the UK's second largest paint and coatings producer.[38]

Beside independent start-ups and the classical evolutional path via 'export, sales agencies, and foreign production', internationalisation based on corporate acquisitions became more and more important. Even in the case of the two chemical fibres producers 'Algemene Kunstzijde Unie Arnhem' (AKU) and 'Vereinigte Glanzstoff-Fabriken AG' (VGF) the two companies agreed on a closer cooperation. When the managements of German VGF and Dutch AKU decided to merge fully in the late 1960s, the cooperation between the two companies had already lasted for more than 40 years. As early as 1921, they had contracted an agreement on the exchange of technical patents and information, and in 1929 the relationship was intensified by the establishment of a joint holding company. After the Second World War the ownership structure had to be renegotiated and was recorded in a new contract between the German and Dutch sides in 1953. Henceforth, AKU and VGF benefited from the rise of synthetic fibres during the European post-war boom.[39]

The creation of the European Economic Community (EEC) had a crucial impact on the business strategies of all companies at that time, since intra-European trade increased enormously. Many companies merged with national or European competitors or set up joint ventures in order to stay competitive on the larger European market. The end of the European post-war boom, the gradual implementation of a common European market (until 1970) and the increased entry of multinational corporations from the US all coincided at the end of the 1960s and created a significant incentive for cross-border cooperation between European companies. Bayer, for example, agreed on a cooperation with the French Rhône-Poulenc about the delimitation of fields of research in the 1960s.[40] In the case of VGF, management appointed a working group which investigated the consequences of a common market as early as 1958.[41] Only some years later, in 1967, an internal study concluded that the reduction of tariffs within the EEC and the end of the polyester patents would bring an increasing integration of the Western European markets and an unprecedented competition between AKU and VGF. The loss of importance of national borders in Western Europe challenged the existing division of labour between the Dutch AKU and the West German VGF. This argument gave weight to the full merger of the two companies.[42] To sum up, until the end of the 1980s the strategy of the chemical companies was more influenced by Europeanisation than by globalisation and it was only in the 1990s that globalisation really gathered momentum. German companies – like Hoechst, BASF, Bayer or Glanzstoff – were central to these two developments. This means that West German institutions and companies were not simply passive recipients of a predetermined development called globalisation, but rather agents of these processes.[43]

In addition to the support of Ernst Hellmut Vits, who had been chairman of the Glanzstoff executive board since 1939, the merger in 1969 was also supported by the supervisory board, headed by Hermann Josef Abs, the longtime CEO of Deutsche Bank.[44] Whereas Dutch AKU was transformed into a holding company, its production operations were integrated into the newly established Enka NV; VGF remained unchanged in its legal structure. The management and supervisory boards of both companies were constituted by the same people, hence the new multinational company was integrated into the Dutch and the German corporate network at once.[45]

In addition to Hoechst and Glanzstoff, other West German chemical and pharmaceutical companies also entered the European and North American markets through FDI. Although the German chemical industry retained its strong export orientation after the post-war boom, the strategies of expansion were increasingly directed to foreign production. FDI showed a significant increase in the late 1960s. While the stock of FDI increased continuously, the annual rates of investment show a less uniform course; single huge acquisitions led to certain amplitudes at industry level (cf. Figure 1). After a sharp increase from 1966/67 onwards, companies were less willing to invest in 1971/72; however, FDI remained at a high, but volatile

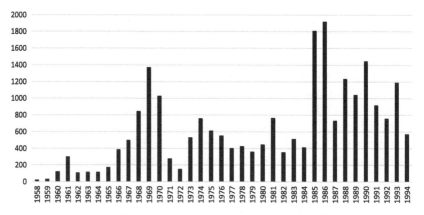

Figure 1. FDI by the West German chemical industry in million DM (1958–1994).
Note: Bundesminister für Wirtschaft, "Runderlasse"; Schreyger, *Direktinvestitionen*, 304–306. Unlike other illustrations, the figure shows not the stock, but the growth on the previous year. The data includes FDI of the pharmaceutical and the chemical fibre industry. Adjusted for inflation by producer prices of commercial products. Cf. Bundesbank: Zeitreihen-Datenbanken / Makroökonomische Zeitreihen / Unternehmen und private Haushalte / Preise / lange Reihen / Erzeugerpreise gewerblicher Produkte (https://www.bundesbank.de/Navigation/DE/Statistiken/Zeitreihen_Datenbanken/zeitreihen_datenbank.html).

level in the coming years and increased once more since from the mid-1980s. The shift from export to FDI had important implications for the corporate network at home because other agents in the economic and political field became relevant to the companies and domestic non-market modes of coordination were not able to control markets abroad.

National governance and international business

In the 1950s, the German economy returned to the world market through its exports and the appropriation of American management and marketing forms, and in the 1960s, internationalisation intensified through the increase of FDI.[46] Nevertheless, the corporate network between industrial companies and banks remained stable until the 1990s. According to the sociologist Paul Windolf, the German corporate network provided an opportunity structure (*Gelegenheitsstruktur*) for the regulation of competition and enabled managers to choose cooperation instead of defection.[47] Long-standing business contacts and solid stockholdings prevented hostile takeovers and enabled continuous financial and business planning. This was a core element of Rhenish capitalism and it was even true for the producers of chemicals, pharmaceuticals and fibres, even though they became engaged abroad sooner and stronger than other industries. It is noteworthy that this institution of Rhenish capitalism persisted for several decades, and the way it worked deserves greater attention, given that this national form of corporate governance was mostly of little use for the regulation of foreign markets.

In the case of AKU/VGF, equal representation on the governing structures in national terms was repeatedly emphasised by the Germans. Even though the German part of the company had more employees (VGF: 27,000; AKU: 15,000), larger capacities and higher sales in 1969, Dutch AKU had been the majority holder of German VGF shares – with exception of some years during the Nazi period – since 1929.[48] With the merger of AKU and KZO into Akzo in 1969, the Germans came into a minority position in the managing bodies.[49] In addition to AKU/Akzo, Deutsche Bank had a sizeable equity stake of VGF and with Hermann Josef Abs (1939–1971), Franz Heinrich Ulrich (1971–1978), and Alfred Herrhausen (1978–1985) also its representatives as chairmen of the supervisory board between 1939 and 1985.[50]

In 1968, in a meeting with the VGF board, Abs stressed that it was necessary to evaluate Glanzstoff's chances of survival without any partner. According to Vits and Vaubel neither VGF nor AKU could persist alone. The German Glanzstoff management had already considered a close cooperation with BASF, but Dutch AKU refused permission and called for a merger of AKU and Glanzstoff.[51] As a consultant of the VGF executive board Abs played a key role during the negotiations. He did not fear an exodus of German customers, nor did he expect any problems with German codetermination regarding the planned cooperation. Rather he assured the managers that the new group could use the German capital market for increases of capital, bonds or loans. In this context, the AKU-chairman Jan van den Brink had already agreed to let Deutsche Bank participate in the new AKU consortium. Furthermore, Abs supported the merger and used his contacts to introduce Vaubel to Shell and Unilever, so that he could gain insights into multinational operating companies. The relationship of VGF and Deutsche Bank provides a manifest example of the close ties between banks and industry within German capitalism.[52]

The VGF board felt vindicated in its decision to merge with AKU when Phrix AG, the fourth largest West German fibre producer, was acquired by BASF in 1967 and competition on the fibre market increased.[53] Abs was not only chairman of the supervisory board of VGF for many years, he had also been a member of the supervisory boards of Deutsche Solvay Werke (DSW) and Kali-Chemie since 1940 and 1949 respectively (in 1953, he became chairman of both boards), and member of the IG Farben/BASF (after reestablishment) supervisory board from 1940 and 1952 respectively.[54] Hence, Abs had a central position in the chemical (fibre) industry for a long time and personalised the high intra-sectoral interlocking within the German corporate network which was typical of German capitalism and which supports the thesis of regulated competition. As a consequence, AKU/VGF asked him to represent the interests of VGF against its competitor Phrix at BASF.[55] This exemplifies that the numerous relations of Deutsche Bank – which had originally arisen from a credit and capital security interest – could lead to a coordination of competitive companies within German capitalism. At the same time, BASF delivered the chemical precursor caprolactam to Glanzstoff for fibre production.[56] Thus, Abs was not only mediating between competitors, but even formed a link between producers and clients. Furthermore, Abs showed that the supervisory board in Germany was not limited to a passive control function, but that it could engage in day-to-day business. According to the economic historian Werner Abelshauser, Abs as chairman of the BASF supervisory board did not restrict himself to advising and monitoring management, but took on entrepreneurial tasks.[57]

The restriction of supervisory board mandates to a maximum of 10 per person and the prohibition of interlocking relations in 1965 – better known as Lex Abs – only brought little change to this, even though the influence of individual bankers and entrepreneurs was limited and the mutual control of companies was prohibited.[58] At VGF as well, Abs was by no means limited to controlling management. In 1962, he was to pull his strings to Daimler-Benz to secure the cooperation with the VGF subsidiary Barmag and some years later in 1966, it was expected that he use his contacts to the state-owned enterprise Deutsche Bahn – as chairman of its board of administration – to prevent closure of certain lines which were important for VGF. Conversely, Abs passed on plans of the city of Gelsenkirchen to the VGF management; after the closure of mines and collieries, favourable labour market conditions and premises were available there in 1966. Furthermore, he put himself forward for mediating in a conflict between AKU/VGF and RWE concerning varying price levels of electricity in Germany and the Netherlands in 1967.[59] Thus Abs' activities within the network increased the planning reliability for all parties and demonstrated the cooperative character of inter-firm relations, which can be interpreted as one major aspect of German capitalism. In 1981 he was asked by the historian Joachim Fest whether he saw no danger in his plenitude of power. Abs replied that while one could not deny that people in leadership positions possess power, he did not have the power to bring other board members to do something against their will. Here Abs was obviously understating his own role in the German corporate network.[60]

The merger of VGF into a multinational company and the transition of leadership to his successors did not fundamentally change this principle, even if Abs had interfered more strongly in the business policy of industrial companies than Ulrich or Herrhausen later did. Thus, Abs, Ulrich and Herrhausen demonstrate the typical permanent relationship between banks and industry within 'Germany Inc.' which facilitated VGF's business finance. Aside from a brief interlude under Vits 1969/70, Deutsche Bank held the chair of Glanzstoff's supervisory board for more than 50 years. Although VGF had business contacts with other financial institutions, Vits stated in 1965 that VGF was effectively married to Deutsche Bank. For example, Dresdner Bank tried to win VGF as a customer and offered its subsidiary Barmag some factories in northern Italy for sale in 1964, but to no effect.[61] The close relationship can also be identified at the level of capital. While AKU held more than three quarters of the shares and a number of shareholders had only held a small proportion in 1962, Deutsche Bank did after all represent 9.44% of the shares registered by utilising the proxy voting right.[62]

In addition to an interlocking in terms of finance, personnel interlocking between German joint-stock companies by their governing bodies was a central characteristic of Rhenish capitalism. Multiple directors coordinated an exchange between large corporations, provided information on technical and organisational innovations and influenced the selection of other top managers. The supervisory boards were a place of relational contracting where orders were negotiated and mergers and acquisitions were discussed.[63] To illustrate this point Table 2 shows the relations of VGF/Enka with other German companies in terms of members of the executive board and the supervisory board from the 1950s to the 1980s. Only longstanding relations of at least two years are listed explicitly, the total number of relations (total) was even higher. The case of VGF/Enka shows the various connections within 'Germany Inc.' and the large number of stable relationships over a long period. This characteristic increased planning reliability for the companies. Despite the involvement of the German company (VGF/Enka)[64] in the multinational AKU/Akzo Group and the great importance of exports, it remained part of the German corporate network until the late 1980s. The number of relationships with other German companies through management and supervisory boards varied between 45 and 84 until the 1990s (cf. Table 3). The increase in 1965 was especially caused by the accumulation of mandates by Abs before the new law came into force. In addition to his position at Deutsche Bank, he had 26 mandates in German administrative or supervisory boards in 1965; in 15 cases he led the chair. Hence, some individual personalities contributed disproportionately to the interconnection of the company: These were the VGF chairmen Ernst Hellmut Vits and Hans Günther Zempelin, and at the VGF supervisory board Abs and his two successors at Deutsche Bank Ulrich and Herrhausen; furthermore, the head of the Klöckner Group Günter Henle, the long-time chairman of Metallgesellschaft Richard Merton, the managing director of Robert Bosch GmbH Hans Lutz Merkle and the CEO of Otto Wolff AG Otto Wolff von Amerongen.

With the exception of the mutual representation of German and Dutch individuals on the governing bodies of the multinational corporation, foreigners remained a rarity in Germany's corporate network. The corporate network in Germany was a national network. This was true for VGF/Enka, but also for the majority of all other German companies. The internationalisation caused neither the entry of foreign managers into German governing bodies, nor was the German network extended to other countries. The latter would have been hardly possible because of the institutional complementarities within different forms of capitalism.[65] In addition to relations with the two subsidiaries Barmag and Kuag and with the main bank (Deutsche Bank), the relationships of VGF/Enka with some insurance companies and potential customers of textile fibres were stable. Internationalisation was moved forward in different steps after 1945, but only when it accelerated in the context of globalisation in the 1990s did economic conditions and demands on companies change fundamentally. Now the national regulatory system lost its importance. The increasing corporate financing on international financial markets had to obey international rules and was accompanied by the rise of institutional owners, whose objectives were determined by the shareholder value principle. Thus, using the example of VGF/Enka some typical characteristics of Rhenish capitalism for the period prior to this change – from World War II to reunification

Table 2. Relations of VGF/Enka to other German companies.

Company	Relations in 1953	Relations in 1965	Relations in 1975	Relations in 1984
Albingia Versicherungs-AG	1	1	0	0
Allianz	0	2	2	1
Bankhaus J. Wichelhaus P. Sohn	0	1	1	0
Barmer Maschinenfabrik-AG (Barmag)	4	3	3	2
BASF	1	2	1	0
Bayer	1	0	1	0
Berliner Handelsgesellschaft und Frankfurter Bank (BHF)	0	0	1	1
Colonia	0	0	1	1
Continental	0	0	1	1
Dahlbusch Verwaltungs-AG	0	0	1	2
Daimler Benz	0	1	2	2
Deutsche Bank	0	5	4	3
Deutsche Linoleum-Werke AG (DLW)	0	1	1	0
Deutsche Lufthansa	0	1	1	1
Deutsche Revisions- und Treuhand-AG	1	1	0	0
Deutsche Solvay-Werke GmbH	0	0	1	1
Deutsche Texaco	0	0	1	1
Deutsche Ueberseeische Bank	1	1	2	0
Dillinger Hüttenwerke	0	1	1	0
Flachglas AG	0	0	1	1
Gewerkschaft Sophia-Jacoba	1	1	0	0
Glanzstoff-Courtaulds GmbH	1	2	0	0
Hermes Kreditversicherung	0	0	1	1
Hoesch AG	0	1	1	1
J.P. Bemberg AG	5	4	0	0
Klöckner & Co.	1	1	0	0
Klöckner-Humboldt-Deutz AG	1	2	1	0
Klöckner-Werke AG	0	1	0	1
Kreditanstalt für Wiederaufbau	1	1	1	1
Kunstseiden Textil AG (Kuag)	3	4	4	2
Mannesmann	1	0	1	0
Metallgesellschaft	1	1	0	0
Neunkirchner Eisenwerk AG, vorm. Gebr. Stumm	0	1	1	0
Philipp Holzmann AG	0	1	1	1
Phoenix Gummiwerke AG	0	1	1	0
PWA Papierwerke Waldhof-Aschaffenburg AG	0	0	1	1
Rheinisch-Westfälische Bank*	2	0	0	0
Rheinisch-Westfälisches Elektrizitätswerk AG (RWE)	0	1	2	1
Robert Bosch GmbH	0	2	1	0
Salamander AG	0	1	1	2
Schwelmer Eisenwerk Müller & Co. GmbH	1	1	0	0
Siemens-Schuckert-Werke	1	1	0	0
Spinnfaser AG	4	4	0	0
Süddeutsche Bank*	2	0	0	0
Süddeutsche Zucker AG	0	1	1	1
Zellstoff-Fabrik Waldhof	1	3	0	0
Total	**45**	**84**	**68**	**48**

Note: The subsidiaries J.P. Bemberg, Spinnfaser AG and Glanzstoff Courtaulds GmbH were merged with the parent company 1967–1971, so these relations disappeared. Rheinisch-Westfälische Bank and Süddeutsche Bank became Deutsche Bank in 1957. All information on corporate networks are based on my own analysis by the following sources: Hoppenstedt & Co., *Leitende Männer*; Vaubel, *Glanzstoff*, 231–250. Nevertheless, the Hoppenstedt handbook does not include information about all companies. For example, Abs was member of the supervisory board of Deutsche Solvay Werke after World War II. Since 1951 this company was organised in form of a GmbH (limited-liability company) which was not listed in the handbook because it had other obligations to publicly disclose than joint-stock companies. Limited-liability companies were included, if they were listed in the handbook. Cf. Gall, *Abs*, 495; Glasemann and Korsch, *Hoffnungswerte*, 187.

Table 3. Relations of BASF, Bayer, Hoechst and VGF/Enka to other German companies.

Company	Degree 1953	Degree 1965	Degree 1975	Degree 1984	Degree 1995
BASF	56	56	61	65	18
Bayer	35	85	76	89	43
Hoechst	78	111	90	86	54
VGF/Enka/AkzoNobel FaserAG	45	84	68	48	9
Total	214	336	295	288	124

– become apparent. Firstly, even if the thesis of the power of banks has been disproved, individual bankers possessed a prominent position in the German corporate network. Secondly, the transition of Vits, Vaubel, Schlange-Schöningen or Zempelin from the executive board to the supervisory board showed the importance of insiders, whose knowledge and social capital were secured for the company in this way. Thirdly, in addition to traditional supply and resource relationships some agents also established relationships with competing companies; Richard Merton and Helmuth Wohlthat were not only on the board of VGF in 1953, but also at Bayer and BASF; Abs was also on the board of BASF, Kali-Chemie and DSW; BASF's Chairman Carl Wurster was also a member of the VGF supervisory board in 1965, and one year later in 1966, Merkle also joined BASF's supervisory body. Unlike a Liberal Market Economy (LME) – and despite increasing internationalisation by FDI since the late 1960s – economic action in West Germany was marked by strong coordination within a national framework until the end of the 1980s.[66]

Some of these structural characteristics of Rhenish capitalism also become apparent through an analysis of Hoechst. While Glanzstoff maintained close relations with Deutsche Bank, Hoechst had close relations to the other two major German banks, Dresdner Bank and Commerzbank. Since the beginning of Hoechst's re-founding at the end of 1951, Hugo Zinßer, CEO of Rhein-Main-Bank AG (successor of Dresdner Bank) had been chairman of Hoechst's supervisory board, followed by Hermann Richter in 1956, a multi board member and industry consultant, who had worked for Dresdner Bank in the 1930s and 1940s. Richter became chairman of the supervisory board of Rhein-Main-Bank in 1952, took over the vice chairmanship of Dresdner Bank afterwards and was chairman of its supervisory body from 1972 to 1978. From 1963 to 1969 he represented the interests of Dresdner Bank at Hoechst as chairman of its supervisory board, subsequently, until 1978, as vice chairman.[67] Paul Lichtenberg (1973–1983), manager of Commerzbank, and Egon Overbeck (1969–1988), chairman of Mannesmann, were members of the supervisory board of Hoechst in 1974. The former Hoechst CEO Winnacker joined Hoechst's supervisory board and also had a seat on the supervisory boards of Mannesmann, Dresdner Bank and Munich Re. Likewise, the new chairman of Hoechst's management board, Rolf Sammet, had seats on the boards of Dresdner Bank and Allianz. These corporate links were maintained in the following years, even when staff were replaced. In 1984, Commerzbank board member Dietrich-Kurt Frowein (1983–1990), Helmut Haeusegen (1978–1988) as chairman of Dresdner Bank and CEO of Munich Re Horst Jannott (1978–1990) had seats on Hoechst's supervisory board. Overbeck upheld the connection to Mannesmann.[68] Here too, long-standing relations between banking and industrial companies increased planning reliability. In 1967, Dresdner Bank took over nominally DM 800,000 in Hoechst shares in exchange for shares of Chemie-Verwaltungs-AG. This package corresponded to 3.5% of Hoechst's share capital, but the bank had no interest in a large industrial investment and reduced its investment to 2.2% by the mid-1970s. Hence, the close personal relations were less based on capital ties, but on a relationship of trust between banks and industry and the function of the bank as a broker of information.[69] Furthermore, the relations of VGF/Enka and Hoechst to the different major German banks demonstrate the competition within the financial sector. There was neither a uniform financial entity nor a complete control of business strategies by banks as the thesis of bank hegemony suggests, and these findings are in line with other results about the power of banks in Germany in the first half of the twentieth century.[70] Even Abelshauser states that, in the case of BASF, bankers – with exception of Abs – had no strong influence on the business policy of management.[71] However, bankers often held the chair on German supervisory boards and had therefore a central position within the corporate network. But it was rather an advisory than a control function and it only lasted until the 1990s when the corporate network dissolved (cf. Table 3).

The fact that a former CEO, first Winnacker and later Sammet, assumed the chair of the supervisory board was typical for the distribution of power in large German companies and illustrates once more the dominant position of insiders. In the case of Hoechst, this prominent position of insiders was underscored by the management holding 'Frankfurter Gesellschaft für Chemiewerte' that acted as a collection point for equity shares and prevented a hostile takeover. It was hardly possible for people outside the German corporate network to influence or to oppose the chosen business strategy. In comparison to other industries, chemical companies initiated less permanent personnel interlocking in the 1970s and 1980s, but these forms existed as well. In the case of Hoechst, the company maintained a long-lasting relationship with the steel company Mannesmann which specialised in the manufacture of water and gas pipelines. This close cooperation included joint ventures like Ruhrchemie. In particular Hoechst's welding division and its engineering contractor subsidiary Uhde were related to the steel industry, and Mannesmann itself became more active as an engineering contractor in the 1970s. Even in the mid-1990s, Mannesmann CEO Werner H. Dieter was a member of the Hoechst supervisory board.[72] In the field of purchasing, the energy-intensive chemical companies chose stronger stabilisation mechanisms in the form of long-term contracts, full integration or joint ventures to secure their most important resource 'energy'.[73]

With regard to internationalisation Hoechst made use of personal contacts as well – as in the case of Peralta in France. Even in the case of Roussel-Uclaf, a relationship of trust between Jean-Claude Roussel and Hoechst board member Kurt Lanz prevented the sale of shares to its West German rival Bayer.[74] But the kind of ties necessary to establish business contacts abroad differed from the corporate network whose importance resided in the mutual exchange of information, in the mutual control of business and in the regulation of competition.[75] From the 1960s to the 1980s, internationalisation had only little impact on the personnel of Hoechst's supervisory board. With the acquisition of Roussel Uclaf, Jean-Claude Roussel entered Hoechst's supervisory board in 1969. After his accidental death in 1972, the interim president of Roussel Uclaf Jacques Brunet filled his position, succeeded from 1973 to 1978 by Jaqueline Roussel President of Compagnie Financière Chimio SA.[76] This was rare. Despite the importance of profits abroad, the governing bodies of Hoechst were almost exclusively occupied by German managers and bankers. Thus, the internationalisation of the group left the existing structures of the Rhenish model intact. One exception was Frederic H. Brandi (until 1976), a banker of Dillon, Read & Co., with whom Hoechst had access to the US capital market.[77]

Hoechst's dependence on petroleum became particularly apparent in the acquisition of a 25% shareholding by the Kuwait Petroleum Corporation after the second oil price crisis in 1982. The entry of a new, non-European major shareholder marked a cut in the history of Hoechst and demonstrated the growing power of oil-producing countries. Commerzbank had arranged the deal between Hoechst and the Kuwaiti company, which also delegated a representative, Abdul Baqi Al-Nouri, onto Hoechst's supervisory board. Up to that time, the share capital of Hoechst had been widely distributed. Now foreign shareholders had 33% of the shares and this proportion increased to 44% in 1986, while the proportion of institutional investors rose from 25% to 58%. This development speaks for the increase of investors with a lower level of tolerance to negative deviations from the expected operating income. It increased the risk of takeover in view of liberalised capital markets and enhanced the orientation of management towards a shareholder corporate policy in the 1990s.[78] Even though Hoechst had a major shareholder from the Middle East and the three major German banks – due to their proxy voting rights – represented about 57% of the share capital at the general meeting in 1986, the threat of takeover and the orientation towards financial markets increased.[79]

The end of Rhenish capitalism?

When globalisation and the liberalisation of world (capital) trade took full effect in the 1990s and West German governments became orientated towards deregulation and privatisation policies, the motif of maintaining interlocking directorates lost importance. The dissolution of the corporate network began.[80] This was also true for other countries – such as the Netherlands[81] – and it was true for the German manufacturers of chemicals, pharmaceuticals and fibres whose corporate structures were transformed as a result of new strategic aims. In the 1990s, the chemical industry was less characterised by acquisitions than by mega mergers and short-term restructuring.[82] Even though Enka could establish a financial reserve in the 1980s, Akzo merged with the Swedish company Nobel Industries to become AkzoNobel in 1994 and integrated the British fibre and paint manufacturer Courtaulds four years later. There were influential figures from the German corporate network represented in the Netherlands, which supported this development, both on the Akzo executive board as well as on its supervisory board – such as Frederick W. Fröhlich, who was responsible for the fibre division in Wuppertal, Hilmar Kopper, head of Deutsche Bank (1989–1997), and Dieter Wendelstadt, chairman of the AXA Group (1991–1998) and former member of the VGF board.[83] After the merger, the synthetic fibre production of AkzoNobel and Courtaulds was outsourced to a new company called Acordis which contained the former Enka divisions. Thereafter Acordis was sold to a private equity and investment company (CVC Capital Partners) and broken apart into individual companies as typical for Liberal Market Economies.[84]

The Hoechst management under CEO Jürgen Dormann (1994–1999) orientated the company rigorously towards the concept of shareholder value and concentrated the portfolio on the most profitable lines. The acquisition of the US pharmaceutical company Marion Merrell Dow (MMD) in 1995 for DM 7.1 billion shows that the US market represented a central point of reference for European chemical and pharmaceutical companies from the 1980s at least and that pharmaceuticals became more important at Hoechst. Dow Chemical wanted to sell its involvement in MMD and to concentrate its portfolio on chemicals from this point, conversely Hoechst wanted to strengthen pharmaceuticals as a core business. In 1996, Hoechst pooled its own pharmaceutical activities as well as Roussel Uclaf, Behringwerke and MMD together and formed the new business division Hoechst Marion Roussel. The business strategy was directed towards life sciences and accompanied by the sale of the specialty chemicals business, by the spin-off of the remaining operating units into independent companies and by the acquisition of the remaining 43% of Roussel Uclaf. Despite this extensive restructuring, Hoechst could not find a suitable business partner in life sciences at first. This happened only in 1998, when Jean-René Fourtou, chairman of Rhône-Poulenc, and Dormann agreed on a merger of their companies. Thus, a new multinational European corporation was formed in the pharmaceutical business.[85] When Dormann took over the chair of the executive board, Hoechst was, in his eyes, too little market-orientated, too introverted, and too academic; all this should change under his leadership. As a consequence, the global workforce of Hoechst was reduced from 172,000 to 97,000 between 1994 and 1999. The cooperative characteristic of West German capitalism lost its importance; cooperative relations within and between companies faded.[86]

Although all chemical companies were confronted with new structural challenges during the 1990s, reactions were not uniform. With its strict adaptation to shareholder value and its relocation of research departments to the US, Hoechst moved significantly further away from the model of Rhenish capitalism than Bayer or BASF.[87] Since 1994, Bayer had become orientated towards shareholder value and had focused on its core competencies as well, but it did not renounce the principle of diversification completely. The previous divisions were transformed into autonomous subgroups (Bayer CropScience, Bayer HealthCare, Bayer Polymers and Bayer Chemicals) under the umbrella of Bayer Holding, other fields of activity were transferred to off-site service companies.[88] At this point a uniform trend became manifest at industry level: a concentration on core competencies and a strengthening of specific chemical divisions. To quote business historian Hartmut Berghoff on the German economy of the 1990s: 'Outsourcing and offshoring of lower-value-added activities became standard.'[89] BASF was an exception. While BASF was orientated towards the financial market in the 1990s, in contrast to its two big German rivals it continued its production within an interlocking operational system (*Verbundchemie*) and even exported the model abroad. Bayer and Hoechst had already moved away from this idea when faced by rising oil prices in the 1970s. Hence, the company's development depended not least on the strategic choice of its corporate decision-makers.[90]

At the same time, the market capitalisation of the three major German chemical companies increased much faster than business numbers or profits: First of all, the market value of Hoechst shares rose significantly by 187% between 1995 and 1999, while concentration on the so-called life sciences led to a decline in surpluses.[91] In contrast to BASF and Bayer, where Allianz as financier of the German economy was still the largest shareholder, the largest equity share of Hoechst was still held by Kuwait Petroleum Corporation.[92] However, the function of this investment had changed significantly in the 1980s: while Kuwait initially wanted to expand to higher-value products, the equity share became a purely financial investment with an interest in an above-average performance. For this reason, Hoechst had to run a more capital market-orientated corporate policy than other companies.[93] Financialisation had become a megatrend since the 1970s which even affected non-financial sectors. More and more corporations were perceived of as portfolios of investment and less as a technical and social unit. This shift began in the US, gained speed in the 1980s with the neoliberal reforms of the US administration, and was embraced in Germany in the 1990s when globalisation and deregulation went into full swing and the European single market was completed by the Treaty of Maastricht in 1992.[94] As a consequence, some authors perceive an erosion of the arrangements that have distinguished CMEs from LMEs, whereas defenders of the classic VoC perspective see the different institutional arrangements as relatively resilient because of its deep historical roots. In this context, Katheleen Thelen points to three different trajectories of change – Varieties of Liberalisation – through deregulation, through dualisation, and through socially embedded flexibilisation. For example, industrial relations in Germany became increasingly bifurcated between a stable a core and a growing periphery by the mid-1990s – a dualisation through institutional drift.[95] In comparison to the political-economic institution of collective bargaining or vocational training, the German corporate network and business finance experienced even a more fundamental change in the 1990s.

Both Hoechst as well as VGF were extreme cases and finally disappeared from the German corporate network. While this was not typical of all German joint-stock companies, this does reveal some remarkable trends within the German corporate governance system. The shareholder value principle at Hoechst, the destruction of VGF by an investment company or the hostile takeover of Mannesmann by Vodafone in 1999 mark the end of a period of transition. While some parts of the German production regime persisted – like the division between the executive board and the supervisory board, the dual education system, or codetermination[96] – other signals suggest an institutional change of the Rhenish model towards a Liberal Market Economy: The decreasing density of the German corporate network, the increasing turnover rates in the context of new financial market laws, the change of ownership structure and the growing influence of investment funds changed business fundamentally.[97] The pertinent question is how much an institutional system needs to change before it constitutes a new model. Some authors say that a stronger orientation to shareholder value was compatible with institutions of codetermination, Hartmut Berghoff and Ulrich Jürgens et al. for example argue that individual shareholding remained low by international standards and that only the large flagship companies became subject to direct stock market pressure.[98] However, the continuation of the model must be questioned if key characteristics have not endured. The social scientists Martin Höpner and Gregory Jackson claim that the institution of codetermination persisted, but what persisted in many cases was only an institutional shell – as Christel Lane puts it. Change in the German corporate governance system has been far reaching since the 1990s. Some protective mechanisms that shielded German companies from market forces have disappeared and the disintegration of the corporate network suggests rather the end of Rhenish capitalism.[99] In contrast, the vocational training system showed a high degree of resilience. Hence, some elements of the set of institutions of Rhenish capitalism were renegotiated while others were left in place.[100]

In the case of the four German companies analysed in this article, the national corporate network retained its form and its functionality during the 1970s and 1980s, even though the social and the political environment as well as market conditions changed within these two decades. It was only in the context of increasing international competition, liberalisation and deregulation in the 1990s when the network lost its importance. The rearrangement of the legal framework facilitated divestments, many banks sold their industry investments, and as a consequence, control by the supervisory board became less important. New institutional investors and a new generation of managers, who were more orientated towards the international capital market, entered the stage and were the agents of this institutional change.[101] According to Lane, German multinationals like Hoechst or Bayer combined domestically generated characteristics with those adopted in host countries into a hybrid form. Nevertheless, several features of German capitalism were upheld and politicians of all kinds, businessmen and trade unions postulated the advantages of German capitalism in the financial crisis between 2007 and 2009.[102]

Conclusion

The literature about corporate networks is often criticised because it is generally based on the membership of managers in governing bodies and therefore only shows the structures and relationships between companies. As it is difficult to discover the content of relations among social actors by analysing the shape of their structural relationship – as Windolf notes –[103] these studies cannot show if and why interests were represented. Explanations of the motives of managers were far and few between – and often more claimed than proved. In contrast, this article has focused on the historical incidents of the German corporate network from the 1950s to the 1990s on the level of the firm and revealed several interlocking logics which were typical of German capitalism. The end of the German corporate network cannot be explained solely by internationalisation, but this process had a great impact on the Rhenish model. The German economy – and especially the producers of chemicals, pharmaceuticals and fibres – had become orientated towards foreign markets since the formation of the German corporate network in the late nineteenth century.[104] However, accelerated multinationalisation from the mid-1960s onwards differed clearly from previous forms of internationalisation. The export boom from a protected home market and the adoption of foreign marketing practices during the 'economic miracle' left the institution of long-standing connections between the banks and industry intact. When the number of multinational companies increased and foreign production emerged after the boom, domestic corporate structures had to be adapted. This was true of the institution of the corporate network, and it was also true of labour relations. It was not until the 1990s that the European Works Council had its breakthrough – and this EC institution had significantly less participation rights than its German counterpart.[105] In addition to domestic expansion, the increase in foreign investments was responsible for the divisionalisation and decentralisation of West German chemical companies in the 1960s and 1970s. This process prepared for the outsourcing of entire business areas and the emergence of a market for corporate control in the 1990s, through which the network lost its function as a coordinating body.[106]

Despite their strong international orientation, Bayer, BASF, Hoechst or VGF/Enka remained part of the German corporate network through their executive and supervisory boards up to the 1980s, reflecting the typical characteristics of the Rhenish model. Hoechst and VGF/Enka chose different networking strategies and worked in one case more strongly with Deutsche Bank, in the other case with Dresdner Bank and Commerzbank. The capital investments of banks remained limited, the close relations between the companies became particularly apparent at the personal level. With Abs, Ulrich and Herrhausen, VGF/Enka had internationally respected bankers on its supervisory board. The Hoechst supervisory board was dominated by representatives of the two other major German banks and former members of Hoechst's executive board.

Such networks could rely on specific dependencies as functional network theories suggest, as well as on longstanding business or personal friendships. But companies were also interested in qualified personnel for their governing bodies. Thus, the initiation and maintenance of such relationships were made for different reasons – as scholars of path dependence frequently emphasise.[107] Deutsche Bank CEO Ulrich stated in an interview in 1972 that some blocks of shares acquired by banks for tax and business reasons had become the character of permanent property.[108] The fragile balance of low profitability, low risk of hostile takeovers and high planning reliability was maintained by a coalition of industrial companies, banks and shareholders – even in the course of increasing internationalisation by multinationals after the boom. As a consequence, the institutional connection between banks and industry in Germany remained stable during the 1970s and 1980s, but it could not be extended into other economies due to institutional constraints. Institutional complementarities prevented a proliferation of the German corporate network into other, especially Liberal Market Economies. However, the increasing international movement of capital generated a stronger orientation to the international capital market and shareholder interests in the 1990s. The importance of traditional corporate and customer relationships faded into the background and the Coordinated Market Economy became more liberal.[109]

Intra-sectoral interlocking between companies of the same industry, as Abs had created between VGF and BASF, were typical for Rhenish capitalism and they were accompanied by cartels in Germany in the first half of the twentieth century. In particular, the German chemical industry was heavily and consistently involved in cartels at that time.[110] While cartels had been banned in West Germany after 1945, many elements of the German corporate governance were left untouched. The corporate network persisted and continued to serve as an institution for market regulation, and German companies still formed predominantly interlocking networks with companies of the same sector.[111] Despite the transfer of technologies as well as political and cultural values from the US in the context of Americanisation after World War II, path dependence was strong and ensured that German capitalism still differed from US capitalism.[112] Up to the 1980s, in times of poor economic development, the idea of counteraction through cartels emerged frequently, as the example of the European structural crisis cartel in the chemical fibre industry illustrates.[113] Nevertheless, the importance of cartels declined in Europe after World War II, particularly in the late 1980s. The idea of competition took possession of Europe, not least because of the antitrust orientated EC policy, rising penalties and the criminalisation of these activities. With the rise of neoliberal ideas in the 1990s, the willingness to cooperate diminished markedly. As cartels faded and the density of the network rapidly declined in the 1990s, two central economic institutions came to an end, which had been crucial for market regulation in Germany in the first half of the century.[114]

Since the 1970s, the financial sector had been upgraded and lost its serving function in the course of neoliberal deregulation. 'The morals of solid banking, together with trust in institutions were lost.'[115] The balance of power and decision-making processes at the top of big companies changed. While the executive boards of industrial corporations – in cooperation with the banks – had a considerable weight against the owners' interests until the 1980s, the return on invested capital and equity prices became more important in the context of rising investment companies and shareholder value. In contrast to long-term corporate strategies even the smallest success differences became decisive. Fund managers, rating agencies, and consulting companies made their decisions on the basis of generally applicable indicators and orientated themselves unilaterally to profit. Hence, the logic of financial markets gained a strong influence on the strategies of German chemical companies in the 1990s. Furthermore, as a consequence of the anti-cartel policies of the EU and increasing global competition, the profit margins of European companies eroded. As a result, most companies focused on core businesses with the potential for profitable growth in order to create (global) quasi-monopolies. The focus on life sciences and the relinquishment of numerous business at Hoechst, the demerger of the fibre division (formerly VGF/Enka) at the Akzo Group or the concentration on health, agriculture and polymers in the case of Bayer were striking examples.[116] Divestments became an integral part of business policy, only BASF with its idea of an interlocking operational system (*Verbundchemie*) remained a – successful – exception.[117] These case studies illustrate that a company's development was not exclusively dependent on institutional constraints. Hoechst's choice of life sciences and shareholder value and BASF's decision in favour of interconnected chemistry demonstrate the range of action, and this fits in well with the point made by Glenn Morgan that the institutionalist argument needs to give greater attention to dynamics at the level of the firm and the power of firms to innovate in new and unexpected ways.[118]

Western Europe only hesitantly followed the Anglo-American neoliberal model and often showed resistance to neoliberal developments. However, Rhenish capitalism faced a great challenge in the rise of the financial sector and deregulation. Even if these changes did not create a full convergence between different forms of capitalism and some institutions experienced only an incremental change, other institutions of West German capitalism changed more fundamentally in the last third of the twentieth century and internationalisation promoted these developments.[119] The examples of four West German producers of chemicals, pharmaceuticals and fibres have impressively demonstrated that the national market had lost its function as a point of reference from the 1970s onwards and that production abroad had gained importance; even if export maintained its importance for domestic plants. The declining role of technical experts on the boards, the rise of new owners without an interest in permanent industrial investments, and new tax and financial market laws facilitated the sale of traditional investments. As a result interlocking directorates between the governing bodies of German joint-stock companies for the control of property and market regulation became obsolete.[120] And no European or global counterpart has emerged until today. However, Albert's supposition that the greater dynamism and cultural attraction of the neoliberal American model would crowd out Rhenish capitalism must be questioned given the resilience of some parts of the Rhenish model – such as co-determination, the vocational training or the dual board system. Particularly by the 1990s, when Hall and Soskice designed their different forms of capitalism, several institutions of Rhenish capitalism as we had long known it in West German history, had been transformed. This did not mean convergence by market pressures, even though some institutional arrangements changed in the wake of deregulation and liberalisation in the direction of Liberal Market Economies, rather different trajectories of change of single political-economic institutions became reality and institutional complementarities had to be rearranged.[121] The financial crisis following 2007 deflated the self-regulating forces of the market, caused a self-demystification of neoliberalism, and cancelled further demands for liberalisation for the time being.[122] The analysis of German producers of chemicals, pharmaceuticals and fibres has shown that the internationalisation of the economy was an irreversible process. Whether the various forms of capitalism will fully converge in the future, however, remains an open question.

Notes

1. Coase, "Firm"; Williamson, *Economic Institutions*.
2. Hall and Soskice, "Introduction," 15.
3. Albert, *Capitalism*; Hall and Soskice, "Introduction"; Hancké and Goyer, "Degrees"; Morgan, "Introduction."
4. Hall and Soskice, "Introduction", 17–21.
5. Hacker, Pierson and Thelen, "Drift." Rational choice institutionalism emphasises the importance of exogenous aspects of preference formation and the functionality of institutions, whereas historical institutionalism mainly stresses endogenous developments as well as norms and culture and sees institutions as the product of concrete temporal processes. Cf. Thelen, "Historical Institutionalism."
6. Albert, *Capitalism*, 111–114; Hall and Soskice, "Introduction," 21–27.
7. David and Westerhuis, *Corporate Networks*.
8. Abelshauser, *Wirtschaftsgeschichte*, 424–430; Doering-Manteuffel and Raphael, *Boom*.
9. Da Rin, "Finance," 87–88, 91–97; Windolf, "Coordination," 444–446.
10. Wengenroth, "German Chemical Industry," 152.
11. Hacker, Pierson and Thelen, "Drift"; Pierson, "Increasing Returns"; Thelen, "Insights"; Thelen, *Political Economy*. Thelen distinguishes between different forms of institutional evolution by drift, layering or conversion.
12. Abelshauser, *Wirtschaftsgeschichte*, 424; Schröter, "Auslandsinvestitionen 1870 bis 1930."
13. Abelshauser, *Wirtschaftsgeschichte*, 424–426; Porter, *Advantage*, 358.
14. Kobrak, *Schering*, 352–354.
15. Chandler, *Industrial Century*, 114.
16. Abelshauser, *Wirtschaftsgeschichte*, 429–430; Chandler, *Industrial Century*, 9–10; Stokes, *Opting*.
17. Erker, "Bayer", 46–47.
18. Chandler, *Industrial Century*, 120–122; Erker, "Bayer," 48; Kleedehn, *Internationalisierung*, 226–231, 267–299, 349–351; Stokes, *Opting*, 131–196.
19. Business Archiv Hoechst, Frankfurt/Main (BAH): Hoe. Ausl. 138, Geschichte verschiedener Hoechst Gesellschaften Ausland, Länderblätter A-L: Brasilien, Frankreich, Großbritannien; Winnacker, *Challenging Years*, 328–332.
20. "Neue Auslandsengagements der Farbwerke Hoechst," in: FAZ 24.09.1965, p. 31; "Gemeinsame Tochter Hoechst-Hercules," in: FAZ 18.05.1966, p. 20; BAH, Hoe. Ausl. 139, Geschichte verschiedener Hoechst Gesellschaften Ausland, Länderblätter M-Z: USA; Klein, *Operation*, 24–31; Vlaanderen, *Hoechst*.
21. Annual Report Hoechst 1965, 16.
22. Abelshauser, "BASF," 491–498; Mittmann, *Industrie*, 254–289; Schreier and Wex, *Hoechst*, 274; Wengenroth, "German Chemical Industry," 153.
23. Johanson and Vahlne, "Learning."
24. Annual Report Hoechst 1970, 72–73, Annual Report Hoechst 1975, 78; "Deutsche Firmen bauen mehr im Ausland," in: Handelsblatt No. 177, 16.09.1970, p. 10.
25. Servan-Schreiber, *Défi Américain*.
26. Loibl, *US-Direktinvestitionen*, 21.
27. Dow Deutschland, *50 Jahre*, 6–8; "Phrix: Gleiche Startbedingung", in: Die Zeit, 11.06.1965; "Wir kaufen die ganze deutsche Industrie", in: Der Spiegel 41/1965, 06.10.1965, pp. 49–64.
28. Chandler, *Industrial Century*, 134–138.
29. Chandler refers to the limits to growth of traditional chemical production, whereas biotechnology and genetic engineering opened new chances. Cf. Chandler, *Industrial Century*, 10.
30. Erker, "Bayer," 48–49; Ferguson et al., *Shock of the Global*.
31. Birke, "Eigen-Sinn"; "Eindringlicher Appell an lohnpolitische Vernunft", in: Handelsblatt No. 178, 17.09.1970, p. 1; "Hoechst diesmal nicht sehr glücklich," in: Handelsblatt No. 184, 25./26.09.1970, p. 11.
32. Wirtschaftswoche No. 24, 06.06.1975. Cited according to Struve, "Konzerne," 313.
33. Dörre, "Globalisierung."

34. Bäumler, *Farben*, 381–386; Schreier and Wex, *Hoechst*, 291; Winnacker, *Challenging Years*, 369–372. At the same time Hoechst opened production plants for Trevira in South Africa, Chile, North Ireland, Brazil and the Netherlands.

35. Wirtschaftswoche No. 20, 10.05.1985, p. 182; Wengenroth, "German Chemical Industry," 154.

36. Hicks, "Hoechst to Acquire Celanese," *New York Times* 04.11.1986; "Fasern und neue Werkstoffe waren der Anreiz," in: FAZ 05.11.1986, p. 16; "Viel Spielraum," *Der Spiegel*, 46/1986, 10.11.1986, pp. 137–138; BAH, USA / AHC / Annual Reports (1971–1986); Klein, *Operation*, 147–207; Schröter, "Competitive Strategy," 67. FDI increased enormously in the 1980s, whereas the quota of foreign trade in the 1970s and 1980s fell into the long-term post-war line. Cf. Ambrosius, "Sektoraler Wandel," 27.

37. Archives Historiques du Groupe Sanofi, Paris: Fonds Roussel Uclaf / RU-26, Stratégie Internationale. Hoechst-Roussel Uclaf 1968–1988. 20 ans de coopération exemplaire. Un état d'esprit européen, in Uclafilm – Revue du Groupe Roussel-Uclaf, Nr. 70, Novembre 1988, pp. 3–5; Bäumler, *Farben*, 297–300; Bayer AG: Corporate History & Archives, Leverkusen (BAL) 387-1 IX Bayer-Vorstandssitzung (07.05.1968, 21.05.1968, 27.06.1968, 16.07.1968); Schreier and Wex, *Hoechst*, 372.

38. Hackney Archives Department, London: Berger, Jenson & Nicholson, D/B/BER/2/2/2, Group Board minute book (08.01.1970); Bäumler, *Farben*, 305–308; Annual Report Hoechst 1967, 19; Annual Report Hoechst 1970, 16; BAH, H0073138, Großbritannien, Berger, Jenson & Nicholsen: Offer to acquire the issued ordinary share capital and warrants of BJN (A085); BAH, H0073141, Großbritannien, Berger, Jenson & Nicholsen: Mitteilung der Rechtsabteilung (14.01.1970), Seligman to Asboth (26.01.1970); "Farbwerke Hoechst: Interesse an britischer Gesellschaft", in: Industriekurier No. 173, 15.11.1969, p. 18; Schreier and Wex, *Hoechst*, 291; Teltschik, *Großchemie*, 223.

39. Vaubel, *Glanzstoff, Bd. 1*; Wicht, *Glanzstoff*, 50–95.

40. BAL 324/3 Kooperation Bayer-Rhône-Poulenc. Forschungsvertrag u. Vorverhandlungen (1963–1965).

41. Stiftung Rheinisch-Westfälisches Wirtschaftsarchiv zu Köln (RWWA) 195-K17-0-3 Notiz für Vits (01.04.1958), Einige Überlegungen zur künftigen Entwicklung der Chemiefaser-Industrie im gemeinsamen Markt (31.12.1958).

42. RWWA 195-A2–53 Gedanken zur möglichen Zusammenarbeit von AKU und Glanzstoff (16.06.1967).

43. Boyer, "Hypothesis"; Boyer and Drache, *States*; Esser, "Germany"; Fligstein and Merand, "Globalization"; Morgan, "Introduction"; Pauly and Reich, "Structures"; Schröter, "Question," 372–374, 392–395, 401–405; Steiner, "Kristallisationspunkt," 43; Wade, "Globalization."

44. Gall, *Abs*; Teltschik, *Großchemie*, 221; Vaubel, *Glanzstoff, Bd. 1*. Though VGF already adopted new methods of management training and marketing from the US in the 1950s, Akzo remained a European enterprise. Cf. Kleinschmidt, "Glanzstoff."

45. Vaubel, *Glanzstoff, Bd. 1*, 155–159. Cf. for the Dutch corporate network: Heemskerk, Mokken, and Fennema, *Corporate Governance Networks* and *Corporate-State Interlocks*.

46. Buchheim, *Wiedereingliederung*; Hilger, *Amerikanisierung*; Kleedehn, *Internationalisierung*; Kleinschmidt, "Glanzstoff" and *Blick*.

47. Windolf, "Corporate Network," 67.

48. RWWA 195-A2–53 Gedanken zur möglichen Zusammenarbeit zwischen AKU und Glanzstoff (16.06.1967); Vaubel, *Glanzstoff*, 160.

49. Vaubel, *Glanzstoff*, 172, 176.

50. In parentheses are the periods of membership in the supervisory board of VGF resp. Hoechst. In 1985 the former CEO of Enka Glanzstoff, Hans Günther Zempelin, became head of the supervisory board. Cf. Vaubel, *Glanzstoff*, 242; Büschgen, "Deutsche Bank."

51. Abelshauser, "BASF", 517–518; RWWA 195-A2–30 Vermerk betr. Besprechung (25.01.1968); Vaubel, *Glanzstoff*, 142.

52. RWWA 195-A2–29 Notiz. Vertraulich! (06.11.1968); RWWA 195-A2–30 Vermerk betr. Besprechung (25.01.1968); Vaubel, *Glanzstoff*, 232; „Wir sind die größte Ohn-Macht der Welt," *Der Spiegel*, 1/1969, p. 37.

53. Abelshauser, "BASF," 527–531, 551–560, 595; Teltschik, *Großchemie*, 221; "Phrix-Werke AG: Nackt und bloß," in: Der Spiegel 33/1970, p. 57; "Phrix-Werke AG: Unerschüttert bergab", in: Der Spiegel 34/1970, pp. 68–69; "Phrix-Werke AG: Unwissend," in: Die Zeit No. 21, 26.05.1967, p. 37.

54. Abelshauser, "BASF," 362–367; Bertrams, "Crisis," 294–295, 316–317; Homburg, "Diversification," 388.

55. RWWA 195-A2–53 Notiz betr. Besprechung (10.04.1967); Windolf, "Coordination," 451–453; Windolf and Beyer, "Co-operative Capitalism," 218–219, 222, Windolf, *Corporate Networks in Europe*, 63–67.

56. Abelshauser, "BASF", 517–518.

57. Abelshauser, "BASF," 402–403.

58. Beyer, "Deutschland AG a.D," 125; Büschgen, "Deutsche Bank," 651–652; Gall, *Abs*, 331–342; "Zwischen Bonn und Banken. Finanzdiplomat Hermann J. Abs," in: Der Spiegel 45/1965, pp. 49–67.

59. RWWA 195-B5–8-2 Barmag an Abs (27.12.1962), VGF an Abs (24.03.1966), Abs an VGF (07.12.1966), Notiz Glanzstoff-Vorstand (25.07.1967).

60. RWWA 195-B5–8-1 Interview mit Hermann Josef Abs von Joachim Fest (19.01.1981).

61. Historical Archives of Commerzbank, Frankfurt/Main (HAC): 500/7,102-2000 Dresdner Bank to Direktion Wuppertal-Elberfeld (21.07.1960, 24.07.1961, 14.08.1962), Aktennotiz betr. VGF (19.11.1964), Aktennotiz betr. Besuch von Herrn Dr. Vits (27.10.1965).

62. Marx, "Internationalisierung"; RWWA 195-B4–1-120/121 Teilnehmerverzeichnis HV VGF (12.07.1962).

63. Windolf, "Corporate Network."

64. The two operating companies Enka and VGF had been connected by a personal union; in 1972 both companies took the uniform name "Enka Glanzstoff" (under German and Dutch law), in 1977 they changed their name into "Enka." In 1991, it became "Akzo Faser AG'; after the merger with Nobel Industries it was renamed 'AkzoNobel Faser AG'. Cf. Vaubel, *Glanzstoff*; RWWA 195-B0–54 Umfirmierung Glanzstoff AG in Enka Glanzstoff AG (1972).

65. Hall and Soskice, "Introduction," 17–21; Hall and Gingerich, *Varieties*.

66. Marx, "Internationalisierung."

67. Erbe, "Richter"; HAC-500/115,634 (138) Dr. Hugo Zinßer (1952–1954); Henke, *Dresdner Bank*, 614; "Ins zweite Glied," *Der Spiegel* 51/1974, 16.12.1974, p. 62.

68. Handbook of German Stock Companies (1970–1990).

69. HAC-500/106,349 Beteiligungsübersichten, Hoechst AG (1974–1975); Marx, "Internationalisierung."

70. Krenn, *Struktur*; Wixforth and Ziegler, "Bankenmacht"; Windolf, *Corporate Networks in Europe*, 220–223; Windolf, "Coordination," 449–451.

71. Abelshauser, "BASF," 401.

72. Gieseler, *Uhde*; Lindner, *Inside IG Farben*, 358–359; Rooij and Homburg, *Plant*, 65, 113–114. Besides Mannesmann and Hoechst, the two mining companies Rheinpreußen and Neue Hoffnung took part in Ruhrchemie; in 1981, Mannesmann sold its stake in Ruhrchemie at Hoechst. Cf. Rasch, "Kohlechemie"; Wessel, *Kontinuität*, 388, 422–423, 439–466.

73. Papenheim-Tockhorn, *Kooperationsbeziehungen*, 262–271; Eckert, "Shareholder Value bei Hoechst," 171.

74. Marx, "Multinationale Unternehmen."

75. Windolf, "Coordination," 444–447.

76. Annual Report Hoechst 1969, 8; Annual Report Hoechst 1978, 57.

77. Annual Report Hoechst 1968, 8; Annual Report Hoechst 1976, 67.

78. Eckert, "Shareholder Value bei Hoechst," 182–183.

79. HA Hauptversammlungen 1985–1987, HV-Vertretung Großbanken (01.06.1987); "Der Multi aus dem Morgenland," *Die Zeit* 41, 08.10.1982, pp. 17–18; Marx, "Internationalisierung." Cf. for the wide distribution of Hoechst share capital: Eckert, "Shareholder Value bei Hoechst," 171.

80. Berghoff, "Financialization," 93–95; Marx, "Internationalisierung"; Windolf, "Corporate Network," 74.

81. Heemskerk, Mokken, and Fennema, *Corporate Governance Networks*.

82. Chandler, *Industrial Century*; Schröter, "Competitive Strategy," 71–79.

83. Annual Reports Akzo 1993–1995.

84. Chandler, *Industrial Century*, 137–138.

85. Berghoff, "Financialization," 90–91; Klein, *Operation*, 218–229; Wehnelt, *Hoechst*, 162–174; "Hoechst bietet 5,2 Milliarden DM für den Rest von Roussel Uclaf'," *Frankfurter Allgemeine Zeitung*, 12.12.1996, p. 21. The new corporation of Hoechst and Rhône-Poulenc was renamed Aventis and in 2004 it formed with Sanofi-Synthélabo the new company Sanofi-Aventis.

86. Berthoin Antal, Krebsbach-Gnath, and Dierkes, *Organizational Learning*; Wengenroth, "German Chemical Industry," 163–164.

87. Annual Report Hoechst 1994, 19; Becker, "Chemie- und Pharmaindustrie," 240.

88. Kädtler, *Umbruch*, 95–109, 143–151, 180–181.

89. Berghoff, "Financialization," 90.

90. Abelshauser, "BASF," 496–499.

91. Becker, "Chemie- und Pharmaindustrie," 235–237.

92. Borscheid, *100 Jahre Allianz*, 430; Beyer, "Deutschland AG a.D," 134.

93. Becker, "Chemie- und Pharmaindustrie," 223, 239–240.

94. Berghoff, "Financialization"; Lane, "Globalization," 218–221; Windolf, "Finanzmarkt-Kapitalismus."

95. Thelen, *Varieties*.

96. Abelshauser, "Produktionsregime."

97. Boyer, "Future"; Streeck, *Re-forming Capitalism*, 77–90; Windolf, "Zukunft"; Windolf, "Corporate Network."

98. Berghoff, "Financialization," 106–107; Jürgens, Naumann, and Rupp, "Shareholder Value."

99. Deeg, "Path Dependency"; Höpner and Jackson, "Markt"; Lane, "Transformation"; Streeck and Höpner, "Einleitung. Macht," 11; Windolf, *Corporate Networks in Europe*, 212–213; Windolf, "Corporate Network."

100. Thelen, "Insights."

101. North, *Institutions*, 83–91.

102. Lane, "Globalization"; David Meiländer, "Wie die Kurzarbeit Jobs gerettet hat,"*Zeit-Online*, 16.06.2010.

103. Windolf, "Unternehmensverflechtung," 201–202.

104. Marx and Krenn, "Kontinuität"; Schröter, "Auslandsinvestitionen 1870 bis 1930"; Streeck, *Re-forming Capitalism*, 187–206.

105. Schröter, "German Model."

106. Wengenroth, "German Chemical Industry," 152–155.

107. Mahoney, "Path Dependence"; Thelen, "Insights," 217–222.

108. Interview mit Franz Heinrich Ulrich 1972, cited according to Büschgen, "Deutsche Bank,"653.

109. Kopper, "Abschied"; Streeck and Höpner, "Einleitung. Macht," 15–17, 27–28; Thelen, *Varieties*.

110. Schröter, "Fields."

111. Kobrak, *Schering*, 353; Windolf and Beyer, "Co-operative Capitalism," 218–219; Windolf, *Corporate Networks in Europe*, 6–7.

112. Berghahn, *Americanisation*; Kleinschmidt, "Resurgence"; Schröter, "Question," 390–392.

113. Marx, "Cartel."

114. Schröter, "Kartellierung," 483–491; Windolf, "Coordination," 446–447.

115. Kocka, *Geschichte des Kapitalismus*, 92–99 [Quote from Iván T. Berend according to Kocka, 94].

116. Kädtler, "Industrieller Kapitalismus".

117. Homburg, "Diversification," 505–527.

118. Morgan, "Complementarities"; Lane, "Globalization," 214–215, 221–224.

119. Abelshauser, *Kulturkampf*; Hall, "Stabilität"; Hall and Soskice, *Varieties*; Kocka, *Geschichte des Kapitalismus*, 117–119; Thelen, *Varieties*.

120. Beyer, "Deutschland AG a.D.", 137–141; Dörre and Brinkmann, "Finanzmarkt-Kapitalismus", 94–95; Fennema and Heemskerk, *Nieuwe Netwerken*; Freye, *Führungswechsel*; Heemskerk, *Decline*; Wengenroth, "German Chemical Industry", 152–159, 166–167; Windolf, "Neuen Eigentümer".

121. Hall and Soskice, *Varieties*; Thelen, *Varieties*.

122. Albert, *Capitalism*; Kocka, *Geschichte des Kapitalismus*, 118; Streeck, *Varieties*, 15–17.

Acknowledgements

The author would like to thank the discussants of the AKKU Annual Conference 'Germany Inc.? Corporations, organisations, and policy maker in West Germany?' (Berlin) in 2011 and of the World Business History Conference (Frankfurt/Main) in 2014, especially Eric Godelier for his comments, Kirsten Petrak-Jones for linguistic help, and the anonymous reviewers of Business History.

Disclosure statement

No potential conflict of interest was reported by the author.

Funding

This work was supported by the Deutsche Forschungsgemeinschaft [grant number DFG RA 469/13-1] and Max-Weber-Stiftung [Gerald D. Feldman Travel Grants].

References

Abelshauser, Werner. "Umbruch und Persistenz: Das deutsche Produktionsregime in historischer Perspektive." *Geschichte und Gesellschaft* 27, no. 4 (2001): 503–523.

Abelshauser, Werner. *Kulturkampf. Der deutsche Weg in die neue Wirtschaft und die amerikanische Herausforderung.* Kulturwissenschaftliche Interventionen; 4. Berlin: Kadmos, 2003.

Abelshauser, Werner. *Werner. Deutsche Wirtschaftsgeschichte. Von 1945 bis zur Gegenwart.* Bonn: BPB, 2011.

Abelshauser, Werner. "BASF since Its Refounding in 1952." In *German Industry and Global Enterprise. BASF: The History of a Company,* edited by Werner Abelshauser, Wolfgang von Hippel, Jeffrey Allan Johnson, and Raymond G. Stokes, 362–620. Cambridge: Cambridge University Press, 2004.

Albert, Michel. *Capitalism against Capitalism.* New York: Wiley, 1993.

Ambrosius, Gerold. "Sektoraler Wandel und internationale Verflechtung. Die bundesdeutsche Wirtschaft im Übergang zu einem Strukturmuster." In *Auf dem Weg in eine neue Moderne? Die Bundesrepublik Deutschland in den siebziger und achtziger Jahren,* edited by Thomas Raithel, Andreas Rödder and Andreas Wirsching. Schriftenreihe der Vierteljahrshefte für Zeitgeschichte. Sondernummer, 17–30. München: Oldenbourg, 2009.

Antal, Berthoin. *Hoechst Challenges Received Wisdom on Organizational Learning.* WZB Discussion Paper. Berlin: WZB, 2003.

Bäumler, Ernst. *Formeln, Forscher. Hoechst und die Geschichte der industriellen Chemie in Deutschland.* München: Piper Verlag, 1989.

Becker, Steffen. "Der Einfluss des Kapitalmarkts und seine Grenzen: Die Chemie- und Pharmaindustrie." In *Alle Macht dem Markt? Fallstudien zur Abwicklung der Deutschland AG,* edited by Wolfgang Streeck and Martin Höpner, 222–248. Frankfurt am Main / New York: Campus, 2003.

Berghahn, Volker R. *The Americanisation of West German Industry, 1945–1973.* New York: Berg, 1986.

Berghoff, Hartmut. "Varieties of Financialization? Evidence from German Industry in the 1990s." *Business History Review* 90, no. 1 (2016): 81–108.

Bertrams, Kenneth. "The Years of Crisis (1914-1950): The Making and Unmaking of International Alliances." In *Solvay. History of a Multinational Family Firm,* edited by Kenneth Bertrams, Nicolas Coupain, and Ernst Homburg, 151–329. Cambridge: Cambridge University Press, 2013.

Beyer, Jürgen. "Deutschland AG a.D.: Deutsche Bank, Allianz und das Verflechtungszentrum des deutschen Kapitalismus." In *Alle Macht dem Markt? Fallstudien zur Abwicklung der Deutschland AG,* edited by Wolfgang Streeck and Martin Höpner, 118–146. Frankfurt am Main / New York: Campus, 2003.

Birke, Peter. "Der Eigen-Sinn der Arbeitskämpfe. Wilde Streiks und Gewerkschaften in der Bundesrepublik vor und nach 1969." In *1968 und die Arbeiter. Studien zum "Proletarischen Mai" in Europa,* edited by Bernd Gehrke and Gerd-Rainer Horn, 53–75. Hamburg: VSA-Verlag, 2007.

Borscheid, Peter. *100 Jahre Allianz. 1890–1990*. München: Allianz, 1990.

Boyer, Robert, and Daniel Drache, eds. *States against Markets. The Limits of Globalization*, Innis Centenary Series. London / New York: Routledge, 1996.

Boyer, Robert. "The Convergence Hypothesis Revisited. Globalization but Still the Century of Nations?". In *National Diversity and Global Capitalism*, edited by Suzanne Berger and Ronald Dore. Conrell Studies in Political Economy, 29–59. Ithaca / London: Cornell University Press, 1996.

Boyer, Robert. "What Is the Future for Codetermination and Corporate Governance in Germany?". In *Transformation des Kapitalismus. Festschrift für Wolfgang Streeck zum sechzigsten Geburtstag*, edited by Jens Beckert, Bernhard Ebbinghaus, Anke Hassel, and Philipp Manow, 135–157. Frankfurt am Main: Campus, 2006.

Buchheim, Christoph. *Die Wiedereingliederung Westdeutschlands in die Weltwirtschaft 1945-1958*. Quellen und Darstellungen zur Zeitgeschichte; 31. München: Oldenbourg, 1990.

Bundesminister für Wirtschaft. Runderlasse Außenwirtschaft Über "Vermögensanlagen Gebietsansässiger in Fremden Wirtschaftsgebieten". *Bundesanzeiger* (1980-1995).

Büschgen, Hans E. "Die Deutsche Bank von 1957 bis zur Gegenwart. Aufstieg zum internationalen Finanzdienstleistungskonzern." In *Die Deutsche Bank 1870-1995*, edited by Lothar Gall, Gerald D. Feldman, Harold James, Carl-Ludwig Holtfrerich, and Hans E. Büschgen, 579–880. München: Beck, 1995.

Chandler, Alfred D. *Shaping the Industrial Century. The Remarkable Story of the Evolution of the Modern Chemical and Pharmaceutical Industries*. Cambridge: Harvard University Press, 2005.

Coase, Ronald H. "The Nature of the Firm." *Economica* 4 (1937): 386–405.

Da Rin, Marco. "Finance and the Chemical Industry." In *Chemicals and Long-Term Economic Growth. Insights from the Chemical Industry*, edited by Ashish Arora, Ralph Landau, and Nathan Rosenberg, 307–339. New York, NY: Wiley, 1998.

David, Thomas, and Gerarda Westerhuis, eds. *The Power of Corporate Networks. A Comparative and Historical Perspective*. New York / Abingdon: Taylor & Francis, 2014.

Deeg, Richard. "Path Dependency, Institutional Complementarity, and Change in National Business Systems." In *Changing Capitalism? Internationalization, Institutional Change, and Systems of Economic Organization*, edited by Glenn Morgan, Richard Whitley and Eli Moen, 21–52. Oxford: Oxford University Press, 2006.

Dow Deutschland Anlagengesellschaft mbH, ed. *50 Jahre Dow in Deutschland. Im Herzen Europas*. Frankfurt am Main: Henrich Druck + Medien, 2010.

Doering-Manteuffel, Anselm, and Lutz Raphael. *Nach dem Boom. Perspektiven auf die Zeitgeschichte seit 1970. 3., ergänzte Auflage*. Göttingen: Vandenhoeck & Ruprecht, 2012.

Dörre, Klaus. "Globalisierung - Eine strategische Option. Internationalisierung von Unternehmen und industrielle Beziehungen in der Bundesrepublik." *Industrielle Beziehungen* 4, no. 4 (1997): 265–290.

Dörre, Klaus, and Ulrich Brinkmann. "Finanzmarkt-Kapitalismus: Triebkraft eines flexiblen Produktionsmodells?" In *Finanzmarkt-Kapitalismus. Analysen zum Wandel von Produktionsregimen*, edited by Paul Windolf. Kölner Zeitschrift für Soziologie und Sozialpsychologie. Sonderheft; 45, 85–116. Wiesbaden: VS, 2005.

Eckert, Stefan. "Auf dem Weg zur Aktionärsorientierung: Shareholder Value bei Hoechst." In *Alle Macht dem Markt? Fallstudien zur Abwicklung der Deutschland AG*, edited by Wolfgang Streeck and Martin Höpner, 169–196. Frankfurt am Main / New York: Campus, 2003.

Erbe, Cornelia. "Richter, Hermann." *Neue Deutsche Biographie* 21 (2003): 532.

Erker, Paul. "Die Bayer AG. Entwicklungsphasen eines Chemiekonzerns im Überblick." In *Stimmt die Chemie? Mitbestimmung und Sozialpolitik in der Geschichte des Bayer-Konzerns*, edited by Klaus Tenfelde, Karl-Otto Czikowsky, Jürgen Mittag, Stefan Moitra, and Rolf Nietzard, 35–56. Essen: Klartext, 2007.

Esser, Josef. "Germany. Challenges to the Old Policy Style." In *Industrial Enterprise and European Integration. From National to International Champions in Western Europe*, edited by Jack Ernest Shalom Hayward, 48–75. Oxford et al.: Oxford University Press, 1995.

Fennema, Meindert, and Eelke M. Heemskerk. *Nieuwe Netwerken. De Elite En De Ondergang Van De NV Nederland*. Amsterdam: Bert Bakker, 2008.

Ferguson, Niall, Charles S. Maier, Erez Manela, and Daniel J. Sargent, eds. *The Shock of the Global. The 1970s in Perspective*. Cambridge: Harvard University Press, 2010.

Fligstein, Neil, and Frederic Merand. "Globalization or Europeanization? Evidence on the European Economy since 1980." *Acta Sociologica* 45, no. 1 (2002): 7–22.

Freye, Saskia. *Führungswechsel. Die Wirtschaftselite und das Ende der Deutschland AG.* Frankfurt am Main: Campus, 2009.

Gall, Lothar. *Der Bankier Hermann Josef Abs. Eine Biographie.* München: Beck, 2004.

Gieseler, Horst. *Von Der Druckerschwärze zum High-Tech Engineering. Die Uhde Story. 75 Years Engineering with Ideas. Uhde, 1921-1996.* Dortmund: Uhde GmbH, 1996.

Glasemann, Hans-Georg, and Ingo Korsch. *Hoffnungswerte. Ungeregelte Ansprüche aus Wertpapieremissionen vor 1945 und ihre Entschädigung nach der Wiedervereinigung.* Wiesbaden: Springer, 1991.

Hacker, Jacob S., Paul Pierson, and Kathleen Thelen. "Drift and conversion: hidden faces of institutional change." In *Advances in Comparative-Historical Analysis*, edited by James Mahoney and Kathleen Thelen, 180–208. Cambridge: Cambridge University Press, 2015.

Hall, Peter A. eds. *Varieties of Capitalism. The Institutional Foundations of Comparative Advantage.* Oxford: Oxford University Press, 2001.

Hall, Peter A., and Daniel W. Gingerich. *Varieties of Capitalism and Institutional Complementarities in the Macroeconomy. An Empirical Analysis.* MPIFG Discussion Paper; 04,5. Köln: MPIFG, 2004.

Hall, Peter A., and David Soskice. "An Introduction to Varieties of Capitalism." In *Varieties of Capitalism. The Institutional Foundations of Comparative Advantage*, edited by Peter A. Hall and David Soskice, 1–68. Oxford: Oxford University Press, 2001.

Hall, Peter A. "Stabilität und Wandel in den Spielarten des Kapitalismus." In *Transformation des Kapitalismus. Festschrift für Wolfgang Streeck zum sechzigsten Geburtstag*, edited by Jens Beckert, Bernhard Ebbinghaus, Anke Hassel, and Philipp Manow, 181–204. Frankfurt am Main: Campus, 2006.

Hancké, Bob, and Michel Goyer. "Degrees of Freedom: Rethinking the Institutional Analysis of Economic Change." In *Changing Capitalism? Internationalization, Institutional Change, and Systems of Economic Organization*, edited by Glenn Morgan, Richard Whiteley, and Eli Moen, 53–77. Oxford: Oxford University Press, 2006.

Heemskerk, Eelke M. *Decline of the Corporate Community. Network Dynamics of the Dutch Business Elite.* Amsterdam: Amsterdam University Press, 2007.

Heemskerk. *Corporate-State Interlocks in the Netherlands: 1969-2006.* Amsterdam: SSRN Electronic Paper Collection, 2008.

Heemskerk, Eelke M., Robert J. Mokken, and Meindert Fennema. *From Stakeholders to Shareholders? Corporate Governance Networks in the Netherlands 1976–1996.* Amsterdam: SSRN Electronic Paper Collection, 2003.

Henke, Klaus-Dietmar, ed. *Die Dresdner Bank im Dritten Reich.* München: Oldenbourg, 2006.

Hilger, Susanne. *"Amerikanisierung" deutscher Unternehmen. Wettbewerbsstrategien und Unternehmenspolitik bei Henkel, Siemens und Daimler-Benz (1945/49-1975).* VSWG, Beihefte; 173. Stuttgart: Steiner 2004.

Homburg, Ernst. "The Era of Diversification and Globalization (1950-2012)." In *Solvay. History of a Multinational Family Firm*, edited by Kenneth Bertrams, Nicolas Coupain, and Ernst Homburg, 333–564. New York, NY: Cambridge University Press, 2013.

Höpner, Martin, and Gregory Jackson. "Entsteht ein Markt für Unternehmenskontrolle? Der Fall Mannesmann." *Leviathan* 29, no. 4 (2001): 544–563.

Hoppenstedt & Co., ed. *Leitende Männer der Wirtschaft.* Darmstadt: Hoppenstedt & Co., 1953, 1965, 1975, 1984, 1995.

Johanson, J., and J. E. Vahlne. "Learning in the Internationalisation Process of Firms. A Model of Knowledge Development and Increasing Foreign Market Commitments." *International Business Studies* 8, no. 1 (1977): 23–32.

Jürgens, Ulrich, Katrin Naumann, and Joachim Rupp. "Shareholder Value in an Adverse Environment. The German Case." *Economy and Society* 29, no. 1 (2000): 54–79.

Kädtler, Jürgen. *Sozialpartnerschaft im Umbruch. Industrielle Beziehungen unter den Bedingungen von Globalisierung und Finanzmarktkapitalismus.* Hamburg: VSA-Verlag, 2006.

Kädtler. "Industrieller Kapitalismus und Finanzmarktrationalität – Am Beispiel des Umbruchs in der (traditionellen) deutschen Großchemie." *Prokla* 169 (2012): 579–599.

Kleedehn, Patrick. *Die Rückkehr auf den Weltmarkt. Die Internationalisierung der Bayer AG Leverkusen nach dem Zweiten Weltkrieg bis zum Jahre 1961.* Beiträge zur Unternehmensgeschichte; 26. Stuttgart: Steiner, 2007.

Klein, Heribert. *Operation Amerika. Hoechst in den USA*. München / Zürich: Piper Verlag, 1996.

Kleinschmidt. *Der Produktive Blick. Wahrnehmung amerikanischer und japanischer Management- und Produktionsmethoden durch deutsche Unternehmer 1950-1985*. Berlin: Akademie Verlag, 2002.

Kleinschmidt, Christian. "An Americanised Company in Germany. The Vereinigte Glanzstoff Fabriken AG in the 1950s." In *The Americanisation of European Business. The Marshall Plan and the Transfer of Us Management Models*, edited by Matthias Kipping and Ove Bjarnar. Routledge Studies in Business History; 5, 171–189. London / New York: Routledge, 1998.

Kleinschmidt. "America and the Resurgence of the German Chemical and Rubber Industry after the Second World War. Hüls, Glanzstoff and Continental." In *German and Japanese Business in the Boom Years. Transforming American Management and Technology Models*, edited by Akira Kudo, Matthias Kipping, and Harm G. Schröter, 161–174. London / New York: Routledge, 2004.

Kobrak, Christopher. *National Cultures and International Competition. The Experience of Schering AG, 1851-1950*. Cambridge: Cambridge University Press, 2002.

Kocka, Jürgen. *Geschichte des Kapitalismus*. München: Beck, 2013.

Kopper, Christopher. "Der langsame Abschied von der Deutschland AG? Die deutschen Banken und die Europäisierung des Kapitalmarkts in den 1980er Jahren." *Archiv für Sozialgeschichte* 52 (2012): 91–110.

Krenn, Karoline. *Alle Macht den Banken? Zur Struktur personaler Netzwerke deutscher Unternehmen am Beginn des 20. Jahrhunderts*. Netzwerkforschung. Wiesbaden: VS, 2012.

Lane, Christel. "Globalization and the German Model of Capitalism - Erosion or Survival?" *The British Journal of Sociology* 51, no. 2 (2000): 207–234.

Lane. "Institutional Transformation and System Change: Changes in the Corporate Governance of German Corporations." In *Changing Capitalism? Internationalization, Institutional Change, and Systems of Economic Organization*, edited by Glenn Morgan, Richard Whiteley, and Eli Moen, 78–109. Oxford: Oxford University Press, 2006.

Lindner, Stephan H. *Inside IG Farben. Hoechst during the Third Reich*. Cambridge: Cambridge University Press, 2008.

Loibl, Klaus-Michael. *US-Direktinvestitionen in der EWG. Das Beispiel der Chemieindustrie*. Wirtschaftspolitische Studien; 22. Göttingen: Vandenhoeck & Ruprecht, 1971.

Mahoney, James. "Path Dependence in Historical Sociology." *Theory and Society* 29 (2000): 507–548.

Marx. "Multinationale Unternehmen in Westeuropa seit dem Ende des Booms. Von der deutsch-französischen Kooperation zwischen Hoechst und Roussel Uclaf zu Sanofi-Aventis (1968-2004)." *Themenportal Europäische Geschichte*. http://www.europa.clio-online.de/2015/Article=728 (2015).

Marx. "A European Structural Crisis Cartel as Solution to a Sectoral Depression? The West European Fibre Industry in the 1970s and 1980s." *Jahrbuch für Wirtschaftsgeschichte / Economic History Yearbook 2017/1* (forthcoming).

Marx, Christian, and Karoline Krenn. "Kontinuität und Wandel in der deutschen Unternehmensverflechtung. Vom Kaiserreich bis zum Nationalsozialismus (1914–1938)." *Geschichte und Gesellschaft* 38, no. 4 (2012): 658–701.

Marx, Christian. "Die Internationalisierung der Chemieindustrie als Herausforderung für die Deutschland AG." In *Die "Deutschland AG". Historische Annäherungen an den bundesdeutschen Kapitalismus*, edited by Ralf Ahrens, Boris Gehlen, and Alfred Reckendrees. Bochumer Schriften zur Unternehmens- und Industriegeschichte; 20, 247–273. Essen: Klartext, 2013.

Mittmann, Detlef. *Die chemische Industrie im nordwestlichen Mitteleuropa in ihrem Strukturwandel*. Kölner Forschungen zur Wirtschafts- und Sozialgeographie; 20. Wiesbaden: Steiner, 1974.

Morgan, Glenn. "Institutional Complementarities, Path Dependency, and the Dynamics of Firms." In *Changing Capitalism? Internationalization, Institutional Change, and Systems of Economic Organization*, edited by Glenn Morgan, Richard Whiteley, and Eli Moen, 415–446. Oxford: Oxford University Press, 2006.

Morgan. "Introduction: Changing Capitalism? Internationalization, Institutional Change, and Systems of Economic Organization." In *Changing Capitalism? Internationalization, Institutional Change, and Systems of Economic Organization*, edited by Glenn Morgan, Richard Whiteley, and Eli Moen, 1–18. Oxford: Oxford University Press, 2006.

North, Douglass C. *Institutions, Institutional Change and Economic Performance*. Cambridge: Cambridge University Press 1990.

Papenheim-Tockhorn, Heike. *Der Aufbau von Kooperationsbeziehungen als Strategisches Instrument. Eine Längsschnittuntersuchung zur Kooperationspolitik deutscher Unternehmen.* Heidelberg: Physica-Verlag, 1995.

Pauly, Louis W., and Simon Reich. "National Structures and Multinational Corporate Behavior. Enduring Differences in the Age of Globalization." *International Organization* 51, no. 1 (1997): 1–30.

Pierson, Paul. "Increasing Returns, Path Dependence, and the Study of Politics." *American Political Science Review* 94 (2000): 251–268.

Porter, Michael E. *The Competitive Advantage of Nations.* London: Macmillan, 1990.

Rasch, Manfred. "Kohlechemie im Ruhrgebiet: Wirtschaft, Technik und Patente. Zur Vor- und Gründungsgeschichte der Ruhrchemie AG 1926–1928." In *Technikgeschichte im Ruhrgebiet – Technikgeschichte für das Ruhrgebiet. Festschrift für Wolfhard Weber zum 65. Geburtstag,* edited by Manfred Rasch and Dietmar Bleidick, 785–815. Essen: Klartext, 2004.

van Rooij, Joannes Wilhelmus, and Ernst Homburg. *Building the Plant. A History of Engineering Contracting in the Netherlands.* Eindhoven: Walburg Pers, 2002.

Schreier, Anna Elisabeth, and Manuela Wex. Chronik der Hoechst Aktiengesellschaft 1863–1988. Frankfurt am Main: Hoechst AG, 1990.

Schreyger, Stefan. *Direktinvestitionen deutscher Unternehmen im Ausland von 1952 bis 1980.* Köln: Universität Köln, 1994.

Schröter, Harm G. "Die Auslandsinvestitionen der deutschen chemischen Industrie 1870 bis 1930." *Zeitschrift für Unternehmensgeschichte* 35, no. 1 (1990): 1–22.

Schröter. "The German Question, the Unification of Europe, and the European Market Strategies of Germany's Chemical and Electrical Industries, 1900–1992." *Business History Review* 67 (1993): 369–405.

Schröter. "Kartellierung und Dekartellierung 1890–1990." *Vierteljahrschrift für Sozial- und Wirtschaftsgeschichte* 81 (1994): 457–493.

Schröter. "European Integration by the German Model? Unions, Multinational Enterprise and Labour Relations since the 1950s." In *Business and European Integration since 1800: Regional, National and International Perspectives,* edited by Ulf Olsson. Meddelanden Fran Ekonomisk-Historiska Institutionen Vid Göteborgs Universitet; 71, 85–99. Göteborg: Graphic Systems, 1997.

Schröter. "Fields of Competition and of Cooperation: Cartel Structures in the International Chemical Industry." In *Competition and Cooperation of Enterprises on National and International Markets (19th-20th Century),* edited by Hans Pohl, 35–56. Stuttgart: Steiner, 1997.

Schröter. "Competitive Strategy of the World's Largest Chemical Companies, 1970-2000." In *The Global Chemical Industry in the Age of the Petrochemical Revolution,* edited by Louis Galambos, Takashi Hikino, and Vera Zamagni, 53–81. New York, NY: Cambridge University Press, 2007.

Servan-Schreiber, Jean-Jacques. *Le Défi Américain.* Paris: Denoël, 1968.

Steiner, André. "Die siebziger Jahre als Kristallisationspunkt des wirtschaftlichen Strukturwandels in West und Ost?" In *Das Ende der Zuversicht? Die siebziger Jahre als Geschichte,* edited by Konrad H. Jarausch, 29–48. Göttingen: Vandenhoeck & Ruprecht, 2008.

Stokes, Raymond G. *Opting for Oil. The Political Economy of Technological Change in the West German Chemical Industry, 1945-1961.* Cambridge: Cambridge University Press, 1994.

Streeck, Wolfgang. *E Pluribus Unum? Varieties and Commonalities of Capitalism.* MPIFG Discussion Paper 10/12. Köln: MPIFG, 2010.

Streeck. *Re-Forming Capitalism. Institutional Change in the German Political Economy.* Oxford: Oxford University Press, 2010.

Streeck, Wolfgang, and Martin Höpner. "Einleitung. Alle Macht dem Markt?". In *Alle Macht dem Markt? Fallstudien zur Abwicklung der Deutschland AG,* edited by Wolfgang Streeck and Martin Höpner, 11–59. Frankfurt am Main / New York: Campus, 2003.

Struve, Petra. "Multinationale Konzerne in der chemischen Industrie der Bundesrepublik Deutschland." In *Multinationale Konzerne. Ihr Einfluss auf die Lage der Beschäftigten,* edited by Klaus Peter Kisker, Rainer Heinrich, Hans-Erich Müller, Rudolf Richter, and Petra Struve, 281–313. Köln: Bund, 1982.

Teltschik, Walter. *Geschichte der deutschen Großchemie. Entwicklung und Einfluß in Staat und Gesellschaft.* Weinheim: VCH, 1992.

Thelen, Kathleen. "Historical Institutionalism in Comparative Politics." *Annual Review of Political Science* 2 (1999): 369–404.

Thelen, Kathleen. *How Institutions Evolve: The Political Economy of Skills in Germany, Britain, the United States, and Japan*. Cambridge: Cambridge University Press, 2004.

Thelen, Kathleen. *Varieties of Liberalization and the New Politics of Social Solidarity*. New York: Cambridge University Press, 2014.

Thelen, Kathleen. "How Institutions Evolve: Insights from Comparative Historical Analysis." In *Comparative Historical Analysis in the Social Sciences*, edited by James Mahoney and Dietrich Rueschemeyer, 208–240. Cambridge: Cambridge University Press, 2003.

Vaubel, Ludwig. *Glanzstoff, Enka, Aku, Akzo. Unternehmensleitung im nationalen und internationalen Spannungsfeld 1929 bis 1978. Band 1*. Wuppertal: Enka AG, 1986.

Vlaanderen, Edward van. *Pronounced Success. America and Hoechst 1953–1978*. Bridgewater, N.J.: American Hoechst Corporation, 1979.

Wade, Robert. "Globalization and Its Limits. Report of the Death of the National Economy Are Greatly Exaggerated." In *National Diversity and Global Capitalism*, edited by Suzanne Berger and Ronald Dore. Conrell Studies in Political Economy, 60–88. Ithaca / London: Cornell University Press, 1996.

Wasserman, Stanley, and Katherine Faust. *Social Network Analysis. Methods and Applications*. Structural Analysis in the Social Sciences; 8. Cambridge: Cambridge University Press, 1994.

Wehnelt, Christoph. *Untergang des deutschen Weltkonzerns*. Lindenberg: Kunstverlag Josef Fink, 2009.

Wengenroth, Ulrich. "The German Chemical Industry after World War II." In *The Global Chemical Industry in the Age of the Petrochemical Revolution*, edited by Louis Galambos, Takashi Hikino, and Vera Zamagni, 141–167. New York, NY: Cambridge University Press, 2007.

Wessel, Horst A. *Kontinuität im Wandel. 100 Jahre Mannesmann 1890-1990*. Gütersloh: Mohndruck, 1990.

Wicht, Wolfgang E. *Glanzstoff. Zur Geschichte der Chemiefaser, eines Unternehmens und seiner Arbeiterschaft*. Bergische Forschungen; 22. Neustadt an der Aisch: Schmidt, 1992.

Williamson, Oliver E. *The Economic Institutions of Capitalism. Firms, Markets, Relational Contracting*. New York, NY: Free Press, 1985.

Windolf, Paul. *Corporate Networks in Europe and the United States*. Oxford: Oxford University Press, 2002.

Windolf, Paul. "Unternehmensverflechtung im Organisierten Kapitalismus. Deutschland und USA im Vergleich 1896–1938." *Zeitschrift für Unternehmensgeschichte* 51, no. 2 (2006): 191–222.

Windolf, Paul. "Coordination and Control in Corporate Networks. United States and Germany in Comparison, 1896–1938." *European Sociological Review* 25 (4) (2009): 443–457.

Windolf, Paul, and Jürgen Beyer. "Co-Operative Capitalism. Corporate Networks in Germany and Britain." *British Journal of Sociology* 47, no. 2 (1996): 205–231.

Windolf, Paul. "Die Neuen Eigentümer." In *Finanzmarkt-Kapitalismus. Analysen zum Wandel von Produktionsregimen*, edited by Paul Windolf. Kölner Zeitschrift für Soziologie und Sozialpsychologie. Sonderheft; 45, 8–19. Wiesbaden: VS, 2005.

Windolf, Paul. "Was ist Finanzmarkt-Kapitalismus?" In *Finanzmarkt-Kapitalismus. Analysen zum Wandel von Produktionsregimen*, edited by Paul Windolf. Kölner Zeitschrift für Soziologie und Sozialpsychologie. Sonderheft; 45, 20–57. Wiesbaden: VS, 2005.

Windolf, Paul. "Die Zukunft des Rheinischen Kapitalismus." In *Organisationssoziologie*, edited by Jutta Allmendinger and Thomas Hinz. Kölner Zeitschrift für Soziologie und Sozialpsychologie. Sonderhefte; 42, 414–442. Wiesbaden: Westdeutscher Verlag, 2002.

Windolf, Paul. "The Corporate Network in Germany, 1896-2010." In *The Power of Corporate Networks. A Comparative and Historical Perspective*, edited by Thomas David and Gerarda Westerhuis, 66-85. New York / London: Routledge, 2014.

Winnacker, Karl. *Challenging Years. My Life in Chemistry*. London: Sidgwick & Jackson, 1972.

Wixforth, Harald, and Dieter Ziegler. "'Bankenmacht'. Universal Banking and German Industry in Historical Perspective." In *The Evolution of Financial Institutions and Markets in Twentieth-Century Europe*, edited by Youssef Cassis, Gerald D. Feldman, and Ulf Olsson, 249–272. Aldershot: Scolar Press, 1995.

Financing Rhenish capitalism: 'bank power' and the business of crisis management in the 1960s and 1970s

Ralf Ahrens

ABSTRACT
The German tradition of Hausbanks financing industrial enterprises over long periods, often accompanied by equity participation and memberships on supervisory boards, is considered a core element of Rhenish capitalism. Reconsidering the discussion about 'bank power' that has often referred to this system of corporate finance, this article explores the opportunities and limits of influence encountered by German big banks vis-à-vis their customers from big industry. Five case studies focusing on the management of financial crises are presented to demonstrate that, in practice, banks could only obtain control in cases of emergency, sometimes even against their will and at high cost.

Introduction

The German tradition of *Hausbanks* financing industrial enterprises over long periods, often accompanied by equity participations and memberships on supervisory boards (also referred to as 'relational banking'),[1] is considered a core element of Rhenish Capitalism. Michel Albert described German industry as being controlled in large part by the few big banks,[2] thus reinforcing more elaborate concepts that started with Rudolf Hilferding's *Finance Capital*.[3] The interpretation of British economist Andrew Shonfield, whose comparative analysis of post-war *Modern Capitalism* identified the big banks as 'prefects' of the German economy, proved even more influential, at least outside the Marxist community: according to Shonfield's findings, corporate law institutions and informal habits generally favoured a tendency towards collaboration between companies, with 'tutelary' banks not only handing out loans, but even acting as a kind of planning board more or less functionally equivalent to public institutions within the French *planification*.[4]

Sociological research on what has been called 'Germany Inc.' (*Deutschland AG*), i.e. the dense personal and capital networks between the largest industrial and financial corporations, also came to the conclusion that asymmetrical distributions of power allowed banks to influence the business strategies of industrial enterprises. It was argued that, until the dissolution of the network since the 1990s, this influence was exercised in industry's favour by accepting moderate but steady shareholders' returns – which, in turn, made it easier to find distributive compromises with trade unions – and by protecting companies against unfriendly takeovers.[5] In the banks' favour, board memberships and proxy voting rights in shareholders' meetings increased their monitoring potential and allowed for interventions if their industrial debtors showed symptoms of crisis. Depending on the individual constellation, the *Hausbank* tradition could either serve as a substitute for trust or enhance trust through continuous personal contacts and privileged access to information about the customers' financial situation and economic perspectives.[6]

Putting the models of Rhenish Capitalism and Germany Inc. to an empirical test, this article will explore the business practice of 'bank power' and its limits by analysing bankers' options and strategies – including the problem of cooperation and competition among banks – in historical situations where large industrial customers were in need of assistance. How and under what conditions did banks try to exert their special influence? What was the underlying rationale? Following a brief sketch of some general characteristics of German banking with regard to industry, it offers five short case studies which are taken from the time when Rhenish Capitalism had to face the gradual passing of the 'economic miracle' and German industry increasingly had to rely on external finance instead of profits[7] (thus presumably further increasing the banks' influence): the failure of the Schlieker concern in 1962; the liquidity crisis of Krupp in 1967; the establishment of the building concern Bilfinger+Berger from 1969 to 1975; the takeover of Demag by Mannesmann between 1972 and 1974; and the financial restructuring of Allgemeine Electricitäts-Gesellschaft AEG-Telefunken (AEG) around 1975. Although these examples were chosen to demonstrate a range of different constellations, their generalisability is limited. Due to the current state of archive-based research in German banking history, they focus for the most part on Dresdner Bank. Measured by enterprise size, amount of equity holdings or number of supervisory board seats, Deutsche Bank was always at the centre of Germany Inc., with Dresdner as a permanent runner-up.[8] But studies focusing on bank–industry relations after 1945 have remained rare up to now even for the market-leader, not to speak of Commerzbank as the third big privately-owned bank or other credit institutions.[9] Moreover, it must be left to future research to put the results in a cross-country comparison.

German (big) banking: institutions and interests

The presence of bankers on the supervisory boards of industrial corporations has a long tradition that dates back to the age of industrialisation. The big German banking corporations founded in the second half of the nineteenth century were 'universal banks', i.e. they took in deposits, handed out both short- and long-term loans, and were also engaged in the securities business. The great importance of this sort of bank for industry was different from the situation in Britain and the US, where – again, for different historical reasons – in a market-based system, separate institutions like investment banks were specialising in corporate finance and raising money on securities markets for this purpose. Germany, like other continental countries, developed a bank-based system of providing industrial enterprises with money for investment or mergers. Banks also acted as co-founders of industrial enterprises and, at least temporarily, took over some of their shares.[10]

In some cases, banks became or remained important shareholders of industrial corporations during much of the twentieth century. Moreover, they held proxy voting rights on behalf of private customers who kept their shares in bank deposits, thus often representing more than 90% of the shares at the corporations' general assemblies. But of much greater importance for corporate control than these large assemblies were the supervisory board meetings. German stock corporation law strictly prescribed dual-board corporate governance. In sharp contrast to the Anglo-American single-board system, German corporations had to establish a supervisory board to monitor and, where necessary, alter the course of the managing board's activities. The principal-agent constellation in corporations generated by the informational advantage of the management thereby shifted in favour of the shareholders. Traditionally, a relatively high proportion of board mandates was held by bank representatives or private bankers. This over-representation (compared to other industries) continued after a reform of the Stock Corporation Act in 1965 limited to 10 the number of seats one banker was permitted to occupy in various companies and prohibited interlocking directorates at the management level (so that a member of the board of managers of an industrial corporation could not join a bank's supervisory board if the reverse connection was already established, or vice versa). In theory, corporate law assigned supervisory boards the right to control management activities on behalf of the shareholders. In practice, the legal framework left a lot of leeway to establish specific rules of control in individual corporations. The relationship between the two boards was determined not only by its charter but also by informal norms, the board members' self-conceptions, and traditional habits which, in turn, were subject to historical change.[11]

Banks thus played an important role within the insider-controlled system of corporate governance. In the outsider-controlled systems of the US or Britain, where corporate finance relied primarily on the capital market and shares were broadly distributed among the public, markets and shareholders monitored the performance of corporations by determining their value on the stock exchange (and, at least indirectly, the managers' incomes). In continental Europe and Japan, equity ownership was dominated much more by major shareholders represented in the supervisory boards, so capital exercised management control from 'within'. In Germany, the big universal banks often held large blocks of shares and compensated a lack of capital supply from the markets with their credits.[12] In the mid-1970s, Deutsche Bank, Dresdner Bank and Commerzbank alone owned 41% of the volume of equity held by German banks in non-bank corporations.[13] The big banks thus generally held a relatively strong insider position from which they could pursue their interests as creditors and as shareholders.

'Germany Inc.' (this term for the dense personal and capital network was probably coined in the 1970s but did not become commonplace until the 1990s) had not been consciously established as some kind of finance capital's commanding height or planning board. Capital participations had evolved over decades for various reasons; informal 'rights' to occupy supervisory mandates could date back to an enterprise's foundation. Nevertheless, the accumulation of network ties and monitoring rights sparked various debates about 'bank power' in Germany during the twentieth century. In particular, the over-representation of the banks with regard to the overall number of supervisory mandates and the large number of interlocking directorates with industrial corporations supported the thesis of bank hegemony. This was a feature that German corporate networks had in common with Switzerland and the Netherlands, whereas other European countries differed in various aspects and for various reasons.[14] The tendency towards some kind of coordinated capitalism stimulated by the network structure with banks at the centre was reflected in relatively 'centralised and cooperative banking associations playing an important role in policy implementation';

politico-administrative supervision was 'centralised and formalised' but at the same time consensus-oriented and reliant on the finance industry's self-control mechanisms.[15]

Banks not only acted as shareholders interested in the short-term maximisation of revenue and stock exchange value. The German system of corporate control was strongly stakehold-er-oriented, and – as some of the following cases will demonstrate – bankers indeed sometimes perceived themselves as agents of common interest: safeguarding the existence of a company might not only mean securing one's own financial engagement, but could also be understood as a societal task. At least partly and to a certain degree, bankers on supervisory boards could share interests with unions and employees, owner families or the state.[16] The model of stakeholder coalition, in turn, corresponded with a traditional long-term business strategy orientation. *Hausbanks* in particular, as a firm's primary banking partner, could hope to gain access to exclusive information about their debtor, and they could expect relatively moderate but steady revenues for credits and services. In return, they were expected to assist their customers in times of (not only financial) crisis and against hostile take-over attacks.[17]

Banks certainly competed for business with large industrial customers, although the German 'three pillar model' of banking groups with partly differing legal bases (private commercial banks, public savings banks and their umbrella institutes on the *Länder* level, credit cooperatives) limited overall competition in the financial sector. On the other hand, they were forced to cooperate not only in the consortia that handled large credits, stock issues or export finance, but also when it came to monitoring their customers. At the same time, single bankers often held several positions in the supervisory boards of other corporations not only because their banks possessed shares or granted credits, but also because they were able to accumulate business contacts and information. Influential private bankers and top managers of the few big banks may even be conceived as a 'class of their own', defined by expert knowledge and networking capabilities, respected as consultants and even mediators in conflicts between companies' owners and managements.[18]

Formal and informal institutions of corporate governance thus supported a certain type of 'organised' or 'managed' capitalism: compared to Great Britain and the US, the German tradition of interlocking directorates and highly concentrated shareholdings favoured cooperative rather than competitive market strategies, i.e. agreements between companies in the same sector to control competition were more probable. While price cartels were forbidden after World War II, business strategies or mergers could still be subject to agreement between leading industrialists and bankers. The intensity, durability and structure of corporate networks (albeit with declining density during the second half of the twentieth century and the first decade of the twenty-first) tended to favour long-term relationships over short-term profits. This held not only for shareholders from the non-financial sectors, but also for the big banks that often owned large shares in non-bank corporations (in contrast to Anglo-American investment funds).[19]

Cooperation in the sense outlined here must, of course, not be confused with the absence of conflict; nor does it mean that banks did not exercise any kind of coercion against their customers in situations of dissent. Depending on the situation, they had to select their activity from different ranges of opportunities. Social scientists tend to analyse the networks of Rhenish Capitalism as 'opportunity structures' *(Gelegenheitsstrukturen)*, focusing more on potential influence than on practices. A historian's task is to take a look inside the black box of individual companies to see how these opportunities were utilised.

Varieties of 'bank power': five case studies

The following brief case studies highlight different constellations of crisis management and the resolution of resulting conflicts. As mentioned, the examples do not cover the German financial industry as a whole, only a few big banks and their customers from big industry. The three universal banks of nationwide importance – Deutsche Bank, Dresdner Bank, and Commerzbank – together had an overall market share of only a little more than 10% around 1970, but they dominated certain fields of business like the stock market or credit transactions with big industry. With regard to their influence on these big customers, the dual-board structure is at the centre of the bank power argument, as banks had above-average representation on the supervisory boards. But again, caution should be exercised when it comes to generalisation. In the mid-1970s, banks' representatives were members of the supervisory board in only one third of approximately 2000 non-bank stock corporations in the Federal Republic (and we know little about the financial relations of even smaller enterprises). But among the 66 biggest corporations listed on the stock exchange, nearly 90% had bankers on their boards, and often more than one – mostly delegated by the three big institutes mentioned above, but also by Bank für Gemeinwirtschaft, Bayerische Vereinsbank and Bayerische Hypotheken- und Wechselbank.[20] Some of the following cases focus on core enterprises in this network. Others were not part of the Germany Inc. network but also provide instructive examples for the way big banks coped with industrial problems in Rhenish Capitalism.

Leaving the ship: Willy Schlieker

Until recently, historical research on the role of banks in the 1960s and 1970s has not devoted much attention to the business practices of banks on the supervisory boards of their customers but has looked, rather, at how they performed their basic economic task, namely granting or denying credits. Considering the spectacular failures of Carl Borgward, Willy Schlieker and the Stinnes brothers in the early 1960s, one may come to the conclusion that the maintenance of close and frequent contacts via supervisory boards encouraged the crucial confidence of banks in their debtors. In these cases, bankers' contacts with industrialists claiming exclusive decision-making authority ('masters of the house') were not very close. Credit policies were strongly influenced by a belief in the ability and will of the company owners to pay back their debts (and maybe also by the long experience of steady and relatively low-risk entrepreneurial successes during the 'economic miracle'). But in times of crisis, trust could rapidly turn into mistrust.[21]

The iron and shipbuilding industrialist Willy H. Schlieker, for example, one of the legendary self-made men of the miracle years, failed in 1962 due to a lack of equity capital. This was ultimately the result of Schlieker's insistence on personal ownership instead of external participants. The ownership structure and internal organisation of his concern were barely transparent to outsiders. The crisis began in his Hamburg shipyard when a rapid intensification of international competition in shipbuilding changed conditions in favour of the ship buyers. The resulting price decrease caused the profitability of the recently modernised shipyard to deteriorate. Schlieker tried to bridge the ensuing shortfalls and liquidity gaps with the profits of other conglomerate enterprises that also functioned as securities for short-term credits. The confusing situation was reflected in highly discrepant estimates of the current liquidity gaps by the concern owner and his creditors. Schlieker's creditors – mainly Dresdner Bank and the two steel companies Phönix-Rheinrohr and Salzgitter – were unwilling to extend loans without more detailed information. Schlieker, for his part, refused to offer any more than his word of honour – which he in fact broke. After their industrial customer had lost his reputation and denied them access to more intense monitoring, the banks finally exercised the exit option and did not renew the credits. The industrial creditors that both had their own competing interests in the ship-building and steel markets followed suit, and took over parts of the Schlieker concern after its failure. The city of Hamburg, where some 5000 jobs were at stake, was asked for backup, but remained very reluctant. In any case, the business potential of political backup should not be overestimated: in the Borgward case, an attempt by the city state of Bremen to rescue the concern by taking equity control and installing new management failed.[22]

Monitoring family business: Krupp

The outcome of the existence-threatening liquidity crisis of Krupp was fundamentally different, though it also had some origins in a lack of trust. The long-established steel concern was entirely the Krupp family's property, which at first sight made the case similar to that of Schlieker. The holding company was organised as a private firm without formal monitoring institutions open to outsiders, and the whole concern was afflicted by structural income weaknesses which the banks involved had long ignored. The sole owner, Alfried Krupp von Bohlen und Halbach, had pursued a strategy of extensive growth since the 1950s and refused to cut back unprofitable parts of the concern. In the mid-1960s the long growth period of the miracle years slackened, and the first true economic crisis of the Federal Republic definitively revealed the principal weaknesses of the concern, in particular, very thin capitalisation. When Krupp nearly suffered illiquidity in 1967, the banks helped out with another large credit. But they only did so after the North-Rhine Westphalian and federal governments had made loan guarantees, and after Alfried Krupp had agreed to transform the holding into Fried. Krupp GmbH, a limited liability company with a supervisory board. Ownership was transferred to the non-profit Alfried Krupp von Bohlen und Halbach Foundation. The transition to modern company structures had become easier after the prospective sole heir of the concern, Arndt von Bohlen und Halbach, had renounced his legacy.

In this case, the banks indeed exercised power through conditional lending (and although they held no capital participations). As a result, their control position was strengthened in terms of formal institutions. The professionalisation of control structures toward the dual-board system was a precondition to bankers exercising their 'voice' option, as were the state guarantees that reduced their risk.[23] But it soon became obvious that their power was highly dependent on how alarming and urgent the liquidity problems were, and that it was limited by the rivalry among them: In 1970, the executor of Alfried Krupp's will, former managing director Berthold Beitz, was able to dissolve Deutsche Bank's Hermann Josef Abs as chairman of the supervisory board and to assume the position himself (and Abs was certainly still one of West Germany's most powerful bankers in terms of supervisory board presence and political connections).[24] Beitz's deputy on the supervisory board, Dresdner Bank spokesman Jürgen Ponto, was later even named one of the 'architects' of Krupp's new business strategies. Given the still highly problematic profit situation of the Krupp concern, one could indeed understand such a prominent banker taking the lead in restructuring the concern in an attempt to improve its earning power. In fact, the banks that were engaged in financing Krupp certainly utilised their monitoring rights, but were only superficially involved in redirecting the still unprofitable concern. Ponto was not even involved in the search for the various new management chairmen hired by Beitz during the 1970s. Contrary to speculations in the press, he was also only informed *ex post* about a spectacular change of ownership structure, i.e. the 25% equity participation of the state of Iran in the concern holding and in the steel company Fried. Krupp Hüttenwerke AG.[25] Nevertheless, Ponto enjoyed a high degree of personal trust and acted as a kind of moderator between Beitz and his top managers, and also mediated conflicts with members of the Krupp family and with the federal minister of science. Though the importance of this task for the performance of an enterprise should not be underestimated, it did not have much to do with bank hegemony. Obviously the banks did not make use of their most important instrument of power, the refusal of credits, during these years. As their behaviour during the severe liquidity crisis in 1967 demonstrated, they did not necessarily operate in a less risk-averse manner here than in the Schlieker case, though Krupp certainly enjoyed a higher, traditional reputation. Ultimately, however – especially without any equity holdings – they were hardly able to control the course of Krupp against the will of a strong personality like Beitz.[26]

Enforcing a merger: Bilfinger+Berger

The third case, the stepwise merger of three medium-sized building companies to become one of the major players in the industry: the Bilfinger+Berger combine (still in existence today as Bilfinger SE), shows a bank really exercising its power and pursuing its own 'industrial policy'. Dresdner Bank held participations in the three merged companies Julius Berger (Wiesbaden), Bauboag (Düsseldorf) and Grün & Bilfinger (Mannheim), and its dominant position was not contested by other credit institutions. Moreover, changing market conditions exerted pressure on smaller building companies when the post-war reconstruction boom faded, competition intensified, and the business became more capital-intensive. The experts at Dresdner Bank had observed these changes and had been aiming at a concentration of assets in the building sector since 1964. But it was only in 1968 that a disastrous slump in Berger's current earnings, combined with insufficient information policies, presented the bank with the opportunity to alter the company's course against the will of its management. Misinformation by the Berger management, i.e. a violation of the shareholders' monitoring rights, provided important leverage.[27] Ponto, the chairman of the supervisory board, sent his own experts to the Berger offices. After they had uncovered grave deficits in management information, the supervisory board unanimously voted for a quick merger with Bauboag and the replacement of Berger's managing director, Max R. Schulz. The two Bauboag managers Kurt Neumann and Martin Klinge thereupon entered the Berger board – both of whom were, in effect, Ponto's delegates. Within a few months in 1969 the merger was organised, with Dresdner Bank ultimately holding 65% of the Berger–Bauboag capital.[28]

Ponto remained chairman of the supervisory board and called insistently for a second merger with Grün & Bilfinger. But it took six more years and another crisis, this time cyclical in nature, before this final step was realised. Even as the Berger–Bauboag merger was still underway, the first talks with Grün & Bilfinger took place. After some strategic discussion, Grün & Bilfinger took over the Berger–Bauboag equity of Dresdner Bank and bought additional shares. For tax purposes, and to limit opposition from the management and employees of both companies, only a cooperation agreement with decisional authority on the part of Grün & Bilfinger was concluded. But at the same time, Klinge and Neumann from Berger–Bauboag were now co-opted into the Grün & Bilfinger board of managers. They were, again, delegated by Ponto, and Dresdner Bank meanwhile owned 45% of the shares. Nevertheless, the final steps to create Bilfinger+Berger Bauaktiengesellschaft in 1975 were only taken when a recession depressed both candidates' revenues.[29]

What we can learn from the Bilfinger+Berger case is that fundamental changes in the structure and governance of industrial enterprises could indeed, under certain conditions, be enforced by banks. In this individual case, however, these changes were highly dependent on the personal commitment of one banker and were backed by substantial capital participations by one bank. And even under these general conditions, it took two economic crises and a lot of time to complete the mergers. Furthermore, the short-term financial interests and mid-term 'industrial policies' of banks should not be conceived as stark opposites: As the different durations of the two merger processes demonstrate, a rapidly increasing risk of credit defaults or even bankruptcy by a customer exerted special pressure on the bank to find a solution.

Negotiating a merger: Mannesmann-Demag

The Bilfinger mergers highlight the importance of the German dual-board system for controlling and sometimes even redirecting corporations. However, things could become complicated if a number of banks had to arrange such strategies among themselves. The take-over of Deutsche Maschinenbau-AG (Demag) by the steel concern Mannesmann demonstrates how they could get into conflict about the ways of their industrial partners when two or more of them were represented on the supervisory board. Demag was the object of a struggle between Mannesmann and Thyssen. Though the two combines had demarcated their primary markets in 1969, they were both pursuing a strategy of diversification into machine building. Demag was one of the larger German machinery companies that was still independent. Mannesmann's chairman of the board Egon Overbeck was aiming at a complete take-over of the machine-building company. His Thyssen counterpart Hans-Günther Sohl, also acting as chairman of Demag's supervisory board, was also interested in strengthening the ties with the company or at least maintaining its independence. For this purpose, Sohl built an alliance with Demag chairman Wolfgang Reuter.[30]

Demag was regarded as a domain of Deutsche Bank, as was Mannesmann. Dresdner Bank's Jürgen Ponto was introduced into the supervisory board as a person of trust for Sohl and Reuter in 1972, while his Deutsche Bank counterpart Franz Heinrich Ulrich backed Overbeck. Ponto had divided loyalties to a certain degree, as he was trying to intensify commercial relations with Mannesmann. Nevertheless, he seriously attempted to establish a pool of shares to defend against the take-over with Sohl and Reuter, only to realise fairly quickly that their initial equity participation was simply too small.[31] The only remaining policy was to avoid open conflicts in order to maintain Demag's solid public image. Until 1974, Overbeck's aggressive strategy succeeded, not least because there were no other big investors willing to rival him. Even Ponto – for simple commercial reasons, not because of his aspirations for business with Mannesmann – was unwilling to let Dresdner Bank buy Demag shares. In addition to the competitive aspect of two (or more) banks on one supervisory board, the Demag case highlights the fact that not only bankers, but also industrialists could try to influence the course of other industrial corporations via the supervisory board. Nevertheless, it was no coincidence that Sohl chose Ponto as his 'man of trust': clearly only a representative of a big bank could attempt to defy someone like Ulrich. The banker, in turn, tried not to disappoint his associate, but knew when it was time to surrender. Loyalty reached its limits when the balance sheet of his own company was affected, and the outcome of the buy-out conflict was clearly determined not by 'bank power' but by the interests and buying potential of industrialists.[32]

Sharing risk: AEG

Finally, the financial restructuring of AEG in the mid-1970s demonstrates the limits, and the risks, of even a more or less concurrent engagement of banks. The electrical equipment concern had expanded rapidly in the 1960s, mainly financed by bank loans and without looking at cost–benefit ratios seriously enough. When dividend payments were stopped in 1973, structural deficiencies became obvious, and they were aggravated by a big loss from the nuclear power branch shortly thereafter. The following international recession put even more pressure on profits and made it obvious that AEG had lost the long-term competition with the other big German electrics concern, Siemens. This was the situation when Jürgen Ponto was appointed chairman of the supervisory board in March 1975 – instead of, as had traditionally been the case, another industrial manager like the displaced Hans Bühler, who had been one of the main initiators of the unlimited growth strategy. Only a banker with a reputation like Ponto's and his financial background seemed to offer a way out of the alarming situation, and Dresdner Bank had for decades been the AEG *Hausbank* and had the lead in its finance consortium.[33]

And indeed, Ponto did what a banker could do best: mobilising money. Under his leadership, the banks took high risks to keep one of Germany's industrial legends alive. In addition to the transformation of short-term into longer-term credits and the maintenance of credit lines, they intensified their commitment as shareholders. This was especially the task of Dresdner Bank, which bought an additional 8% of AEG equity from General Electric in 1976. But Ponto also convinced the other banks to agree on a considerable capital increase (from 704 to 930 million Deutschmarks) and to buy the new shares themselves at a fairly high price, as they were practically unsellable on the stock market.[34] This reaction by the banks was obviously not the kind of short-term market-oriented behaviour one would expect from shareholder value-oriented financial institutions: Instead of minimising their risk, they in fact increased it, thereby demonstrating their will to stabilise a big player in the Germany Inc. network in times of crisis and their faith in long-term recovery. The banks opted for an active commitment that required tight cooperation and trust among themselves – in other words, the constellation was the opposite of the Mannesmann-Demag case.

Providing loans and financing the issue of new shares were, of course, core tasks of the banks that, in the German system of corporate finance, no other institution could shoulder. However, as in the Bilfinger+Berger case, Ponto went beyond financial measures and became deeply involved in the restructuring of the industrial combine. He took the distress sale of AEG's 50% share of Kraftwerk Union (KWU) – West Germany's most important producer of power plants – into his own hands. But the deal with competitor Siemens proved costly, as AEG still had to guarantee damages from older KWU plants. And the installation of a new chairman of managers, the former director general of Gelsenberg AG, Walter Cipa, was a bad decision with grave consequences. Again, Ponto's intimate Sohl, who was also chairman of the Gelsenberg supervisory board, played a crucial role in this decision. The idea of recruiting a reforming manager from another branch seemed at first sight to make sense, and Cipa's programme of reorganising the opaque structure of the concern and increasing the controlling potential of the top management was widely approved. But the supervisory board soon had to watch shop morale slump on account of his sharp reorganisation measures, factory closings and autocratic leadership style; important top managers left the concern. In addition to the brain drain, Cipa's earnings announcements remained over-optimistic, to say the least. When AEG was still unable to distribute dividends in 1977, the supervisory board soon became plainly aware of how weak was its potential to monitor the covered risks and to put a leash on an obstinate manager. After losses in the following years, a recapitalisation in 1979 also had to be borne in large part by the banks.[35] The monitoring potential of the banks remained low; their only power in the last instance was lending money or spending it on shares. But the exercise of this sort of 'bank power' certainly did not guarantee the stabilisation of an industrial customer: The banks exercised their 'voice' option only to see AEG going further downhill over the next few years and offering a settlement in 1982 in which they suffered high damages – especially the *Hausbank* Dresdner, which at the time owned 21.5% of the shares.[36]

In the case of AEG, even an extraordinarily strong supervisory position with the chairman taking drastic measures did not generate mistrust at the right moment. Though it was certainly not a case of 'complicity' between managers and supervisors,[37] the quality of monitoring and control was not adequate for the amount of capital that was at stake. The reputation and magnitude of the customer, but also personal misjudgement played a role. On the other hand, this case demonstrates the high degree to which German bankers were still available to help their industrial customers out of crisis – at least if the customer was such a flagship of West German industry as AEG. Apparent weaknesses in times of intensifying competition and dwindling general growth rates were not, per se, reasons to retreat from risk. Rather, the banks' acquisition of new shares in fact intensified a capital network. A precondition was trustful cooperation among the banks involved as long as they decided not to exit. The networks of Germany Inc. suggested a strategy of 'voice',[38] though the attempts to co-direct the course of AEG ultimately failed.

Conclusion: limits and prospects of bank power

Looking into the black box of German bank–industry relations in times of crisis revealed some behavioural patterns of general importance. The examples from the 1960s and 1970s outlined in this article demonstrate that banks did not act as prefects of the economy in Shonfield's sense when the cost was too high (and certainly did not practise any kind of collective central planning). West German big industry was facing structural deficiencies and sometimes dramatic crises that required far-reaching reorganisations and the provision of external capital or credit by banks. In general, banks seem to have preferred a policy of intervention and assistance vis-à-vis their customers rather than a short-term reduction of losses in situations of crisis. The Schlieker failure nevertheless demonstrates that this inclination was of course limited by risk analyses, and that trust in big debtors could rapidly turn into mistrust.

It may therefore be misleading to conceive personal or reputational trust only as an *alternative* to institutionalised monitoring rights when banks had to decide about credit lines or other financial risks.[39] At least in critical situations, trust *required* a minimum of control, and the banks' monitoring potential was increased by the dual-board system, where bankers acted as supervisors of industrial managers and might also become friends with them. The presence of banks' representatives on supervisory boards, ideally in the position of chairman, was also a precondition to being able to exert influence beyond the simple 'power' to lend money or not (which was not power, per se, as long as there were competitors willing to step into the breach for whatever reason). The presence of various banks on the supervisory board of one customer firm generally strengthened their influence, but – as the Demag case demonstrates – it could, under certain circumstances, also split them into factions. Their influence was exercised largely through the choice of management personnel, and also through the approval or denial of bigger investment projects. But it was only in times of severe crises that banks really tried to govern industrial companies in the sense of prescribing management decisions. In general, they were neither qualified for industrial management nor interested in it. The basic interest of West German big banks with regard to their industrial customers was the maintenance of long-term business relations in their various fields of activity.

Moreover, the cases of Bilfinger Berger and AEG demonstrate that crisis alone was not a sufficient circumstance to successfully enforce a bank's interest: In the first case, the *Hausbank* could enforce a merger and thereby initiate effective restructuring; in the second, a massive collaborative intervention by the banks ultimately resulted in big losses. In a situation like this, the banks were able to take over additional shares of an industrial enterprise, thus increasing their potential hegemony over the management and the other shareholders. But they also bore additional risks, and their potential to redirect management strategies and control their implementation was limited. Where there were no acute financial problems, as in the case of Krupp after 1967, influence on corporate policy was even more strictly limited. In terms of historical practice, bank power was indeed exercised in Rhenish Capitalism – but only on occasion, and sometimes at high cost as the banks' monitoring potential had its limits.

To check the validity of these results from West German examples, future research should emphasize international comparison. Such studies should probably focus more on bank–industry relations in other continental, Coordinated Market Economies to describe potential 'Varieties of Rhenish Capitalism' than on their obvious differences to Liberal Market Economies.[40] Nevertheless, it might be interesting to ask for convergences of these models in practice as well. The decades under review here were also a period of internationalisation for German banks and industrial companies. Regarding the financial industry, this did not become manifest so much in different attitudes like in the public conflict between Deutsche Bank and Dresdner Bank about the sale of Daimler-Benz shares to Kuwait or Iran in 1974/75.[41] All in all, the freedom of capital flows was uncontroversial as it created new markets for the big banks. But during the 1970s and 1980s, German non-bank enterprises also demonstrated a growing degree of self-finance as competition in the supply of capital and credits grew. At the same time, banks began to reduce equity stakes in non-bank corporations to some degree. The opportunities to exercise bank power generally decreased.[42] Economic and sociological research has observed the dissolution of Germany Inc. and some convergence towards the Anglo-American model of competitive capitalism and market-oriented corporate governance on an increased scale since the mid-1990s. The big banks sold large parts of their equity participations and reduced personal ties with other corporations.[43]

However, it remains to be explored how far-reaching and enduring these trends will prove to be – especially since the financial crisis, beginning in 2008, has redirected attention towards the benefits of industry-based coordinated capitalism. Prior to this, the American model of shareholder value, i.e. corporate control with a short-term financial orientation, did not simply replace traditional business culture, but was to a certain degree incorporated into the stakeholder model. The result was a 'German variant' that could be described as 'negotiated shareholder value'.[44] Limits to competition between banking groups were removed by harmonising the legal framework for the various banking groups and extending international regulation, and capital markets gained importance both in financial interme-diation and on the political agenda.[45] But the degree of financialisation, with its often assumed effects of destabilising institutionalised company networks and fostering the con-vergence of national market economies towards the neoliberal model, remained relatively low in Germany even before the crisis. Despite spectacular turns by some big banks towards international investment banking and the loosening of their network ties, the vast majority remained engaged in relational banking (though formal credit ranking became much more important in financing industry and trade, thus partly replacing informal trust). The GDP share of bank revenues rose only slightly, and household savings still went, to a very high degree, into bank deposits instead of securities. In terms of the Varieties of Capitalism approach, the country still remained a variant of Coordinated Market Economy compared to the American liberal model.[46] In other words, it remained an example of Rhenish Capitalism's flexibility and openness to institutional reform without throwing core charac-teristics overboard.

Notes

1. The (anglicised) German term 'Hausbank' will be used in this article because neither the uncommon literal translation 'house bank' nor related terms like 'principal' or 'primary bank' really cover the content and semantics. For a brief discussion of characteristic features, see Elsas and Krahnen, "Universal Banks and Relationships with Firms," 211–213.
2. Albert, *Capitalism Against Capitalism*, 106–113.
3. Hilferding, *Das Finanzkapital*.
4. Shonfield, *Modern Capitalism*, 246–250.
5. Streeck and Höpner, *Alle Macht dem Markt?* (esp. the article by Beyer, "Deutschland AG a.D."); Streeck, *Re-forming Capitalism*, 77–89.
6. Cf. Tilly, "Trust and Mistrust," esp. 113.
7. See Plumpe, "Das Ende des deutschen Kapitalismus"; Köhler, "Havarie der 'Schönwetterkapitäne'?"; Tilly, "Geschäftsbanken und Wirtschaft". See also the general overviews by Giersch, Paqué and Schmieding, *The Fading Miracle*; Carlin, "West German Growth."
8. Beyer, "Deutschland AG a.D.," 123.
9. The basic reference for most of the case studies is Ahrens and Bähr, *Jürgen Ponto*, partly relying on my own research of the papers of Dresdner Bank's spokesman now held at Commerzbank Historical Archives, Frankfurt a.M. (HAC). Ponto's papers offer uncommonly broad insights into his supervisory mandates. Other relevant works based on internal material (including Dresdner Bank files) are Stier and Krauß, *Drei Wurzeln*; Tilly, "Trust and Mistrust" and *Willy H. Schlieker*; Gall, "Von der Entlassung."
10. For detail on the roots of the German system of corporate finance in the nineteenth century, see especially Fohlin, *Finance Capitalism*. Fohlin argues that banks' stock holdings were typically

temporary and did not result in long-term equity stakes in industrial enterprises' (27); for the evidence, see Ibid., 106–120. For an overview on the twentieth century, focusing on aspects of inter-bank competition, see Deeg, *Finance Capitalism Unveiled*, 29–72. Important German studies analysing the influence of banks on their industrial customers in earlier decades are Wellhöner, *Großbanken und Großindustrie*; Wixforth, *Banken und Schwerindustrie;* and the sociological network analysis by Krenn, *Alle Macht den Banken?* For a short description of the classical distinction between market-based and bank-based systems of corporate finance, see Grossman, *Unsettled Account*, 157–62; Vitols, "The Origins"; on the traditions of universal banking in different countries see Tilly, "Universal Banking."

11. See Gehlen, "Aktienrecht und Unternehmenskontrolle."
12. Cf., for example, Schmidt, "Corporate Governance in Germany"; Hackethal, *Banken, Unternehmensfinanzierung und Finanzsysteme*, 153–183; Früh, *Die Rolle der Banken*. Even in the 1990s, 'bank loans constituted close to 80% of long-term external funding to business in Germany' compared to 12% in the US; Schmidt, "Corporate Governance in Germany," 395.
13. Together with their affiliates in West Berlin, where these institutes were not present after 1945 for political reasons; Krümmel, "German Universal Banking Scrutinized," 47. During this investigation, 336 banks were interviewed about participations exceeding 10%.
14. Scott, "Intercorporate Structures," esp. 222–224; Windolf and Beyer, "Co-operative Capitalism," 219–223. Overviews in English on the German debates about 'bank power' focusing on the decades after 1945 include Esser, "Bank Power" and Busch, *Banking Regulation and Globalization*, 85–120.
15. Busch, *Banking Regulation and Globalization,* 115, 224–225; cf. Lütz, *Der Staat*.
16. For example, Schmidt, "Corporate Governance in Germany," 396.
17. See, from a current economic perspective, Elsas and Krahnen, "Universal Banks and Relationships."
18. Berghoff and Köhler, "Redesigning a Class."
19. Windolf and Beyer, "Co-operative Capitalism"; Windolf, "The Corporate Network."
20. *Bericht der Studienkommission "Grundsatzfragen,"* 2–3, 116–130, 440–441. For a network analysis focusing on the 1970s, cf. Ziegler, Bender and Biehler, "Industry and Banking." A recent contribution on corporate finance in a smaller company from a business history perspective is Lesczenski, "Zwischen Kooperation"; also Elsas and Kranen, "Universal Banks and Relationships," 208–226.
21. Tilly, "Trust and Mistrust," 113–122, 134.
22. Ibid., 115–120; Tilly, *Willy H. Schlieker*, 137–171.
23. Cf. Lothar Gall, "Von der Entlassung," 558–575, 581–584; James, *Krupp*, 260–268.
24. Käppner, *Berthold Beitz*, 343–348. On Abs, see Gall, *Der Bankier*.
25. Letter from Ponto to Beitz, 27 Oct. 1976, HAC-500/8094-2002.
26. Käppner, *Berthold Beitz,* 393–402; Ahrens and Bähr, *Jürgen Ponto*, 150–159.
27. Minutes of a meeting of Berger supervisory board on 12 Dec. 1968, HAC-500/17812-2000.
28. Stier and Krauß, *Drei Wurzeln*, 364–461; Ahrens and Bähr, *Jürgen Ponto,* 161–163.
29. Ibid., 163–165; Stier and Krauß, *Drei Wurzeln*, 483–520.
30. Cf. Uebbing, *Wege und Wegmarken*, 82–84; Wessel, *Kontinuität im Wandel*, 439–448; Sohl, *Notizen*, 242–243.
31. Ponto, Betr.: DEMAG, 22. Aug. 1972, HAC-500/18123-2000.
32. Ahrens and Bähr, *Jürgen Ponto*, 137–141.
33. See Strunk, *AEG*, 78–105; Ipsen and Pfitzinger, "Krise," 63–78 and 84–86.
34. Strunk, *AEG*, 110; "Krach im großen Haus," in *Der Spiegel*, 20 Jan. 1975, 41.
35. Strunk, *AEG*, 108–115; Ahrens and Bähr, *Jürgen Ponto*, 174–178 (the respective chapter written by Bähr); Sohl, *Notizen*, 196–197.
36. Ipsen and Pfitzinger, "Krise," 80.
37. For this argument, cf. Tilly, "Trust and Mistrust," 134.
38. Cf. Windolf and Beyer, "Co-operative Capitalism," 211.
39. Tilly, "Trust and Mistrust," 109, n. 9.
40. For definitions, see Hall and Soskice, "Introduction."
41. Ahrens and Bähr, *Jürgen Ponto*, 181–193.

42. Deeg, *Finance Capitalism Unveiled,* 79–86, 96–102.
43. On the dissolution of corporate networks since the 1990s and consequences for corporate control, see for example Beyer and Höpner, "The Disintegration"; Beyer, "Die Strukturen."
44. Vitols, "Negotiated Shareholder Value."
45. Lütz, "The Finance Sector"; Deeg, *Finance Capitalism Unveiled,* 87–93.
46. Deeg, "Financialization and Institutional Change"; cf. Lütz, "The Finance Sector," 38–40.

Disclosure statement

No potential conflict of interest was reported by the author.

References

Ahrens, Ralf, and Johannes Bähr. *Jürgen Ponto. Bankier und Bürger. Eine Biografie.* München: Beck, 2013.
Albert, Michel. *Capitalism against Capitalism.* London: Whurr, 1993.
Berghoff, Hartmut, and Ingo Köhler. "Redesigning a class of its own: social and human capital formation in the German banking elite, 1870–1990." *Financial History Review* 14 (2007): 63–87.
Beyer, Jürgen, and Martin Höpner. "The disintegration of organised capitalism: German corporate governance in the 1990s." *West European Politics* 26, no. 4 (2003): 179–198.
Beyer, Jürgen. "Deutschland AG a.D.: Deutsche Bank, Allianz und das Verflechtungszentrum des deutschen Kapitalismus." In *Alle Macht dem Markt? Fallstudien zur Abwicklung der Deutschland AG,* edited by Wolfgang Streeck and Martin Höpner. Frankfurt: Campus, 2003, 118–146.
Beyer, Jürgen. "Die Strukturen der Deutschland AG. Rückblick auf ein Modell der Unternehmenskontrolle." In *Die "Deutschland AG". Historische Annäherungen an den bundesdeutschen Kapitalismus,* edited by Ralf Ahrens, Boris Gehlen and Alfred Reckendrees. Essen: Klartext 2013, 31–56.
Busch, Andreas. *Banking Regulation and Globalization.* Oxford: Oxford University Press, 2009.
Carlin, Wendy. "West German growth and institutions, 1945–90." In *Economic growth in Europe since 1945,* edited by Nicholas Crafts and Gianni Toniolo, 455–497. Cambridge: Cambridge University Press, 1996.
Deeg, Richard. *Finance Capitalism Unveiled.* Ann Arbor: University of Michigan Press, 1999.
Deeg, Richard. "Financialization and Institutional Change in Capitalism: A Comparison of the US and Germany." *The Journal of Comparative Economic Studies* 9 (2014): 47–68.
Elsas, Ralf and Jan Pieter Krahnen. "Universal Banks and Relationships with Firms." In *The German Financial System,* edited by Jan Pieter Krahnen and Reinhard H. Schmidt, 197–232.
Esser, Josef. "Bank Power in West Germany Revisited." *West European Politics* 13 (1990): 17–32.
Bundesministerium der Finanzen (ed.). *Bericht der Studienkommission "Grundsatzfragen der Kreditwirtschaft".* Bonn: Stollfuss, 1979.
Fohlin, Caroline. *Finance Capitalism and Germany's Rise to Industrial Power.* New York, NY: Cambridge University Press, 2007.
Früh, Hans-Gereon. *Die Rolle der Banken in der Corporate Governance.* Ein Erklärungsansatz der Neuen Institutionellen Ökonomie. Bern: Haupt, 1999.
Gall, Lothar. *Der Bankier. Hermann Josef Abs. Eine Biographie.* München: Beck, 2004.

Gall, Lothar. "Von der Entlassung Alfried Krupp von Bohlen und Halbachs bis zur Errichtung seiner Stiftung 1951 bis 1967/68" in *Krupp im 20. Jahrhundert. Die Geschichte des Unternehmens vom Ersten Weltkrieg bis zur Gründung der Stiftung*, edited by Lothar Gall. Berlin 2002 (1951): 473–589.

Gehlen, Boris. "Aktienrecht und Unternehmenskontrolle. Normative Vorgaben und unternehmerische Praxis in der Hochphase der Deutschland AG" in *Die "Deutschland AG". Historische Annäherungen an den bundesdeutschen Kapitalismus*, edited by Ralf Ahrens, Boris Gehlen and Alfred Reckendrees. Essen: Klartext 2013, 165–193.

Giersch, Herbert, Karl-Heinz Paqué, and Holger Schmieding. *The fading miracle*. Four decades of market economy in Germany. Cambridge: Cambridge University Press, 1994.

Grossman, Richard S. *Unsettled Account. The Evolution of Banking in the Industrialized World since 1800*. Princeton: Princeton University Press, 2010.

Hackethal, Andreas. *Banken, Unternehmensfinanzierung und Finanzsysteme*. Frankfurt: Lang, 2000.

Hall, Peter A. and David Soskice. "An Introduction to Varieties of Capitalism" in *Varieties of Capitalism*, edited by Peter A. Hall and David Soskice, Oxford: Oxford University Press, 2001, 1–68.

Hilferding, Rudolf. *Das Finanzkapital. Eine Studie über die jüngste Entwicklung des Kapitalismus*. Wien: Verlag der Wiener Volksbuchhandlung, 1910 (*Finance Capital. A Study of the Latest Phase of Capitalist Development*. Edited by Tom Bottomore. London: Routledge & Kegan Paul, 1981).

Ipsen, Dirk, and Jens Pfitzinger. "Krise in der Deutschland AG: Der Fall AEG." In *Alle Macht dem Markt? Fallstudien zur Abwicklung der Deutschland AG*, edited by Wolfgang Streeck and Martin Höpner, 60–92. Frankfurt: Campus, 2003.

James, Harold. *Krupp A History of the Legendary German Firm*. Princeton: Princeton University Press, 2012.

Käppner, Joachim. *Berthold Beitz. Die Biographie*. Berlin: Berlin Verlag, 2010.

Köhler, Ingo. "Havarie der "Schönwetterkapitäne"? Die Wirtschaftswunder-Unternehmer in den 1970er Jahren", in *Pleitiers und Bankrotteure. Geschichte des ökonomischen Scheiterns vom 18. bis 20. Jahrhundert*, edited by Ingo Köhler and Roman Rossfeld. Frankfurt: Campus, 2012, 251–283.

Krenn, Karoline. *Alle Macht den Banken? Zur Struktur personeller Netzwerke deutscher Unternehmen am Beginn des 20. Jahrhunderts*. Wiesbaden: Springer VS, 2012.

Krümmel, Hans-Jacob. "German Universal Banking Scrutinized. Some Remarks Concerning the Gessler Report." *Journal of Banking and Finance* 4 (1980): 33–55.

Lesczenski, Jörg. "Zwischen Kooperation, Krise und Aufbruch. Messer Griesheim, Hoechst und die Auflösung der Deutschland AG (1965–2004)." In *Die "Deutschland AG". Historische Annäherungen an den bundesdeutschen Kapitalismus*, edited by Ralf Ahrens, Boris Gehlen and Alfred Reckendrees. Essen: Klartext 2013, 351–376.

Lütz, Susanne. *Der Staat und die Globalisierung von Finanzmärkten. Regulative Politik in Deutschland, Großbritannien und den USA*. Frankfurt: Campus, 2002.

Lütz, Susanne. "The Finance Sector in Transition: A Motor for Economic Reform?" In *The Politics of Economic Reform in Germany: Global, Rhineland or Hybrid Capitalism?*, edited by Kenneth Dyson and Stephen Padgett, 26–42. London: Routledge, 2006.

Plumpe, Werner. "Das Ende des deutschen Kapitalismus." *Westend. Neue Zeitschrift für Sozialforschung* 2, no. 2 (2005): 3–26.

Schmidt, Reinhard H. "Corporate Governance in Germany: An Economic Perspective." In *The German Financial System*, edited by Jan Pieter Krahnen and Reinhard H. Schmidt. Oxford: Oxford University Press, 2004, 386–424.

Scott, John. "Intercorporate Structures in Western Europe: A Comparative Historical Analysis." In *Intercorporate Relations. The Structural Analysis of Business*, edited by Mark S. Mizruchi and Michael Schwartz. Cambridge: Cambridge University Press, 1987, 208–232.

Shonfield, Andrew. *Modern Capitalism. The Changing Balance of Public and Private Power*. London: Oxford University Press, 1969 (first ed. 1965).

Sohl, Hans-Günther. *Notizen*. Düsseldorf: Sohl, 1983.

Stier, Bernhard and Martin Krauß. *Drei Wurzeln – ein Unternehmen. 125 Jahre Bilfinger Berger AG*. Heidelberg: ifu, 2005.

Streeck, Wolfgang. *Re-Forming Capitalism. Institutional Change in the German Political Economy*. Oxford: Oxford University Press, 2010.

Streeck, Wolfgang, and Martin Höpner (eds.). *Alle Macht dem Markt?. Campus: Fallstudien zur Abwicklung der Deutschland AG*. Frankfurt, 2003.

Strunk, Peter. *AEG. Aufstieg und Niedergang einer Industrielegende*. Berlin: Nicolai, 2000.

Tilly, Richard. "Universal Banking in Historical Perspective." *Journal of Institutional and Theoretical Economics* 154 (1998): 7–32.

Tilly, Richard. "Trust and Mistrust: Banks, Giant Debtors, and Enterprise Crises in Germany, 1960–2002", *Jahrbuch für Wirtschaftsgeschichte/Economic History Yearbook*, no. 1 (2005): 107–135.

Tilly, Richard. *Willy H. Schlieker. Aufstieg und Fall eines Unternehmers (1914–1980)*. Berlin: Akademie, 2008.

Tilly, Richard H. "Geschäftsbanken und Wirtschaft in Westdeutschland seit dem Zweiten Weltkrieg." In *Geld und Währung vom 16. Jahrhundert bis zur Gegenwart*, edited by Eckart Schremmer. Stuttgart: Steiner, 1993, 315–343.

Uebbing, Helmut. *Wege und Wegmarken. 100 Jahre Thyssen*. Berlin: Siedler, 1991.

Vitols, Sigurd. "Negotiated shareholder value: the German variant of an Anglo-American practice." *Competition & Change* 8 (2004): 357–374.

Vitols, Sigurd. "The Origins of Bank-Based and Market-Based Financial Systems: Germany, Japan, and the United States." In *The Origins of Nonliberal Capitalism.Germany and Japan in Comparison*, edited by Wolfgang Streeck and Kozo Yamamura. Ithaca: Cornell University Press, 2001, 171–199.

Wellhöner, Volker. *Großbanken und Großindustrie im Kaiserreich*. Göttingen: Vandenhoeck & Ruprecht, 1989.

Wessel, Horst A. *Kontinuität im Wandel. 100 Jahre Mannesmann 1890–1990*. Düsseldorf: Mannesmann-AG, 1990.

Windolf, Paul, and Jürgen Beyer. "Co-operative Capitalism: Corporate Networks in Germany and Britain." *The British Journal of Sociology* 47, no. 2 (1996): 205–231.

Windolf, Paul. "The Corporate Network in Germany," 1896–2010, in *The Power of Corporate Networks. A Comparative and Historical Perspective*, edited by Thomas David and Gerarda Westerhuis. New York: Routledge, 2014, 66–86.

Wixforth, Harald. *Banken und Schwerindustrie in der Weimarer Republik*. Köln: Böhlau, 1995.

Ziegler, Rolf, Donald Bender and Hermann Biehler. "Industry and Banking in the German Corporate Network", in *Networks of Corporate Power. A Comparative Analysis of Ten Countries*, edited by Frans N. Stokman, Rolf Ziegler and John Scott. Cambridge: Polity Press, 1985, 91–111.

Supplier relations within the German automobile industry. The case of Daimler-Benz, 1950–1980

Stephanie Tilly

ABSTRACT

The German automobile industry is often described by the maintenance of stable relationships between automakers and their suppliers. According to the varieties of capitalism approach, many firms in coordinated market economies (CME) cultivated strong inter-company relations. The article incorporates this idea and reflects on the supply relationship in the German automobile industry from the 1950s to the 1980s. The rapid increase in automobile production during the phase of growth demanded increasing capacities in the supplier industries and had some conflict potential, but at the same time supply structures were characterised by great continuity. At the end of the boom the coordinating culture of relations came under pressure and the existing rules of the game were modified.

Introduction

'We also know the saying to live and let live – because a dead supplier is of no use for us.' This statement was made by Otto Jacob, the head of the purchasing department at Daimler-Benz in the early 1960s, when he outlined the basic principles of the purchasing philosophy held by the long-established auto producer.[1] Nevertheless, as early as in the beginning of the 1970s Daimler-Benz strengthened its attempts to buy automotive parts and components not only in the accustomed German market but also in foreign countries. Throughout the previous decade, this kind of approach had been successful only to a certain extent. It seems there were some differences of expectations regarding the securing of supplies which rendered inter-firm relationships not easily interchangeable.[2]

Discourse about the 'varieties of capitalism' has also touched upon the peculiarities of inter-company-relations. In their seminal book on the topic, Peter Hall and David Soskice hint at differences in the way in which inter-firm relationships may be structured in different types of economic systems. Within the range of varieties of capitalism, the Liberal Market Economies (LME) and Coordinated Market Economies (CME) represent two stylised versions. In simplified terms, LMEs may tend to contentious labour relations and corporate governance driven by capital interests, whereas CMEs may have governance structures characterised by labour participation, cooperative industrial relations and regulatory law. In this view, CMEs like Germany are often marked by close relationships between manufacturers and their supplier base.[3] According to this perspective the set of institutions given in a coordinated economy seems to ease the building up of long-term, non-market relationships with suppliers.[4] Thus, for instance the existence of business associations might foster the cooperation of firms along the value chain or with other companies on the same level. Moreover, the legal framework is seen as a support to long-term inter-firm relations, since contract law limits the options of action in case the contractual parties are unequal partners.[5]

In fact, there may be variations in the way in which the automobile industry dealt with its suppliers in particular political economies. For instance, Susan Helper's research on auto suppliers showed that the connections US automobile producers held with firms in upstream sectors can be characterised as arm's length relationships, driven by price competition and short-term considerations which made suppliers quite easily replaceable for the customer.[6] General Motors had a history of particularly contentious relations with its suppliers. 'GM's stance towards … its suppliers had been deeply adversarial.'[7] Helper's comparison of the US automobile industry with the Japanese case pointed out differences in realising the automotive supply and underlined the trust-based, long-term cooperation that seemed to be a distinctive feature of the Japanese automotive network,[8] an attribute that seemed to be missing in the case of some of the big American auto producers, first and foremost GM, which had evolved a 'legacy of mistrust', ending in an 'uneasy collaboration without trust' later on.[9]

In contrast to this, the German automobile industry is reckoned to be marked by the maintenance of stable relationships between automakers and their suppliers. This dissimilarity between 'spot' relationships and close long-term relationships seems to fit quite well into the varieties of capitalism framework and the stylised distinction between LME and CME – respectively Rhine Capitalism.[10]

This article offers an historical perspective on supplier relationships within the German automobile industry in the period from the 1950s to the 1980s. Its approach turns on a double question. How were the relationships between a large producer and its suppliers in this industry structured? What type of relationship culture emerges from a study of available archival materials? Since the prevalence of steady long-run relationships qualifies as an element of Rhine Capitalism, the question of their stability becomes an important one. The following discussion thus focuses on the 'stability propensity' of supplier relationships, i.e. on the longevity and robustness of the relationships. 'Stable relationships' are here defined as relationships that persist and continue to function in spite of structural imbalances in the relative bargaining positions of the partners and in spite of conflicts of interest in negotiations between them. This focus suggests further questions: How were conflicts of interest resolved? Did they lead to collapse or interruption of the relationships? Is it possible to identify constellations that promoted or hindered cooperative behaviour?

The empirical evidence will be drawn mostly from the Daimler-Benz business archives. That puts an important actor of the German automobile industry in the center of analysis. In this period, we must remember, the West German automobile market was oligopolistic. Four firms – 'The Big Four' (Ford, Opel, Daimler-Benz, and Volkswagen) – dominated the industry, in 1958 with two-thirds of the market, which by the mid-sixties had risen to over three-quarters. [11]

By looking closely at Daimler-Benz, the study offers a particularly instructive example. Daimler-Benz automobile production drew on an extraordinarily large number of components, both manufactured in-house and by external suppliers.[12] A cursory discussion of Volkswagen and its suppliers supplements the analysis.

Hence, the following narrative does not aim at a systematic comparison of supplier relations in 'liberal' or 'coordinated' market economies, but it will try to describe practices of supplier relations by means of a German case example within a period of growth and adaptation of the German automobile industry. The heterogeneity of the products involved suggests an extremely wide range of business relations, a concrete story with contradictions that underline the contingent elements in the historical process of relationship-building. That might preclude clear-cut generalisation. Nevertheless, the analysis of inter-company relations during a period of change that follows will reveal the persistence of elements that support the thesis of a positive connection between the robustness of those relations and Rhine Capitalism.

The first section starts with a short outline of the automotive sector in the above-cited period. The next chapter will take a closer look at cases of conflict and cooperation in supplier relations. In addition, this subdivision will try to show aspects of change within the period. A conclusion will summarise the findings.

The significance of supplier relations in the automobile industry

The automobile industry can be regarded as a quite heterogeneous branch of industry. According to one contemporary definition of the Association of the Automobile Industry (*Verband der Automobilindustrie* [VDA]), the term 'automobile industry' included not only the production of private motorcars and utility vehicles but also involved the manufacture of parts or families of parts.[13] It was estimated that one private motorcar was made up of roughly 6000 to 12,000 parts.[14] In the 1960s and 1970s supplied parts already represented more than half of the gross production value of a single motorcar.[15]

'Given that each vehicle is made out of many thousands of single parts, automobile factories cannot possibly produce all these parts themselves,' as the Frankfurter Allgemeine Zeitung commented in the early 1950s. 'Otherwise their production plants would have to take on huge proportions, they would have to carry out research and development in an immense number of fields. ... This method of decentralized production ... has not only proved its worth but is of great significance with regard to the preservation of small and medium-sized firms.'[16] What seems to be an almost imploring observation points to the role played by the automobile supplier industry in the exceptional growth of the automobile industry after 1945.[17] A substantial part of the car boom was carried by the supplier industry or through outsourcing.[18] However, an overall characterisation of automobile suppliers is not straightforward as the supplier industry not only included the 'parts and accessories industry' but could include firms in plastics processing and steel forming as well as the iron-working, sheet metal- and metal- processing industries, and equally big companies in the electrical goods or tyre industry.[19] Corresponding to this broad spectrum, quite varied patterns of relations can be identified within the automobile industry. Given that domestic automobile production was dominated by only a few big automakers, a manageable number of customers was a typical but also problematic characteristic of the original equipment (OE) market for regular automobile production – contemporaries were already concerned about 'the power of demand' and its possible abuse.[20] While the number of those companies linked to automakers through general supply relations could be very high,[21] the number of established OE suppliers was, depending on the production structure of the automaker in question, probably more likely to be between 600 and 2000 firms.[22]

The Fordist automobile factory, which was able to manufacture many families of parts itself, was the model of modern automobile production aspired to during the boom years. Experts on this branch of industry highlighted the example of the company Adam Opel AG because it also manufactured technically elaborate modules, such as carburettors, itself.[23] While the contemporary economic press identified signs of a trend to 'a greater concentration of production' and feared a general increase in the depth of production within the automobile industry,[24] a contemporary survey of the early 1960s came to the conclusion that the degree to which producers were integrated had in general terms remained unchanged.[25] Internal analyses of the depth of production at Daimler-Benz also pointed to a relatively constant development of this factor during the period of time from the 1960s to 1980.[26] Nevertheless, it is difficult to define this factor precisely.[27] From the mid-1970s onwards, the depth of production in other German automobile producers experienced a slight drop in terms of the so-called Adelman Index – an approximative indicator for vertical integration by the ratio of value added to sales.[28] The drop in in-house-production was most pronounced at Opel and Ford as US subsidiaries.[29] This trend to reduce the depth of manufacturing continued to mark German automobile producers in the 1980s.

The strategic decision, whether to buy or produce a needed input, represents a classic problem of entrepreneurial choice in complex companies. Excluding a takeover of the supplier by the automobile producer, the possibility that the latter could begin to produce the input itself introduces an element of uncertainty and conflict potential into the supplier–producer relationship. The above-mentioned consideration that the aggregated data for the 1960s do not clearly suggest a significant increase in the production depth does not mean that the risks related to 'in-sourcing' did not exist; and for certain product categories those risks made themselves felt. The complex make-or-buy calculations of the automobile producers not only involved cost considerations but also labour market issues, as the production of parts for the after-sales market could be an effective buffer in order to maintain jobs in phases of economic stagnation.[30]

The period of time focused on here between the late 1950s and the early 1980s experienced both phases of boom as well as a slowing of the dynamic. Up to the mid-1960s, growth in the automobile industry – carried by the impetus of motorisation – was unbroken. In the course of the 1970s the German automobile industry had to increasingly face up to changes in the competitive environment which led to critical setbacks in the automobile markets. The changes in economic conditions certainly played a very significant role in the development of business relations between automakers and their suppliers. At the same time, it will also become evident that during phases of growth or relative stability a continual re-balancing of relations was also necessary.

Cases of conflict and cooperation in supplier relations, 1950–1980

The changes in the economic climate in terms of growth and structural change confronted business partners with the necessity to adapt in different ways which repeatedly involved a new allocation of risks and tasks. The rapid increase in automobile production during the phase of growth demanded that production volumes be increased in the supplier industries too, which soon brought these up to full capacity. Numerous suppliers were faced by the alternative of either expanding capacities in the uncertain hope of lasting perspectives – or losing possible options for growth to competitors. The option of producing in series was very popular but also cut both ways: On the one hand, OE business represented a big order volume as series size grew, on the other hand, this also increased the risk of suppliers becoming dependent on only a few big customers in relation to a substantial proportion of turnover.[31] At the same time, the contractual basis for business relations between automakers and suppliers did not in most cases represent a formal commitment for the future – at least not in terms of a planning horizon which extended beyond the coming year. It was customary for the big automobile producers to sign annual contracts for supplies – mostly in the autumn – preceded by lengthy exploratory talks and negotiations. These agreements did not normally include a fixed allocation of supplier products but agreed quotas of the production volume of a planned series, i.e. part of the economic risk was passed on to the suppliers.[32]

Overall it had become customary in the automobile industry to stipulate the conditions of contract in one standard form as the basis for supplies to the customer. This involved the General Terms and Conditions of Procurement of the automaker concerned. Usually the supplier had to accept the customer's purchasing conditions upon the finalisation of the contract if it wanted to secure the tender.[33] In some cases these could be modified depending on the market position of the supplier company. For example, supplier companies with a particularly strong market position were able to impose their own 'sales conditions' – but the majority of suppliers had to recognise the General Terms and Conditions of Purchasing in their entirety which limited the rights of the supplier in special clauses.[34] This included, for example, the delivery commitment which guaranteed the customer the exclusive right of purchase for all products which involved joint research and development on the part of the supplier and the customer. In addition, procedures for product control were increasingly passed on to suppliers. For the legal obligation to 'test for and notify' product defects also affected the relations between automobile producers and their suppliers. In the supplier agreements clauses were common that freed the automobile producers from the need to test for product defects. Instead, it placed the burden of proof on the supplier. This made the latter worse off than the rules of general liability, which obligated buyers to examine products supplied.[35]

Against this background, the phase of growth in automobile markets which had been labelled as relatively harmonious in terms of competition between automakers,[36] did in fact have quite some conflict potential regarding supplier relations along the value chain. The expansion of capacities in the automobile industry was sometimes accompanied by difficult negotiating processes between parties, the result of which was dependent on the individual power resources of those actors involved. Focusing on this conflict potential provides insights into whether certain forms of inter-company relations can be linked to a certain type of capitalism.

One supplier of Volkswagen who manufactured forged parts for Beetle production, for example, had substantially expanded its facilities during the course of the 1950s, confident of future orders. However, a large part of these capacities were not utilised because Volkswagen – totally unexpectedly for the supplier – brought in another supplier for the accounting period of 1957.[37] This action was quite in line with customary procurement principles and also not unusual.[38] Moreover, it was not seldom the case that supplier companies were themselves included in the search for a second supplier and in the discussion of how the quota should be shared.[39] Nevertheless, the differing perspectives of supplier and customer clashed on this issue. Although the business partners initially strove to reach a compromise at board-room level – VW general director Heinrich Nordhoff urged the responsible buyer in the VW purchasing department to consider providing the firm in question with additional orders – the VW-purchasing department was not prepared to comply with this suggestion as in its view the supplier had simply held up more productive capacities than had been agreed upon. While the exact details of the agreement cannot be reconstructed, it remains significant for the context examined here why the head of procurement at VW seemingly wanted to face the conflict head on and not indirectly work on a cooperative solution: The very fact that the company belonged to the "Schmiedering" – a group of forging companies which aimed at facilitating the regular transfer of information – was sufficient cause for distrust.[40] The VW purchasing department had already in the past suspected price-fixing within this network. At the same time it should be remembered that the forging industry belonged – in structural terms – to a group of suppliers with a particularly big risk of dependence as manufacturing was mainly based on their customer's technical drawings. They had only an advantage of specialisation regarding manufacturing know-how. Nor did they have any competitive edge.[41] This constellation meant that supplier companies were easily exchangeable and, in addition, also by implication at a high risk of being substituted by the customer's own manufacturing process as soon as a certain product technology was openly available on the market. This became apparent in the early 1960s as the Volkswagen plants actually began to set up their own drop forging department in Kassel with which the firm could cover roughly half of its own demand for gear wheels. The Volkswagen plant in Kassel had acquired 'hot masters', American 'state-of-the-art' drop forging machines. As a consequence, a part of the operations of drop-forging companies in southern Westphalia was made obsolete. In this particular case, a company which had just expanded its facilities had invested in the embodiment of a technology which – without those 'hot masters' – was effectively out of date before it was ready to produce. 'The young people from Kassel', as was noted in a memorandum at the wheel maker Kronprinz on these developments, 'have calculated huge savings'.[42] In this case the comparative cost advantage of the supplier was thus too small, the efficiency gain from vertical integration too large for the relationship to continue.

Against the background of the structural risk of dependency faced by the drop-forging industry, it appears understandable that this branch of industry cultivated a historically evolved, fully functioning organisation within which it was able to formulate its interests. This may have promoted the exchange of information within the forging industry which perhaps temporarily compensated for certain asymmetries in relations between an individual company and customer. Structural imbalances need not exclude stable relationships. Yet in the above-mentioned case, the existence of a horizontal network seems not to have promoted cooperation with the automobile producer – indeed, this institutional characteristic seems to have represented more of a special incentive for the customer to terminate relations in certain product groups.

It can be regarded as a characteristic of the supply function in the automobile industry that the supplier not only competed with other companies within the same branch and specialisation but also with their customers. Not least, the threat of a customer taking on production itself was a tactical manoeuvre as well, used during buying negotiations in order to push through price cuts or to gain insight into the supplier's calculation base.[43]

The public discussion of make-or-buy gained new impetus during the first half of the 1960s when General Motors and Ford made bigger investments into in-house production at their European subsidiaries. Within the Association of the Automobile Industry which in line with its organisational structure not only brought automobile producers together but also companies in the parts and accessories industry, representatives of the latter industry tried to suggest 'talks with the automobile industry', 'in order to combat the concept of in-house production'.[44] Management at the wheel suppliers Kronprinz however remained rather sceptical about the initiative: 'We must wait and see how far these ideas have success. But until now all such talks with the automakers have failed.' These doubts reflect how the VDA, which traditionally represented big industry and one part of the supplier industries, only had limited powers of integration with regard to the interests of the business partners involved.

Nevertheless, the basic readiness to talk, visible on both sides, is by no means a trivial matter, for it may be seen as an indicator that inter-company relations were not based exclusively on market rules. On several different levels, vital organisational structures existed which facilitated exchange of viewpoints, especially important where conflicts of interest were involved. The maintenance of continued dialogue within the association may be interpreted as an index of the functional viability of German Corporatism.

The concept of 'supplier loyalty'

The decision of automobile producers to follow the trend to greater factory integration did not necessarily have to lead to conflict with its regular suppliers. This can be illustrated by a further example: The company Kronprinz AG in Solingen which supplied Volkswagen with wheels lost most of this business because VW introduced the in-house production of wheels in 1959/60.[45] Yet this was not to the detriment of relations between these business partners as advance warning of in-house production had been given several years before – and in addition compensatory business had been agreed upon. Instead of wheels, VW now bought precision tubes from Kronprinz. At Kronprinz, the head of sales recorded in his personal notes: 'VW has kept its word: instead of orders for wheels now stainless steel tubes.'[46] The compensatory business transaction can be seen as a trust-building measure, as a sign of commitment to business relations. This example clearly underlines the search for consensus and suggests a vision of business relationships built on the goals of continuity and stability.

That Volkswagen's management recognised the fundamental importance of cooperation with suppliers is reflected in comments made by Julius Paulsen in the annual report for 1960:

'We should not forget that our production needs are enormous, involving billions, repeatedly call for deliveries from the same suppliers, and that even in the case of large enterprises our needs absorb 50 percent or even more of their capacity. We are thus dependent on a trustworthy, cooperative relationship, for, should conflicts arise, we could not immediately respond by changing suppliers.'[47] The idea of 'trustworthy cooperation' that emerges here, appeared to have no alternative, corresponding as it did to the structural features of the period.

The procurement division at Daimler-Benz also saw the question of capacities in component manufacturing during the boom as problematic at some points – probably because some suppliers had be to motivated to expand their facilities, even when it was already clear according to Daimler-Benz's own investment plans that such production capacities were going to be created on its own premises.[48] Given such conflicting aims, rules had to be found according to which both sides retained a certain scope for action and which still allowed investment incentives. In one case, the customer suggested the supplier expand capacities, but at the same time offered an unusually long-term supply contract in order to guarantee the supplier a degree of planning security despite the plans for in-house production.[49]

Thus, possible alternatives to business relations were being sought even during the phase of growth. Overall, the continual make-or-buy calculation revealed that the customer did indeed think about possible exit strategies in those cases where trade with a supplier could not be regarded as exclusive in the long-term on the basis of patents or know-how. The automobile producer's continual search for new suppliers which was part of routine pro-curement procedure can also be interpreted in this sense.[50]

At the same time, the supply structures within the automobile industry during the period examined here were also characterised by great continuity. The list of Daimler's most impor-tant suppliers included the names of many companies which could look back on business relations over many decades, which means that several companies had worked with Daimler-Benz AG since pre-war times.[51] This suggests a cooperative and not market-based arrange-ment of inter-firm relations. Daimler-Benz AG had made the long-term approach to supplier relations a fundamental tenet. "Loyalty to suppliers is not an empty slogan but is something taken seriously at DB [Daimler-Benz]," seriously enough, at least to appear in guidelines written for the purchasing department in the late 1950s.

'It is not our wish to switch suppliers just because of repeated complaints about goods. These complaints … should be dealt with by the responsible parties of both works (supplier and customer). Only in persistent cases is a switch necessary.'[52]

This model of relations was a frequently quoted principle of the company's purchasing policy. None the less, it was based on a cost calculation as a supplier went through a kind of educative process before being allowed into the circle of "regular suppliers":[53] "We are aware … of the costs involved in the 'education' of a new supplier," as procurement director Otto Jacob explained, "as we have to practically start from scratch in each case."[54] By means of this "educational process", Daimler-Benz thus transformed its relationship with certain suppliers into a closer connection based on something more than simple market forces.

At the same time, the idea of trust-based relations was related to the market segment in which the company operated as a producer of top-of–the-range cars and long-lasting com-mercial vehicles. Thus, the guiding principle proved surprisingly robust throughout the boom years and beyond. "Supplier loyalty to qualified vendors is one of our firm principles," as one member of staff in the Daimler-Benz materials department still emphasised in the early 1980s, identifying this as a definite contrast to the demands of a market of volume. [55] "In our case, optimum prices are not the lowest prices, but more reasonable prices at which the required qualitative factors such as development know-how and potential, product quality and reliability also in terms of keeping delivery deadlines, can be obtained."[56] Over the course of time, the principle of loyalty to suppliers had thickened into a web of considerable expec-tations regarding supplier performance. The customer expected the suppliers to be up-to-date in terms of development, quality, reliability and ingenuity.

It seems reasonable to assume that this culture of relations came under pressure to adapt in the face of a changing competitive environment. The slump of the recession in 1966/67 represented an initial test of endurance which severely depressed car sales but did not put all producers in equal difficulties. On the basis of a sample survey on supplier relations in the commercial vehicles division, the Research Institute for Medium-sized Firms (*Institut für Mittelstandsforschung*) concluded: 'most suppliers [spoke] of an exceptional loyalty of their customers during the recession.'[57]

Daimler-Benz also weathered the first recession relatively well;[58] it continued relations to most regular suppliers without change, although it had to admit that under the pressure of rising costs and the market's shrinking absorptive capacity it had not always remained true to its own principles. 'Today DB is still accused of not having behaved fairly', as one purchasing manager at Daimler-Benz noted, looking back on the recession of 1966/67.[59] Daimler-Benz had guaranteed its suppliers that it would only begin in-house production for substantial reasons. These included, for example, questions of quality, price considerations, the question of capacity or lastly – and here the choice of attribute in this memorandum begs interpretation – 'if behaviour was improper'.[60] 'But any changes would always – as claimed by DB AG – be announced in the long-term and carried out in general agreement. In 1967/68 we did not act in this manner but demanded, even without consideration of our own production costs … changes in the short-term.'[61] At the beginning of the recession the management thought that the new policy might affect the significant number of 90 supplier companies. In fact, this was not necessary because the economic dip was quickly overcome and the new boom lowered the pressure. Nevertheless, the changes which were actually implemented had hit a few supplier companies severely. Some of them had, coerced by circumstance, bound themselves to other (foreign) customers, such as, for example, the gear producer Zahnradfabrik Friedrichshafen (ZF), which took on some five-year contracts with customers such as Volvo, Berliet, and Ford.

The 'auto-crisis' of 1974/75

In 1974/75 the automobile sector faced an all-time low. With the emergence of new competitors on the world market and changes in consumer preference, previously unknown changes had to be faced by the 'growth industry in retirement', as one trade paper ironically labelled the automobile industry.[62] In addition there were general factors of uncertainty to face such as exchange rate fluctuations, changes in traffic policy and conflicts with employee organisations. Not least, the changed economic conditions after the 'Golden Age'[63] represented a problem in terms of costs for automobile producers. As a result, automakers focused on the savings potential in the purchasing costs for supplies more strongly than before.

Yet, looking back, the Federal Ministry for Economic Affairs (*Bundeswirtschaftsministerium*) interpreted the downward trend not as an industry-wide crisis but as the crisis of individual producers.[64] Daimler-Benz in this crisis displayed relatively little susceptibility to external influences but the gap between costs and returns had grown to a worrying extent.[65] It was thought that the pricing policy on the procurement side should accommodate this fact more strongly. This is reflected by the measures formulated by top management with regard to trading negotiations for the year of 1976. According to these, buyers were to remember that 'DB AG can boast stable or indeed rising numbers of programs. This stability has made us the undeniable No. 1 for our suppliers and this is a position which should be exploited in negotiations *without arrogance* but with the *appropriate pressure*. It can be assumed that this structural stability can also be guaranteed in the future.'[66] Management continued to lift the recommended upper levels for procurement abroad which had been valid up to this point. These measures finally closed with a savings target in comparison to the previous year – which given the general rise in prices represented a thoroughly ambitious project. 'The aim is – in overall terms – to achieve a minus result compared to 1975'.[67]

As events were to show, conditions were such that this change of course could not be realised in this form, a fact which soon had to be recognised by the automakers themselves as well. Looking back, it was thus noted within the department for materials management at Daimler Benz AG,[68] that the automobile producer had applied 'strict, perhaps stricter standards' on transactions with suppliers in the business year of 1976.[69] The reflections on these procedures were summarised in a note for the files. In contrast to former practice, DB had as a customer attempted to systematically profit more from the competition between suppliers. At the same time the internal note also warned not to 'overstep the mark', because – as the customer indeed recognised – some suppliers were now fighting for their very existence under the increasing pressure on prices.[70]

One part of the supplier industry, and in particular the part concerned with steel and plastics processing, was indeed in an unfavorable intermediate position, in a kind of dilemma between the producers of raw materials and automobile manufacturers.[71] While this 'sandwich position' between two branches of industry, dominated by big production units and a tendency to structural oligopoly, had, for suppliers,[72] this intermediate position became particularly problematic during the auto crisis: Due to the rather small degree of price competition in the raw materials industry, prices for raw materials could be kept high in some cases despite the general market tendencies, so that the costs for raw materials paid by the supplier industry went up while their returns – in correspondence to the weakness of the sales market – diminished.[73] The price-cutting pressure created by customers increased this discrepancy between costs and returns.

Unofficial observations and comments reveal that the automakers did indeed recognise the structural worries of the suppliers.[74] In this situation Daimler-Benz AG decided to concede additional price increases of 2% to 4% to a group of suppliers – and in this manner corrected existing contracts to the benefit of its suppliers.[75]

With this measure the automobile manufacturer probably also hoped to win back the trust of suppliers and, as was stated in an internal memo, '[to] increase the credibility of future negotiations' and '[to] strengthen the trust of suppliers in a loyal approach ... [to] contracts'.[76] The long-term character of the commitment in supplier relationships is obvious here. The observation of conditions in the supplier industry and careful emphasis on the customer's reputation further supported the continuity of the relationship. Such practices have been described by Susan Helper as 'trust-building' measures in the cultivation of inter-company relations.[77]

On the basis of the source material examined so far, it is difficult to assess the role of the various supplier associations and the VDA in the settlement of this conflict. On the one hand, some supplier associations – inter alia the associations of the iron-, metal sheet- and metal-working industries, foundries, drawing shops and cold rolling mills – proposed a discussion within the VDA about the difficulties faced by the supplier industry following the auto crisis and the increasing pressure on costs.[78] But the VDA wanted to avoid an official debate about the 'relations of the suppliers to the automobile industry' as far as possible and for the time being to leave aside concrete questions as to the purchasing policies of individual producers.[79] To some extent this was due to the unusual structure of the organisation: The VDA – as already mentioned above – represented in its producer groups I and III automakers as well as companies from the supplier industry which of course narrowed its scope for action in socio-political terms when faced by real conflicts. Not surprisingly DB was also critical of discussion of its purchasing policy within the associations. 'We don't believe it to be … appropriate, if suppliers who consciously undercut their competitors in order to secure orders now want to mobilize their associations in order to complain about the purchasing morals of their opposite number.'[80] Instead, discussion within the VDA focused on producer liability.

To understand the underlying conflict potential it is necessary to explain what the issue 'producer liability' involved. The term corresponded to the legal obligation of manufacturers to offer safe products. It makes both auto producers and their suppliers liable for damages to buyers or to ultimate consumers originating from the product sold. The specific cause of the damage was seen as irrelevant. What the industry stressed was the safeness of the entire 'automobile package'. Such emphasis thus obscured the truly central issue: the conflict of interest between producer and suppliers and the determination of who was (and is) responsible at which point in time for the necessary control of the quality and safeness of the product? [81] Here it is also becomes clear that the associations' efforts aimed at preservation of dialogue in the relations between the main actors. Their hinge function became fruitful in a long-run perspective.

At first, the discussion regarding liability questions did not develop either because another automaker – VW – wanted to push the most important aspects to one side. The background to this initiative was that VW had wanted to push through a change in its procurement conditions (in the opinion of the Stuttgart premium manufacturers 'in their typically casual way', although 'in essence fully justified')[82] and had thus faced criticism. The foundries and drawing shops, the iron-working, sheet metal- and metalworking industries and the non-ferrous metalworking industry mobilised their associations in order to combat changes. With the help of the associations' legal experts, it was thus possible to negotiate that 'with regard to testing methods and volume of supplied tests, the costs and risks cannot be carried by the supplier alone.'[83] Here the associations' efforts proved effective as a factor in the shaping of the future institutional framework.

In the following years, discussion about the actual distribution of costs and responsibilities in many areas of business relations was controversial and the attempt was made to adapt the established rules of the game to the changed conditions or to define these more precisely.[84] The actors within the automobile industry recognised that they were experiencing a phase of transformation which restricted the range of action previously possible and reflected upon the fact that certain market asymmetries had to be taken account of 'more than before'.[85] The Confederation of German Industry (Bundesverband der Deutschen Industrie [BDI]) also set up a working group for questions of supply in the latter half of the 1970s, under the impression of the controversial debate about competition and on the suggestion of member associations. This committee not only focused on the automobile industry but also aimed at assessing the range of interests involved in business relations between suppliers and buyers and to suggest some solutions to critical questions.[86] The concluding paper reveals in which areas the basis for a consensus could be found but also where there were limits to balancing out of interests. Several practices for example – such as the automatic adaptation of agreed prices to lower competitive prices or the exploitation of prices, calculated on the basis of bigger order volumes, for smaller ones – were commonly rejected as an abuse of power on the demand side. With regard to the questions of guarantee and producers' liability no agreement could be reached.[87]

Product-based supplier structures

Since the mid-1970s, DB had begun an internal, systematic examination of its own supplier structures. No doubt the aim was to gain a better understanding of the competitive relations across the various areas of supply. The desire to understand the company's own supply structures may have grown with the realisation that during the recession a totally new course with a tougher stance had not functioned and that it was necessary to be aware of the nuances of supply relations. Here we see that the model of long-run stable inter-company relations was more than a phrase, but a relevant practical guide. That offers support for the thesis stressing stable relationships as a characteristic of Rhine Capitalism.

The internal analysis revealed that big companies played the biggest part in terms of the overall volume purchased.[88] The author made the point that in the case of some product groups 'competition is in a sorry state and should be reactivated'. In addition, the structural analysis listed those suppliers of finished parts which used high proportions of their total capacities for DB orders (i.e. in some case more than half), sometimes entailing substantial order volumes, which was concomitant to a 'corresponding dependence' of the supplier. Conversely, dependencies on the side of DB could be assumed if a supplied part could for example only be provided by one supplier. Yet here it was also a question of looking at each case in practice. The conclusion emphasised 'that the number of suppliers per materials group … does not alone allow assumptions about the actual influences on competition'. Neither was the company size of a supplier alone a criterion for the actual market constellation. The report concluded: 'It is not possible to say that we only have successful or less successful suppliers. Suppliers of a broad product range have successful and less successful products. A development which suggests that amongst other things the product is decisive.'[89]

Thus, several factors could be of decisive importance for business relations: whether the development and manufacture of a product required specialised know-how; how and whether this know-how was protected if necessary; how valuable and how customer-tailored the product was; the size of the company being supplied; whether the product range of this supplier company included different supply products; whether many suppliers with comparable products existed within this market segment and how high the turnover share of the biggest customer was.[90]

Conclusion

It seems at this point not an easy task to turn the cases of supplier relations in the automobile industry highlighted here into a unified body of results. Nevertheless, despite the variety of individual constellations, it is possible to recognise common characteristics. This is true, for example, of the basic principle guiding supplier relations: the goal was to maintain a stable, long-run relationship. Apart from its mention as an ideal, in many practical situations, even difficult ones requiring adaptation to changing circumstances, the effort to maintain a stable supplier relationship prevailed. The introduction raised the question of the business culture which characterised the German automobile industry. The answer is 'stability oriented'.

'Stable' does not mean 'static', however. The stability orientation observed cannot be confused with unchanging relations. On the contrary, it is only recognisable as a principle guiding adaptation to changed conditions. Rigidly cemented relationships are vulnerable ones.

The few examples presented here already illustrate the following: During the very phase in which the industry slumped and the network of relations in the automobile industry also came under pressure to adapt, the actors involved used existing organisation structures in order to formulate their standpoint of political interests, to denounce 'bad practices' involving the exploitation of advantageous market constellations and to find a consensus on non-negotiable 'limits to business transactions between suppliers and purchasers'.[91] Here we observe the actors – in keeping with the views of Rhine Capitalism – busy in a dialogue searching for a consensus which could shield the relationship from purely market forces. In the process, the legal basis to business relations was subjected to systematic assessment and interpretation.

Within the German automobile industry, long-term supplier relations were in fact common despite the great potential for conflict. So can we assume – as an inversion of the 'legacy of distrust' identified by Susan Helper for the American case of General Motors[92] – a 'legacy of trust' in the case of the West German automobile industry after 1945 or at least in the case of supplier relations? A conclusive answer remains problematic although the elements reconstructed above do provide some indications.

In the case of Daimler-Benz, some of the fundamental criteria identified by Helper as catalysts for the creation of trust seem to have been realised: long-term commitment, information exchange, technical assistance, and customer reputation.[93] The course correction undertaken by Daimler-Benz through the retrospective raising of purchasing prices following the auto crisis can be understood as a conscious measure to maintain customer reputation. At the same time, the strict quality orientation of the final product also worked towards a reproduction of existing business relations.

The case study of Daimler-Benz, of course, offers no more than a sample of relationships in the German automobile industry. Given the latter's oligopolistic market structure, however, it is surely a relevant one. How it executed its purchasing activities had a kind of signal function within the branch. Moreover, discussions took place within the business associations which also touched on fundamental questions of supplier relationships, and these were important for the entire industry. In addition, the cursory comments on Volkswagen showed that though this company's approach to supplier relationships differed somewhat from that of Daimler-Benz, its guiding principle was similar. The differences had to do with certain conditions of the business volume, that is, with details, while the basic principles were the same.

What were the conditions that facilitated the development of stable relationships not always in conformity with market conditions? It certainly seems plausible that the institutional setting played a role in this development.

In several instances business associations provided an arena for the formation of opinion and the discussion of conflicts between the contracting parties. Within the Varieties-of-Capitalism framework this is seen as a feature of CMEs, among which Rhine Capitalism is a typical model. The institutional setting seems to have fostered the cooperation of firms of the same level and along the value-added chain – in contrast to spot relationships.

Beyond the formal institutional or organisational framework business culture represents an important dimension of the process by which stable inter-company relations were established and perpetuated. Business culture implies expectations and experiences of the involved actors concerning the ways of doing business, about compliance, the entrepreneurial scope of action – and possible escalation levels in case of conflict. Accordingly it can be interpreted as a set of informal rules of the game, which provide an orientation function.[94] This is consistent with the observations of Susan Helper who, in her study of automobile producers after the establishment of the model of 'lean production', has doubts about the hypothesis that institutional differences in the economic order provide sufficient explanation for different developments in different countries. Thus she concludes that the 'success of the … German automotive firms in the US' offers grounds for rejecting the importance of the institutional framework as a decisive factor. Nevertheless, Helper's study does admit that historical experience with relationship-building could be a crucially important asset.[95]

In fact, the form of inter-company relations cannot be understood or interpreted independently from their origination. The perspective of the cases discussed above also suggests that the individual actors' scope for action should be taken seriously. During the phase of growth, a continual balancing out of relations was already evident. Despite the long-term nature of the relational culture, customers did have the real possibility of opting out for a number of supplier products. The transition to new competitive conditions in the course of the 1970s seemed to ultimately culminate in a reorientation process for the actors in which the existing rules of the game were modified. Here the creativity of those actors searching for 'alternatives to existing arrangements' was already able to appear.[96]

Overall, the wide range of supplier structures found in the period examined here is an indication of the great heterogeneity of constellation in inter-company relations even within the same institutional context and across different phases of the industry's history. The period up to the first setbacks to growth, or indeed up to the so-called 'Japan shock' of the 1980s, is sometimes remembered by contemporaries in an idealised way as a kind of 'gentlemen's capitalism'. Other studies see in this period a pattern of 'old style' supply chains which tended to focus on price instead of long-term relations whereas the setting in the period after 1980 changed markedly in terms of relationship-building.[97] Examining the economic history of the period suggests that both labels have their blind spots.

The structural closeness of shared business operations was not a sufficient condition for the continuance of business relations of which changeability was demanded. Or, to put it differently, stable supplier relationships were not an automatic reflex of the organisation of production in the automotive industry. The way frictions concerning the division of labour in automotive industry were resolved indicated the stability of inter-company relations in the period investigated and so often associated with Rhenish Capitalism.

Notes

1. Mercedes-Benz Classic, Archive (quoted in the following as MBCA), 1 P PS 03 0027, lecture Otto Jacob held at Rationalisierungskuratorium der deutschen Wirtschaft, 1962, p. 11.
2. Regarding buying activities abroad (which had been pursued as early as in the1950s) the purchase department of the Volkswagen-Werke stated in 1966: 'When those offers resulted in only few orders for the current series, this was because often quality or workmanship of the provided samples did not meet VW regulations nor corresponded to the drawings.'Volkswagen-Konzernarchiv (quoted in the following as VW-KA), 174-2366, 1949–1968, Jahresbericht über den Einkauf und die Materialabteilung für 1965.
3. Hall and Soskice, *Varieties,* 26; Schröder, *Varianten,* 105.

4. Hall and Soskice, *Varieties,* 37. See also how Susan Helper puts the idea of Hall and Soskice: *Management Practices,* 68.
5. Hall and Soskice, *Varieties,* 26s.
6. Helper, *Management Practices,* 57s.
7. Helper, *Management Practices,* 62.
8. Sako and Helper, "Determinants of Trust," 387–417.
9. Helper and Sako, "Management Innovation," 412.
10. Still, some of the arguments enunciated within the debate about varieties of capitalism have aroused criticism. For instance, Gary Herrigel doubts the claim that institutional advantages apparent in a society can convincingly explain differences of supplier relations in different locations: 'it is unclear to us that even the cooperation observable in German OEM-supplier relations is in any significant way traceable to the "beneficial constraints" of the institutional architecture in the German coordinated market economy.' Herrigel and Wittke, "Varieties," 328. Moreover, critics indicate that the stylisations add up to an overemphasis of dissimilarities between different institutional settings, overlooking the 'remarkable heterogeneity over time' even within individual political economies, see Herrigel and Zeitlin, "Alternatives to Varieties,"
11. Beckmann, Käfer, Goggos, Heckflossen. "Eine retrospektive Studie über die westdeutschen Automobilmärkte in den Jahren der beginnenden Massenmotorisierung", Vaihingen/Enz 2006, 310.
12. See also See MBCA, Werner Reich, Bericht ueber meine Untersuchung bei der. Daimler-Benz AG, Stuttgart-Untertuerkheim, n.d., presumably 1963.
13. As for example Verband der Automobilindustrie (VDA), Tatsachen und Zahlen (quoted in the following as TuZ), 1964, p. 4; VDA, Jahresbericht Auto, 1973/74, 15.
14. As estimated by the VDA at the end of the 1970s, cf. Tilly, "Das Zulieferproblem," 137.
15. Union des Industries de la Communauté Européenne (Unice), Die industrielle Zuliefertätigkeit in der Bundesrepublik. Ausarbeitung der deutschen Delegation des Unice-Ausschusses zum Studium der Probleme der kleinen und mittleren Unternehmen in der EWG vom 25.8.1965, Brüssel [n.d., manuscript], 2.
16. "Steuer und Konzentration", in: Frankfurter Allgemeine Zeitung, 23.7.1953, 11.
17. On the growth in automobile industry cf. Tilly and Triebel, "Automobilwirtschaft nach 1945", 2ss.
18. Scherner, Streb and Tilly, "Supplier Networks," 996–1020.
19. See also Kunz, *Die Marktstellung,* 33; also Tilly, "Kooperation," 159.
20. See for example Gellner, *Wird die kleinere*; Monopolkommission, Sondergutachten 7: Mißbräuche der Nachfragemacht und Möglichkeiten zu ihrer Kontrolle im Rahmen des Gesetzes gegen Wettbewerbsbeschränkungen, Baden-Baden 1977; also Geck and Petry, *Nachfragemacht gegenüber Zulieferern*; Hamer, *Zuliefererdiskriminierung*; Kessen, *Nachfragemacht der Automobilindustrie*.
21. The total number of suppliers to Daimler-Benz increased from around 14,000 in 1955 to roughly 27,000 in 1979. MBCA, 1 E 01 1629.
22. The figures vary. For the early 1980s 850 to 2000 companies were estimated, cf. Iber-Schade, Auswirkungen des Strukturwandels.
23. Jeske, "Die stummen," 3.
24. "Steuer und Konzentration," in: Frankfurter Allgemeine Zeitung, 23.7.1953, 11.
25. Bericht über das Ergebnis einer Untersuchung der Konzentration in der Wirtschaft vom 29. Februar 1964, erstattet vom Bundesamt für gewerbliche Wirtschaft in Frankfurt am Main, in: Deutscher Bundestag, IV. Wahlperiode, Drucksache IV 2320, 164.
26. Proportion of materials cost on average 51.4% 1963–1982, cf. also development of in-house/ outsourced proportions within the same period, MBCA, 1 E 01 0567 (Wirtschaftsausschuss 1983, "Fremdfirmenbeschäftigung insgesamt und insbesondere Umfang der Auswärtsfertigung bzw. –bearbeitung".
27. This ratio is said to be somewhat problematic, among other things because changes in purchasing- and sales prices and shifts in the product portfolio (for example, shifts to more material-intensive models) can cause a bias.

28. Cf. the discussion in Dirrheimer, Zur Meßbarkeit, 5–16; see also Matthews, "Fordism, Flexibility and Regional Productivity Growth," Arizona State University 1996, 64s.
29. Dirrheimer and Hübner, "Economic Consequences."
30. See Jeske, "Die stummen," for this argument.
31. Cf. also Jeske, "Die stummen."
32. Cf. e.g. the purchasing contracts of Daimler-Benz AG, see point 'F.' of the guidelines of the materials department of 20.2.1961, 5, MBCA, 1 E 01 0203. See also Laleike, *Struktur*, 141. Monopolkommission, Sondergutachten, 73. Some suppliers also functioned merely as stop-gaps for peak operations and reserved capacities for those product groups for which automakers also had in-house production but bought additional capacities during phase of boom as capacity limits were reached.
33. Monopolkommission, Sondergutachten 7: Missbräuche der Nachfragemacht und Möglichkeiten zu ihrer Kontrolle im Rahmen des Gesetzes gegen Wettbewerbsbeschränkungen, Baden-Baden 1977, 77.
34. Cf. for a discussion of purchasing conditions, Grote, "Zulieferer, Partner der Großen?," 42.
35. Monopolkommission, Missbräuche., 78.
36. Berg called this a "Phase der friedlichen Koexistenz"; Berg, *Konzentration und Wettbewerb*.
37. Cf. for the background to the management of drop-forged parts VW-KA 1974/434/3, correspondence Paulsen and Nordhoff , July 15, 1957 and August 6 1957. For background to the case involving the Deutsche Edelstahlwerke (DEW) in Remscheid cf. also Westfälisches Wirtschafts-Archiv (WWA), Bestand F 189, Nr. 273, Bd. 1, Hausmitteilungen, August 14, 1952; and Salzgitter Konzernarchiv (quoted in the following as SKA) M.19031, Briefwechsel und Notizen Goossens/Eisenbraun/Albert im August und September 1963.
38. Cf. general principles formulated by Nordhoff, in: VW-KA 1974/434/3, note, 8.3.1957.
39. Cf. also Jeske on Cooperation.
40. A line of continuity goes back to the organisational structures of the war economy, to the 'Sonderring Gesenkschmiedestücke', which belonged to the main body ('Hauptring') 'Iron and Steel'. For an organisational chart referring to November 1943 see WWA, F. 189, file No. 245. See also WWA, Bestand F 189, Nr. 273, Bd. 1, Hausmitteilungen, August, 14th 1952.
41. Cf. the portrayal by someone on the 'frontline' Industriemagazin März 1977, in: MBCA, 1 E 01 1629.
42. Note, September, 4 1963, 'betreffend Eigenfabrikation von geschweißten Rohren beim VWW', in: SKA, M. 19031.
43. This was still the case in the early 1980s – cf. Geck/Petry.
44. SKA, M. 19031, minutes of Direktor Goossens concerning advisory board meeting of 'Herstellergruppe Teile und Zubehör im VDA', April 15, 1964, Frankfurt/Main.
45. SKA, M. 19031, note concerning supervisory board meeting of Kronprinz AG (January 27 1959), October 29 1959.
46. Ibid.; see also a similar arrangement between the wheel manufacturer and the European Ford Works in SKA, M. 19030, Niederschrift Nr. 19, managing board meeting December 8 1964.
47. VW-KA, JB Einkauf, 174/2366 (1949–1968), hier: Jahresbericht über den Einkauf und die Materialabteilung für 1960.
48. MBCA, 1 V 14 0489.
49. But this did represent a certain limitation on investment planning, cf. ibid.
50. Cf. for example the guidelines set up by Daimler-Benz, MBCA, 1 E 01 0203, Richtlinien der Materialwirtschaft.
51. Cf. Streb, Scherner, Tilly, Supplier Networks, 1010 and 1012. Cf. also MBCA, 1 E 01 1622, "Lieferanten mit Millionenumsätzen 1951–1965".
52. MBCA, 1 E 01 0203, Richtlinien der Materialwirtschaft, Richtlinien vom 9.6.1958, 9.
53. Cf. Daimler Benz AG, Das Großunternehmen und der industrielle Mittelstand. Eine Untersuchung über die klein- und mittelbetrieblichen Zulieferer der Daimler Benz AG, Stuttgart 1962. This study speaks of 16,500 suppliers – but the group of regular suppliers must have been significantly smaller, see Iber-Schade, "Auswirkungen des Strukturwandels."
54. MBCA, 1 E 01 0202, Jacob, Rede "Automatisierung der Einkaufsarbeit," 12.

55. MBCA, 1 E 01 1620, Unterabschnitt: Binder 1/83.
56. Ibid.
57. Helga Grote, "Zulieferer," 45. See also for more details F.W. Meyer and H. Grote, Möglichkeiten einer Untersuchung der Funktionen und der Wettbewerbslage kleiner und mittlerer Zulieferunternehmen in der Bundesrepublik Deutschland. Eine Untersuchung erstellt im Auftrag des Bundesministers für Wirtschaft, Bonn 1970.
58. E. Grunow-Osswald, Wirtschaftskrisen – Wendepunkte für den Konzern? In Tilly and Triebel, Automobilindustrie 1945–2000, 77–110.
59. MBCA, 1 E 01 0559, August, 5th 1970, Programm-Entwicklung, Investierungen und Mehrkosten.
60. Ibid.
61. MBCA, 1 E 01 0559, August, 5th 1970, Programm-Entwicklung, Investierungen und Mehrkosten. DF.
62. Automobilwirtschaft, October 1973, 219.
63. Cf. Eric Hobsbawm, The Age of Extremes, 225; Marglin and Schor, The Golden Age of Capitalism.
64. Bundesarchiv (BA), B 102-204347, Informationsvermerk, 14.3.1980 für den Besuch VDA.
65. Grunow-Osswald, 95; on the ‚crisis-sensitivity' of the company cf. Dominik Fischer, Krisen und Krisenbewältigung bei der Daimler Benz AG, Vaihingen/Enz 2010.
66. MBCA, 1 E 01 1649, extract from the minutes of the 'MAL/MEL-meeting' on October 3, 1975, original emphasis.
67. Ibid.
68. MBCA, 1 V 14 0489, here: Wolters to v. Harling on February 13, 1976.
69. Ibid.
70. Ibid.
71. Cf. MBCA, 1 V 14 0489, here: Dr. Prinz to F. Ulrich on July 1, 1976, annex "Vermerk Einkaufssituation Mitte 1976", 2.
72. See for example Kunz, Marktstellung, 20; cf. also Grote, Partner der Großen.
73. Cf. MBCA, 1 V 14 0489, here: Dr Prinz to F. Ulrich on 1 July 1976, annex: "Vermerk Einkaufssituation Mitte 1976," 2; 7f. and ibid., Einkaufsbericht der Firma Bosch, March 26, 1976, 2.
74. Cf. various correspondences in MBCA, 1 V 14 0489, for example Wolters to v. Harling, February, 13th, 1976.
75. Monopolkommission, 71. Cf. MBCA, 1 V 14 0489, Vermerk Einkaufssituation Mitte 1976.
76. MBCA, 1 V 14 0489, Vermerk Einkaufssituation Mitte 1976, 5.
77. Helper and Sako, "Determinants of Trust," 404.
78. The Wirtschaftsvereinigung Metalle promoted the proposal as well, MBCA, 1 V 14 0489, January 20, 1976.
79. MBCA, 1 V 14 0489, here: Reuter to Zahn February 3, 1976. Representatives of the automakers argued in the same vein that problems in the crisis-ridden supplier industry should not be solved in fundamental but in individual terms.
80. 'Official talks on this subject are of no use to anyone; it is far more the case that we in future want to be available for talks with individual suppliers who have overstretched their product range and fallen into serious difficulties.' MBCA, 1 V 14 0489, Wolters to v. Harling, February, 13th, 1976.
81. MBCA, 1 V 14 0489, February 3, 1976, Reuter to Zahn regarding 'Einkaufsmacht'.
82. MBCA, 1 V 14 0489, February 3 1976, Reuter to Zahn regarding ‚Einkaufsmacht'.
83. Cf. Industriemagazin März 1977, MBCA, 1 E 01 1629.
84. Cf. for the discussion also Tilly, Kooperation.
85. MBCA 1 V 14 0489, Vermerk Einkaufssituation Mitte 1976.
86. MBCA, 1 E 01 1674, Ergebnisbericht des BDI-Arbeitskreises Zulieferfragen, Anlage zu Schreiben BDI (Benisch/Minet) July 6, 1979.
87. MBCA, 1 E 01 1674, Ergebnisbericht des BDI-Arbeitskreises Zulieferfragen, Anlage zu Schreiben BDI (Benisch/Minet) July 6, 1979.
88. MBCA, 1 E 01 1629 (36.8% of the total purchased related to 76 firms with more than 5000 employees or were big groups).
89. MBCA, 1 E 01 1629.
90. Cf. also the criteria of dependence in Geck/Petry as well as Freiling, Abhängigkeit der Zulieferer.

91. MBCA, 1 E 01 1674, Ergebnisbericht des BDI-Arbeitskreises Zulieferfragen, Anlage zu Schreiben BDI (Benisch/Minet) July 6, 1979.
92. Helper and Sako, "Management Innovation," 412.
93. Helper and Sako, "Determinants of Trust," 404.
94. Concerning formal and informal institutions cf. Douglass North, Institutionen, institutioneller Wandel und Wirtschaftsleistung, Tübingen 1993 43ss., 55ss.
95. Helper, "Management Practices," 68.
96. Herrigel and Zeitlin, "Alternatives to Varieties of Capitalism," 672.
97. Herrigel and Wittke could be interpreted in this manner: 'on the whole, price was the determining factor for sales in old style manufacturing supply chains in the US and Germany. OEMS were very vertically integrated and supplier structures in both countries tended to be divided between a relatively small number of large standard component producers, such as Robert Bosch or Borg Warner in the automobile industry and multitudes of small and medium sized contract shops engaged in capacity subcontracting' (Herrigel and Wittke, "Varieties of Vertical Disintegration," 329).

Acknowledgements

Many thanks are due to Wolfgang Rabus (Mercedes-Benz Classic, Archives) for his energetic support of my research, and to the editors and reviewers for their helpful suggestions on the paper. I would like to thank Kirsten Petrak-Jones for precious linguistic help and Richard Tilly for insightful remarks.

Disclosure statement

No potential conflict of interest was reported by the author.

References

Berg, Hartmut, Konzentration und Wettbewerb im Gemeinsamen Markt: Das Beispiel der Automobilindustrie, in: Wirtschaftsdienst, Vol. 4, 1967, 202-208.
Daimler Benz AG, Das Großunternehmen und der industrielle Mittelstand. Eine Untersuchung über die klein- und mittelbetrieblichen Zulieferer der Daimler Benz AG, Stuttgart 1962.
Dirrheimer, Manfred, Zur Messbarkeit der vertikalen Integration, Berlin 1980 (International Institute of Management, Wissenschaftszentrum Berlin, discussion paper series 80-2)
Dirrheimer, Manfred/ Hübner, Thomas, Economic Consequences of different component- and car producer relationships, manuscript, Science Center Berlin, Graduate School of Management, University Berlin.
Fischer, Dominik, Krisen und Krisenbewältigung bei der Daimler Benz AG, Vaihingen/Enz 2010.
Freiling, Jörg. Die Abhängigkeit der Zulieferer. Wiesbaden: Ein strategisches Problem, 1995.
Geck, Hinrich-Matthias, and Günther Petry. Nachfragemacht gegenüber Zulieferern. Eine Untersuchung am Beispiel der Automobil- und der elektrotechnischen Industrie: Köln u.a, 1983.
Gellner, Berthold, Wird die kleinere und mittlere industrielle Unternehmung diskriminiert? Eine Untersuchung über die wirtschaftspolitische Bedeutung der Klein- und Mittelindustrie der Bundesrepublik Deutschland, Berlin 1968.

Grote, Helga, Zulieferer. Partner der Großen? in: *Automobilwirtschaft*, Februar 1971, 42-46.

Grote, Helga, and Fritz W. Meyer. *Möglichkeiten einer Untersuchung der Funktionen und der Wettbewerbslage kleiner und mittlerer Zulieferunternehmen in der Bundesrepublik Deutschland*. Bonn: Eine Untersuchung erstellt im Auftrag des Bundesministers für Wirtschaft, 1970.

Grunow-Osswald, Elfriede. "Wirtschaftskrisen. Wendepunkte für den Konzern?" In *Automobilindustrie 1945–2000*, edited by Stephanie Tilly and Florian Triebel, 77–110. München: Eine Schlüsselindustrie zwischen Boom und Krise, 2013.

Hall, Peter and Soskice, David, eds. Varieties of capitalism. *The institutional foundations of comparative advantage*, Oxford 2001.

Hamer, Eberhard, Zuliefererdiskriminierung, *Minden* 1988.

Helper, Susan. "Management Practices." *Relational Contracts, and the Decline of General Motors, in: Journal of Economic Perspectives* 28, no. 1 (2014): 49–72.

Helper, Susan/Sako, Mari, Determinants of trust in supplier relations: Evidence from the automotive industry in Japan and the United States, in: *Journal of Economic Behavior and Organization*, Vol. 34, 1998, 387-417.

Helper, Susan, and Mari Sako. "Management innovation in supply chain." *Industrial and Corporate Change* 19, no. 2 (2010): 399–429.

Herrigel, Gary/Zeitlin, Jonathan, Alternatives to Varieties of Capitalism, in: "Varieties of Capitalism" *Roundtable, Business History Review*, Vol. 84, 2010, 667-674.

Herrigel, Gary/Wittke, Volker, Varieties of Vertical Disintegration. The Global Trend Toward Heterogeneous Supply Relations and the Reproduction of Difference in US and German Manufacturing, in: Morgan, Glenn/ Moen, Eli/ Whitley, Richard: *Changing Capitalisms. Internationalization, Institutional Change and Systems of Economic Organization*, Oxford 2005, 312-351.

Hobsbawm, Eric, The Age of Extremes. *The short twentieth century 1914-1991, London Repr.* 2010.

Iber-Schade, Annerose, Auswirkungen des Strukturwandels in der Automobilindustrie auf Kfz-Zulieferunternehmen, in: Röper, Burkhardt (Ed.), *Strukturpolitische Probleme der Automobilindustrie unter dem Aspekt des Wettbewerbs*, Berlin 1985, 95-127.

Jeske, Jürgen, Die stummen Diener der Automobilindustrie, in: Blick durch die Wirtschaft, 17. 2.1964.

Kessen, Holger. *Nachfragemacht der Automobilindustrie*. Eine Analyse unter den Gesichtspunkten Kartellrecht, AGB-Recht und Konzernrecht: Frankfurt a.M, 1993.

Kunz, D. *Die Marktstellung der mittelständischen Zulieferer*. Stuttgart: Eine Untersuchung der Zulieferverhältnisse in der gewerblichen Wirtschaft Baden-Württembergs, 1972.

Laleike, Klaus, Struktur und Wettbewerbsprobleme der Kraftfahrzeug-Teile-Wirtschaft, *Aachen* 1965.

Marglin, Stephen/Juliet Schor, The Golden Age of Capitalism, Oxford 1990. *Monopolkommission, Sondergutachten 7: Mißbräuche der Nachfragemacht und Möglichkeiten zu ihrer Kontrolle im Rahmen des Gesetzes gegen Wettbewerbsbeschränkungen*, Baden-Baden 1977.

Scherner, Jonas, Jochen Streb, and Stephanie Tilly. "Supplier networks in the German aircraft industry during World War II and their long-term effects on West Germany's automobile industry during the 'Wirtschaftswunder.'" *Business History* 56, no. 6 (2014): 996–1020.

Schröder, Martin. *Varianten des Kapitalismus*. Wiesbaden: Die Unterschiede liberaler und koordinierter Marktwirtschaften, 2014.

Tilly, Stephanie, Das Zulieferproblem aus institutionenökonomischer Sicht. Die westdeutsche Automobil-Zulieferindustrie zwischen Produktions- und Marktorientierung (1960-1980), in: Jahrbuch für Wirtschaftsgeschichte, Vol. 1, Nr.0, 2010, 137-161.

Tilly, Stephanie, Kooperation in der Krise? Beziehungspraktiken in der deutschen Automobilindustrie von den fünfziger bis zu den siebziger Jahren des 20. Jahrhunderts, in: idem/Triebel, Florian (Ed.): Automobilindustrie 1945-2000. *Eine Schlüsselindustrie zwischen Boom und Krise, München* 2013, 155-184.

Tilly, Stephanie/Triebel, Florian, Automobilwirtschaft nach 1945. Kontinuität, Krise, Wandel. Eine Einführung, in: idem (Ed.), Automobilindustrie 1945-2000. *Eine Schlüsselindustrie zwischen Boom und Krise, München* 2013, 1-21.

Whitley, Richard, Business History and the Comparative Analysis of Capitalisms, in: "Varieties of Capitalism" *Roundtable, Business History Review*, Vol. 84, 2010, 648-652.

Confrontational coordination: The rearrangement of public relations in the automotive industry during the 1970s

Ingo Köhler

ABSTRACT

The article stresses the importance of communication processes as a fundamental basis for interest coordination in Rhenish Capitalism. Using the example of public relations work of the German automotive industry during the 1960s and 1970s, the article shows that a long dominant consensus about automobility as a guarantee for economic growth and social prosperity began to unravel as the negative aspects of mass motorisation came under public scrutiny. Older asymmetric concepts of corporate communication based on manipulative lobbying efforts and agenda setting strategies were superseded by an 'issue management' approach that took the collective interests of the public seriously. These confrontational but also responsive patterns of communication strengthened the institutional arrangements in the long run.

Introduction

The success story of the German automobile industry is a textbook case for the economic efficiency of Rhenish Capitalism. The case of Volkswagen in particular serves as a role model for the close partnership between state and industry with regard to its semi-private owner-ship structure. Powerful collective bargaining associations, strong traditions of corporate co-determination, and carefully balanced wage and employment policies, however, have been typical features of the entire industry for many decades. According to the economic sociologist Wolfgang Streeck, such 'beneficial constraints'[1] of corporate governance are supposed to be the main reason for the economic strength of the German carmakers. Striving constantly for cooperative governance and compromises allowed the firms to implement profit strategies compatible with the national income distribution and the (West-)German growth system.[2] The mere fact that the German automobile industry managed to withstand the restructuring of the global car market more successfully than their British or American competitors in the 1970s and 1980s has been considered a strong indicator for competitive advantages which the firms were able to draw from coordinated market systems.

Yet, there is neither a best production regime nor the one best way to organise capitalism – from a historical perspective at least this should be seen as the most significant result of the recent *Varieties of Capitalism* (VoC) debates.[3] This approach to political economy by Hall and

Soskice highlights the importance of institutional arrangements as the basis of all economic activities. In this view, economic growth depends on the ability of all economic agents – politicians, entrepreneurs, workers, consumers, and their associations – to find a mode of interaction which covers their respective interests in the best manner possible. Hall and Soskice distinguish two types of institutional arrangements: on the one hand, *Liberal Market Economies* based on market competition, and on the other, *Coordinated Market Economies* based on cooperative strategic interaction. According to this approach, Rhenish Capitalism established itself after 1945 in Western Germany as a highly coordinated system building on older traditions of an 'Organised Capitalism'. As the French Economist Michel Albert puts it in 1991, Rhenish Capitalism was not only characterised by strong personal and capital ties between industry, banks and insurance companies. Strong tripartite contracts of business, labour, and state affiliations facilitated cooperative interaction geared to the principle of a socially balanced economy.[4] In recent years, much research has directed our attention to the concept and its distinctive institutional framework. These studies frequently refer to the historical roots of the German Model, but they remain strongly attached to the macro-economic level.[5] Studies which provide us with insights into the bargaining processes between companies and their stakeholders are, by contrast, almost absent from the literature. Following the hypothesis that the German automobile industry received fundamental growth impulses from the quality of its institutional relationships, this article sets out to locate micro-level practices of interaction and to put them at the centre of analysis.

Strategic interaction means, above all, strategic communication.[6] The agents involved need to share information about their interests, their expectations and, finally, their scope of action. These are fundamental requirements for cooperative problem solving. But, we know much too little about the semantic patterns and practices of communication on which such negotiation processes are based. To close this research gap, this article focuses on the public relations work of the car companies and automotive associations in the 1960s and 1970s as an exemplary case for the communication patterns of Rhenish Capitalism. It examines the companies' strategies to influence the political decision-making process by generating public understanding for business issues. Public relations, however, meant more than political lobbying. Adapting the concept from American textbooks for the first time during the 1950s, German management scholar Carl Hundhausen defined public relations as a way of 'soliciting public confidence'.[7]

German managers, Hundhausen advised, should provide the public with credible information about their companies as well as about their ideas regarding current economic, social and political issues. His mainly theoretical considerations referred to the originally American notion of 'corporate citizenship' which fit very well with German notions of cooperative coordination.[8] Both in theory and practice, however, public relations also carried connotations of 'opinion-forming'. In this sense PR activities intended to manipulate the public opinion and strengthen the firms' position in the bargaining processes regarding institutional arrangements.[9] As will be shown below, by the late 1960s automotive industry leaders used public relations tools primarily not to balance interests, but as strategic instruments in the controversy over the positive and negative effects of mass motorisation.

Before we can integrate the issues of corporate communication and public relations into VoC theory, however, we first must clear-up a common misconception. While Rhenish Capitalism has received much praise for its well-managed consensus, this does not necessarily mean that the process of interest coordination was always free of friction.[10] Quite to the contrary, the German example suggests that coordinated market economies received positive impulses from an endless quarrel over the power to frame the discourse and from constant renegotiations of economic and social compromises. According to Peter Hall, unexpected economic crises or gradual social or political transitions have the potential to destabilise existing institutional arrangements.[11] The economic actors lose their 'common knowledge set of beliefs' and their 'confidence in the trustworthiness of the relevant institutions'.[12] Political objectives shift and have to be redefined. Thus, the institutional framework of Rhenish Capitalism becomes subject to a constant process of transformation, a struggle for power and for the framing of issues. In this sense, the overall stability of the German coordinated economy was based strongly on a co-evolution of institutions and a flexible mutual alignment of formal and informal rules. Analysing the practices and semantics of communication may provide us with new insights into the historical processes of renegotiating the principles of socio-economic order.[13]

After the economic boom of the first two post-war decades, the West German automotive industry had to cope simultaneously with economic, social, and political challenges during the 1970s. These fundamental changes in its business environments make the industry ideally suited for a closer look at its public relations work – in an effort to analyse the linkages between corporate communication strategies and the transition of the institutional set up of Rhenish Capitalism. The study sets out at the beginning of the 1960s, a phase when the car was one of the most accepted and highly coveted goods of Germany's emerging consumer society. In its second part, the article shows how public relations then became a central element of corporate crisis management during the 1970s. As the public consensus about the social and economic benefits of individual mobility was rapidly unraveling, PR activities were modernised and professionalised. The external shock of the oil price crises and, equally important, the increasing visibility of the long-term social and environmental costs of mass motorisation threw the sector into a 'double crisis'. The firms' media and PR departments found themselves in a struggle against a growing tide of political and media criticism. Alarmed by the threat of regulation, I will argue, the companies decided to change the methods and instruments of their public relations work. They had to rebuild public confidence and to accentuate their economic and social responsiveness. The well-established practices of consensual coordination were replaced by more confrontational forms of corporative bargaining.

Consensus of automobility: freedom, consumption, and cars

The effort to expand individualised transportation after 1945 was supported by most, if not all, of German society. The private car became a symbol of economic and social progress. 'There would be no economic upswing, no prosperity without the car',[14] such was the motto for the joint project of motorisation. Indeed, the automotive industry generated strong multiplier effects for the overall economic reconstruction and recovery of West Germany. Due to their success in export markets German carmakers became an important source of foreign currency. Rapidly expanding automobile factories created jobs and ensured a proper income for many new workers. According to the ideas of Fordism, which became a very popular concept in Germany at this time, economic growth in this sector became equated with a democratic promise for a growing number of people to participate in the new-found prosperity and to a share in the expanded array of consumption opportunities. The

Allgemeine Deutsche Automobil-Club (ADAC), Germany's largest association of car owners, described the motor vehicle as the perhaps most valuable instrument to raise the public acceptance of the Social Market Economy (*soziale Marktwirtschaft*). We have to consider the enormous spread of private cars as a 'clearly visible sign … for the advancing democratization process in West Germany', the ADAC stated in 1959.[15]

German opinion leaders in politics, science, culture, and the media shared this assessment. According to Minister of Economic Affairs Ludwig Erhard, the automobile would help the German people to enjoy 'a much better and, by far, freer life'.[16] In this view, the freedom of individual mobility, the opportunity of moving fast, comfortably and autonomously through cities and open spaces by car, was reinterpreted as a representation of the new-found liberties of the Western political system. Following the model of the US, German elites emphasised the importance of a democratisation of consumption as a prerequisite for the successful implementation of the capitalist social order. Moreover, many German journalists stylised the individualistic car as the most effective weapon against the nation's totalitarian past.[17]

Based on such mutually reinforcing economic and socio-political expectations, a stable institutional arrangement arose within the German political economy which tended to push mass automobility as far as possible. State and industry coordinated their activities by task-sharing: The automobile manufacturers focused on the expansion of their production capacities. They aimed to satisfy the fast-growing demand, particularly in the small car segments of the market. They invested their profits into modern production facilities, and passed significant parts of their earnings over to the workers in the form of moderate, but steadily rising wages – company policies closely coordinated with employee representatives. Rising quantities of production, increased productivity and cost degression effects enabled firms to keep the sales prices low. The list prices for a standard 'entry-level' car, such as a Volkswagen Beetle, only increased at an overall rate of 3% between 1955 and 1966. If one considers that at the same time the annual inflation rate was nearly about 2%, this amounted to a steady decline in prices. The growing purchasing power and the willingness of German consumers to join the ranks of motorised society lead to greater demand and hence increased production.[18]

The government promoted this joint project of 'one car for everybody' by means of transport and tax policies. While industry made cars available, government's most important task was to provide adequate traffic infrastructure which the growing motorisation of private households required. During the 1950s and 1960s, politicians awarded road-building projects the right-of-way over investments in public transport systems. State governments and local authorities started radical urban renewal programs based on the notion of a 'car-friendly city'.[19] At the same time, federal authorities completed several major projects to extend the national motorway (*Autobahn*) network. By the end of the 1960s the government drew up an ambitious plan to improve motorway density up to a point where every German had motorway access within a distance of 25 km from his or her residence. This so called 'Leber-Plan' – named after the German Minister of Transport Georg Leber – as well as all other federal highway projects were financed with the revenues from gasoline tax which had been earmarked exclusively for the purpose of road construction. All these infrastructural measures were considered to be a 'service from the public to the public'.[20]

In addition, the government established strong tax incentives for the purchase of private vehicles. The tax reform of 1955 abolished older luxury taxes, which had been imposed on car ownership during the Weimar Republic. Now, car owners not only benefitted from very low automobile taxes but also gained a privileged status through new forms of tax reliefs. The use of one's own private car for commuting was encouraged by a fixed tax-deductible mileage flat rate of 0.50 DM per kilometer. Most importantly, the strongest indicator that the government was truly committed to the freedom of mobility paradigm was its 1952 suspension of all forms of speed limits for passenger cars. This, however, proved to be too liberal even for German car drivers. Due to a massive increase in traffic accidents caused by cars, the authorities had to withdraw the suspension five years later.[21] Yet, the lax treatment of speed limits on the German motorway to this day remains a relic of the appeals to unin-hibited self-determination in a new, democratic society of car consumers on which the automobile consensus of the post-war period had been built.

Going back to the question of institutional arrangements, we must consider that there was not yet an established public arena to handle conflicts because the social and economic importance of the automobile industry was rarely called into question. Only a few outsiders exposed the problems arising from the rapidly growing traffic. But these critical voices were effectively drowned out by a unanimous chorus of voices from industry, politics, media, and consumers all supporting automobility and mass motorisation. Neither corporate nor polit-ical communicators, furthermore, adopted the guidelines of public relations theory regarding a transparent information policy. Instead, following established traditions and routines of German corporatism, state and industry coordinated their activities in backroom deals behind closed doors. One central characteristics of Adenauer's in some ways liberal, but in others still quite authoritarian 'chancellor democracy' was that relevant economic and socio-political issues were discussed privately in close personal contact among the elites. Managers and officials of the corporatist organisations were welcome guests in the back rooms of government buildings.

Within this peculiar system of bargaining, the German Automobile Industry Association (*Verband der Deutschen Automobilindustrie [VDA]*) played an important role as a mediation authority. The CEOs of Volkswagen, Daimler, Opel, BMW or Ford of Germany met with high-ranking politicians at so-called 'fireside chats' or 'gentlemen's dinners' which the VDA regularly organised.[22] Personal talks, one of the VDA officials admitted quite frankly in 1967, were the most effective way to pursue the political agenda of the car industry.[23] At the same time, the association supplied political authorities at their request with data on the auto-mobile sector and with their ideas and concepts for designing the future of the automobile society. These informal patterns of strategic cooperation resulted in a regulatory regime in which the boundaries between consulting, mediation, and political interference became blurred. Lobbying was a widely accepted instrument within the German Social Market Economy in its early stages – or, as a critical journalist put in 1974, the coordinating activities were all too often deliberately shrouded in secrecy to improve the effectiveness of the insti-tutional decision-making process.[24]

German carmakers, furthermore, delegated certain parts of the negotiations with state authorities to the representatives of the automobile association. Looking at the negligible presence of business leaders in the media, PR expert Carl Hundhausen considered German managers to be 'pathologically publicity-shy'. He suggested that the traditional ideal of the honorable businessman with its implied code of conduct was responsible for their reserva-tions vis-à-vis public exposure. According to Hundhausen's view, what had appeared rea-sonable in the past increasingly became an obstacle for the spread of modern American public relations strategies. Hundhausen, however, interpreted this behaviour of German

managers as a systematic 'strategy of conflict avoidance'. In fact, the importance of negotiating consensus should be regarded as a key distinctive feature of corporate governance in
Rhenish Capitalism.[25]

Most of the German car companies began to establish specialised press departments
during the 1920s. They provided journalists with figures and facts about the firms, informed
them about the launch of new car models, technical innovations or the development of
production and sales. Comments on current political or social issues, however, were published only by the industry association. The public relations work of the companies was
heavily coordinated and centralised. At the beginning of the 1960s, a joint press committee
was founded in which the spokesmen of the firms and professional VDA media experts met
regularly to coordinate their activities. Here, every public statement was discussed in detail
before it was released to the press. The VDA coordinated these processes of intra-industry
opinion-formation which preceded any external communication. The committee set the
agenda for company level public relations activities and served as a platform for the exchange
of information about the business environment among firms. In the context of the negotiations with state authorities about the Leber-plan in 1968, for example, the VDA stated
explicitly that it was 'mandated [by the German automobile executives] to enlighten the
public about the dire need of motorway building'.[26] Despite the fact that the companies
competed on the more and more volatile and global car markets they strove to speak with
one voice in political issues. This underscores the high degree of self-organisation of the
industry. Their common goal was to combine their efforts to pursue their interests in the
public opinion-making process.

Accordingly, the companies' conceptions of public communication were largely identical
with one another. Both in corporate marketing and in public relations, asymmetric concepts
of communication with the stakeholders were dominant.[27] The German carmakers believed
themselves to be in a powerful position due to the fact that, in the public's eyes, they were
hailed as the guarantors of the economic and social reconstruction of the nation. In 1967,
on the occasion of a formal dinner introducing a new car model, a BMW spokesman referred
to the high-ranking politicians and journalists in attendance as 'trusted partners of our public
relations activities'.[28] On the one hand, this statement can be read as a reaffirmation of
cooperation and, ultimately, of the institutionalised consensus around the automobile. On
the other hand, however, it serves as an example of the one-dimensional PR approach of
the industry. The companies were not really striving for an open dialogue about the interests
of their stakeholders. Instead, they primarily defined their objectives and formulated expectations and demands towards their environment. The notion of an impartial exchange of
views was superseded by unilateral attempts to push one's own agenda.[29]

It is especially striking to note how limited the role of the media as a critical voice and a
check on institutional arrangements was among the actors of Rhenish Capitalism in the first
two post-war decades. Journalists were considered simple, uncritical disseminators of the
reports and of the promotional images the industry wanted to get into the papers.

While scholars established high ethical standards for public relations work, in practice a
strong network of informal and almost corrupt structures of cooperation between companies
and the press emerged. The 'Wine-and-Dine-Era'[30] of corporate communication encom-
passed a wide array of dubious practices. An internal BMW report from 1966 allows us greater
insight into the techniques of the spin-doctors: In the run-up to press conferences the company compiled questionnaires. BMW 'handed them out to trusted people from the press

with the request of asking these very questions. This is the way to arrange matters in accordance with our companies' objectives. ... Funny little gifts and personal invitations' should strengthen the personal ties and 'put the firm in good standing with the journalists'.[31] Now and then, journalists and politicians would find gratuities or small tokens in their hotel rooms, the liberal parliamentarian Karl-Herrmann Flach noted in outrage in 1967.[32] At the same time, the press department of Ford in Germany was instructed by the Detroit parent company 'to establish a one-to-one-relationship ... and keep the writers happy. ... Nothing impresses a writer more than being flown in a company plane'.[33] Enclosed with this directive the PR-specialists got a list of potential giveaways and personal advantages supposed to be suitable for 'optimising' test reports of their new car models. Moreover, it became a common practice of corporate PR to hand over exclusive, completely enjoined press articles to the journalists with the aim of an unfiltered dissemination of information. In 1968, the German news magazine *Der Spiegel* examined these methods critically for the first time under the headline: 'Public Relations: Padded Promotion'.[34] The report did not primarily denounce the – under economic aspects more or less reasonable – attempts of the industry to team up with the press, but rather condemned in the harshest of terms the undemocratic German media culture which allowed such manipulation of the press.

To sum up from an analytical rather than a moral perspective, interpersonal alliances between industry, state, and media facilitated and stabilised the process of institutional cooperation. In the political economy of early West Germany, these close ties have to be considered not only as a prerequisite for strategic interaction but also as a result of the presence of institutional complementarities,[35] as well as the actors' reliance on the informal mechanisms of Rhenish Capitalism.

Automobile dissensions: pollution, consumerism, and crisis communication

At the end of the 1960s, the corporate public relations work had to be adjusted to a new set of circumstances. The automobile consensus was unravelling and along with it the balance of strategic coordination. The more cars clogged the roads, the harder it became to deny the obvious ecological and social problems of mass motorisation. Just at the point when the automobile became a universally accessible consumer item in Germany, its benefits were called into question. Put in a larger context, the car can be seen as one example for an overall process of socio-economic change which the well-known German sociologist Ulrich Beck described in 1986 as the rise of the 'risk society'. According to Beck, the shared focus of the immediate post-war decades had been on economic prosperity and the improvement of individual living standards. As society had reached these goals, the risks and collective costs of the modern consumer society came to public attention by the 1970s.[36]

In analysing this phenomenon we have to keep in mind the fact that this did not by any means lead to a point where consumers lost their individual desire for cars. Rates of private motorisation were still progressing further throughout this decade. Only in 1973/74 did car sales stagnate due to the economic uncertainties of the oil price crisis. Afterwards, the automobile industry posted new sales records. What did change, however, were consumer preferences and the structure of demand. Emotional buying motives such as social distinction and representation lost importance while more rational and functional criteria were on the rise. Much more than in consumer behaviour, the 'disenchantment of the automobile'[37] could be found in the political, scientific, and media debates about the dangers of private automobility.

The car and its producers came under criticism for a variety of reasons. First, a growing number of road accidents alarmed politicians, automobile associations, traffic engineers and the media. Between 1955 and 1970 the number of car crashes increased from 0.6 to 1.4 million. To some degree, this could be attributed to the similarly massive increase in car registrations, but casualty figures rose at a disproportionately high rate. For the first time, almost 20,000 people died, and more than half a million were severely injured on German streets each year.[38] These numbers set off a public debate about traffic regulations, and the social costs of the automobile society came under intense scrutiny. With articles headlined 'Battlefield Road', or 'Scourge of Mankind' the political press dissociated itself from the erst-while symbol of prosperity.[39] Secondly, the environmental issues of noise nuisance and exhaust pollutions became a subject of discussion. Especially in Germany's urban areas the traffic flow was getting choked by thousands of new vehicles which also increased the volume of dirt and harmful gas emissions. Here, car drivers derived their benefits of individual mobility at the public expense of millions of city dwellers – a fact that exemplified the issue of an equitable distribution of the social risks in mass consumption societies.

Until the mid-1960s protests against the externalities of the automotive boom had remained isolated and unorganised and limited to citizens directly affected. The German Federal Ministry of Transport downplayed the environmental hazards in 1959 by calling them 'unfortunate, but unavoidable side-effects of motorisation'.[40] This statement must be considered not simply as a sign of an ignorant attitude among political leaders, but also as an indication of naivety of Germany's social elites more broadly. In the 1950s only a handful of scientific studies on the potential health risks of traffic noise or vehicle exhaust fumes were available. Distressing reports about smog alerts in Los Angeles and, along with that, the debates about the governmental regulations of the Clear Air Act in the US in 1966 sparked a growing sensitivity towards environmental issues in Germany as well. Now, for the first time, scientific long-term studies about toxic effects of car exhaust were commissioned by federal and local authorities. At the same time, the media started to focus a great deal of attention on these topics. Newspapers, union magazines, community newsletters, church bulletins and even the ADAC's own member magazine, raised the question of how to deal with the problem of exhaust gases.[41] This broad-based media coverage put politicians and companies under pressure to take action.

By the end of the 1960s, critiques of the automobile became more encompassing. The manufacturers of the most symbolic product of liberal Western lifestyle found themselves at the centre of debates about consumer protection and the downsides of modern consumer culture. They did not really feel challenged by the intellectual anti-capitalist attacks of social philosophers or by the student protests of the generation of 1968 – the fundamental of the existing social order in Western Germany seemed too strong to be a threat in the eyes of the industry. Much more alarming for the companies was the fact that their common marketing and PR strategies took a lot of heat. A growing coalition composed of journalists, social scientists, and politicians started to call out the automotive industry (alongside other producers of consumer goods) for their manipulative strategies which were considered to be open attempts to restrict the autonomy and freedom of consumers. Following the concept of the countervailing power of demand, which had become very popular in Germany at the beginning of the 1970s, the Consumers' Associations (*Arbeitsgemeinschaft der Verbraucherverbände* [AgV]*)*, an association of public consumer councils, stated in 1973: 'Measures of consumer policy should increase the power of consumers to influence the economic process in general and to reestablish their sovereignty of individual decision-making. In this sense, strengthening the position of the consumer is a continuous task of public policy.'[42]

As Christian Kleinschmidt has already emphasised in his work on the rise of organised consumerism, the implication here is that consumer protection in Germany would be to a much lesser extent reliant on grassroots private initiatives or a self-organised consumer movement.[43] In contrast to the US, the German consumer movement was primarily institutionalised through public or semi-public associations. For the councils representing the consumer interests on the national and regional level, collective bargaining with the competing industrial associations was a central function. According to the VoC approach, here again the traditional institutional order of the German model of Rhenish Capitalism was reproduced, but at the same time filled up with new actors and issues.

The creation of *Stiftung Warentest* was another important government impulse for consumer protection in Germany as well as a milestone in creating market transparency for consumers. This publicly financed foundation of engineers and scientific marketing experts started to publish impartial test reports of consumer products in 1966. Giving the consumer the opportunity of gathering product information provided not by the companies, but by an alternative, objective source, the foundation aimed at enhancing consumer sovereignty. Assisted by the press, the message these measures sent out to the companies was quite clear. The firms were called upon to give up manipulative advertising and to improve their efforts of paying serious attention to the consumer's interests by providing them with fair and accurate product information. The public pressured producers to truly serve consumers, instead of looking at them as nothing more than anonymous and passive objects of corporate sales tactics and profit seeking.[44]

Thus, already some years before the oil price shock, German carmakers had to face a severe social acceptance crisis of their management strategies and products. The institutional arrangements of the boom years of individual mass motorisation were shaken-up in three respects:

First, German state authorities withdrew from the political-economic alliance and no longer continued their unqualified preferential support of individual transport. The change of the established political procedures was closely connected with a change of the political make-up of the federal government. For the first time after the Second World War, a coalition of Social Democrats and Liberals came into power in the autumn of 1969. Following the slogan *'Mehr Demokratie wagen'* (literally: 'Let's dare more democracy') the new Federal Chancellor Willy Brandt initiated a programme of reforms. These aimed at social liberalisation and, in questions where collective public interest collided with individual economic goals, a tighter framework of regulation and state intervention.[45] The conflicts between individual mobility on the one hand and environmental and consumer protection on the other became exemplary cases for the latter scenario.

Second, the number of stakeholders involved grew. More and more actors and groups stepped into the public arena and formulated their demands towards products and management. Consumer associations and environmentalists, physicians, transport experts, sociologists and publicists critical of modern mass consumption turned to the problems of automobility. The established growth model and the political priorities of the so-called

German economic miracle (*Wirtschaftswunder*) were called into question from various corners of society.

Third, the press redefined its position in the strategic interaction processes of the political economy. With a lot more self-confidence, journalists now dedicated their work to monitoring and critically assessing current social conditions. They, too, distanced themselves from their former uncritical positions towards automobility and became important instigators of the politicisation of the car.

Against this backdrop, the automobile industry executives for the first time lost their power to shape public opinion and they saw themselves in a situation of a communicative rivalry with their stakeholders. The basis of common expectations which had guaranteed the established balance of interests got lost as the actors developed significantly different views with regards to the pros and cons of mass motorisation. In this situation, they lost their trust in the established rules and practices of cooperative coordination. They had to rearrange themselves to once again stabilise an unbalanced political situation.[46]

For the car companies the areas of debate were new and unfamiliar. Under pressure from external critics they called into question the effectiveness of their existing communication strategies. For public relations work it was imperative to take an unequivocal stand on the concerns of the stakeholders. Charges of a lack of seriousness levelled at companies had tarnished corporate images, which made them market-relevant problems. Public relations evolved from a mere advertising tool towards a holistic concept of 'issue management'.[47] Again, the VDA coordinated the public response of the industry. The press committee developed a dual strategy of crisis communication: On the one hand its intention was to underline the companies' positions vis-a-vis the critics clearly and effectively. On the other hand, the industry signaled to its political and social counterparts its willingness to cooperate in the process of solving the problems.

With this two-pronged approach, the association first tried to win back its influence on public opinion by means of a flood of new publications and press releases. Part of the vast PR campaign was the start of a new series of scientific publications in 1969. Up to eight books and papers per year presented results of research projects, most of which were commissioned or funded in full by the automobile industry. The publications covered a broad range of issues starting with traffic development plans, innovations in motor engineering and safety technologies, all the way to public health surveys and environmental analyses.[48] At the same time the VDA redesigned its annual membership magazine to a glossy brochure, addressed to all 'friends of the automobile' and those interested in subjects concerning modern automobility. Starting with the 1971 issue, the rather stodgy statistical facts about the economic developments of the industry gradually gave way to readable essays under the rubrics such as 'State', 'Road safety' or 'Environment'. The pithy statements were aimed to provide the public relations departments of member firms with talking points for the public debate. With these aids at hand, the VDA urged, they had to defend the automobile industry by speaking with one voice against 'the enemies of the existing social order'.[49] At the same time the VDA turned its attention directly to an audience outside their interest group for the first time.

Public relations work started to focus strongly on mediated communication strategies. Through their own publications and through radio and TV interviews the VDA tried to enhance the visibility of its positions in the public arena and to show off their competence and responsibility when it came to questions concerning the future of the modern mobile society. Still, direct lobbying remained an important element of their bundle of PR strategies. Starting in 1972 the automobile association launched a direct mailing campaign addressing all members of federal and state parliaments. Once a month each of them received the *autotelegramm*, an informational brochure with opinion pieces of high ranking representatives of the automotive industry on current social and economic issues – cherishing the hope of being able to reestablish the old cooperative relationship sometime in the future.[50]

Similarly, their line of reasoning referred to the basic foundations of the socio-economic arrangements of the past. 'Every seventh [German] lives off of the automobile'[51] was an argument put forward by the industries' PR strategists. The key message promoted not only the economic importance of the automotive sector, but also appealed to the economic senses and the social responsibilities of the political decision-makers. The car makers took a clear stand on the political debates about product or car market regulations. Their message was that they would be forced to charge higher sales prices to cover the installation costs for every safety or environmental product requirements imposed by government regulations. As a consequence, this would not only weaken the competitive position of the German manufactures on the world market. It was also presented as a question of whether politicians were willing to exclude families with lower income, which were not motorised yet, from their fundamental right of being able to afford a private car.[52] In this respect, the companies revived the argumentative associations between democracy and freedom of consumption. In doing so, they tried to conceal their own economic interests cleverly behind the legitimate needs and wishes of the consumers.

The communication strategy of the companies is indicative of another aspect of Germany's political economy. The representatives of the automobile industry presented their interests to the state authorities with a lot of self-confidence. At the same time, however, they tried to strengthen their positions by building coalitions with other social groups. Their aim was to mitigate conflicts and make offers for new forms of cooperation. In our example, the companies were closing ranks with consumers and employee representatives, in order to put politicians under public pressure. But it was clear that these partial institutional coalitions were fragile, and that the institutional arrangements of Rhenish Capitalism needed a more general readjustment based on the willingness of every party involved to balance out individual and collective interests. Here, the industrial representatives realised that they, too, had to make concessions to the state. The only question was, how many concessions had to be made and how hard-won any new compromise would prove to be.

The political debates over car market regulations offer us greater insight into the struggles for discursive dominance. Faced with indisputable scientific results, automobile firms widely acknowledged the health hazards which had their origins in the million-fold use of cars. Still, they jumped on every chance to minimise their own responsibility. From the viewpoint of the VDA many problems were, for example, 'the direct result of insufficient and, therefore, overloaded traffic areas'. In other cases they concluded, 'unfavorable weather conditions' combined with 'human inadequacies' in operating the vehicles had to be held responsible.[53] Allegations of potential mechanical defects or shortcomings in the product construction were categorically rejected by the car companies. Nonetheless, they signalled their readiness to improve the automotive engineering in order to do their bit for a safer and cleaner environment.

Offering forms of voluntary self-restraint and self-control, companies asked political authorities in return to abstain from their regulation plans. VDA president Achim Diekmann urged political leaders to return to a jointly coordinated economic policy. In the spring of 1971 he pleaded for a 'concerted action' of all parties involved. 'We have to harmonise public and private interest' and to 'ease the tensions' between economy and ecology based on cooperation.[54] The only way 'to retrieve an acceptable standard of living in a reasonable time frame', the VDA stated little later, would be a coordinated step-by-step plan in which 'the financial obligations of the federal government, states, municipalities, industry, car owners, and private households' were seriously taken into account.[55]

This suggestion hardly went far enough for the governing social-liberal coalition. Given the fact that corporate profits had increased to a new record-setting level in 1971 the government had different ideas about a fair distribution of costs and benefits. Following the American model, political authorities insisted on a polluter-pay-principle. They enacted a law in August of 1971 to reduce the lead additives of passenger car fuel.[56] One month later, they presented an 'environmental programme' to the public. In it, the Federal Government announced its plans for setting up strict legal limits for the toxic car exhaust emissions and raised the spectre of further technical regulations, including requirements for safety belt systems and catalytic converters.[57] In the summer of 1973, finally, the debates between state and industry came to a head in a sharp and public dispute. On the occasion of the traditional 'gentlemen's dinner' at the opening of the International Automobile Fair (IAA) of Frankfurt/M., German Transport Minister Lauritz Lauritzen took the chance to present his polemic pamphlet 'Right of way for the people'[58] which he had published only few weeks prior to the most important European car exhibition. The minister advocated more technical regimentation for the production of automobiles, and furthermore called for redirecting big parts of the transportation budget towards public transport.

This sparked a severe controversy between government and industry which increasingly involved more general aspects regarding regulative policy in the Social Market Economy. The VDA and the directors of the German car companies attacked the government harshly. They warned the public of a reckless dirigisme that would turn back time to a 'command society'.[59] They considered the consumers and themselves as producers to be patronised by a nanny state. In a time when industry was being criticised for manipulating society with simple advertisements, the association argued, some anti-capitalist dissidents and self-proclaimed consumer protectors were succeeding in infecting public opinion with their 'anti-automobile-hysterics'. The companies viewed any form of government interference as a fundamental challenge to the liberal principles of the market economy. The debates more and more became a competitive power play between the state and the industry conveyed via the press.[61]

The conflict-oriented style of the political bargaining process was toned down only with the economic downturn of 1974/75. This, again, was a common pattern of behaviour in the German variety of capitalism. In response to an unexpected change of the economic framework, competing institutions moved together and started searching for cooperative ways of solving the problems. If nothing else, at least in this respect the oil price crisis had one positive effect for the industry. Due to urgent economic problems, the government now placed their ambitious ecological and regulatory reforms at the bottom of the political agenda while economic considerations took their place as top priorities. During the crisis, policymakers sought to keep the key sector for an overall economic recovery, the automobile industry, free from financial burdens of additional state regulation.[62] This way, it was hoped the dangers of a long-lasting industry-wide crisis with severe consequences for the German job market could be reduced. Under such conditions it was easy for the car executives and their association to legitimise their interests. The Daimler CEO Joachim Zahn emphasised in his 1973 Christmas address to the employees that efforts of politicians and journalists to 'restore a climate of trust' had been stepped up.[63] He himself pleaded for a more reasoned and objective discussion on the future of transport, and he renewed the industry's offer of voluntarily promoting the collective environmental concerns of the society.[64]

Indeed, there were strong indications that the effort to implement new transport and environmental policies had run out of steam since 1974. It would be wrong to conclude, however, that the consensus of automobility of the 1950s and 1960s was completely rees-tablished without modification. The social externalities of the automobile were now securely anchored in the collective mind and had to be permanently integrated into the institutional arrangements. To achieve this aim, state authorities did not rely primarily on direct regimen-tations – and if they did, they showed consideration for the capacities of industry to accom-modate them. Together with the European partners, the German government intensified the exhaust regulations only slightly after 1975. The much stricter US-limits were introduced in Germany not before 1983, catalytic converters only in 1986.[65]

Instead of regulations, the state attached great importance to the idea of consumers countervailing power. Searching for new ways of balancing out individual and collective interests, the government focused on strengthening the cooperation with the consumers. The oil price shock made it easy for them to find points of contact. Individual interests in reducing the fuel consumption dovetailed well with public goals of resource-efficiency and of lowering of noxious fume emissions. Due to increasing gas prices, the consumer tried to cut their operating costs. The consumer preferences accordingly shifted towards more fuel-efficient cars which were, at the same time, less harmful to the environment. Better than any regulation the incentives of demand put pressure on producers to adjust their product policy to the wishes of the consumers. In the mid-1970s new small and compact car models like the *Volkswagen Polo*, *Opel Corsa* or *Ford Fiesta* were launched with a big market success. To no small degree, this was also a favourable development for the purposes of environmental protection.[66]

At the same time the government tried to sensitise the consumers for a more responsible handling of cars. This policy concept was derived from the idea of the 'sovereign consumer' who would make reasoned use of his or her autonomy, as long as he or she was thoroughly informed about the pros and cons of automobility.[67] This principle fit well into the overall concept of Rhenish Capitalism. The state had proven its willingness to intervene pro-actively into the markets in order to safeguard public interest in the period between 1970 and 1973. Subsequently, since 1974, the foundation of the new political-economic compromise was that the government would withdraw from regulatory measures if all the institutions involved willingly stand up for road safety education, consumer protection and environmental aware-ness. Of course, the limited scope of these forms of symbolic socio-political actions need to be stressed. For the automobile industry, for example, public declarations of its new sense of corporate social responsibility often served merely as fig leaves for their individual profit strategies. Nevertheless, they had to adjust their PR strategies to suit more open and trans-parent forms of communication with their stakeholders to win back public acceptance and to improve the image of their companies and products.[68]

Already in 1969, the automobile industry, federal and local authorities, the ADAC, insur-ance companies, unions, and churches had jointly initiated the road safety education programme called 'Hello partner – Thank you!' which promoted respectful traffic behaviour. A similar form of cooperation between firms, social associations and the state emerged in the campaign 'Click - buckle up before you start' which advocated the voluntary use of seat belts. On that issue the state once again prescribed half-hearted regulations. Safety belt systems were to be installed only in new cars, and the drivers had the free choice of using it without any sanctions until 1984.[69] During the oil price crisis, in November 1973, the German government imposed speed limits and a driving ban on four Sundays. These measures served as a moral appeal to the public for joint efforts of crisis management. The media, the automobile industry and almost all social groups supported the state initiative, but only for a while. When the oil shortages ended, the regulations lost their justification. Most parts of the society and, not surprisingly, the carmakers urged the state promptly and unanimously to restore the peoples' freedom of mobility.[70] 'Free Driving for Free Citizens',[71] they demanded.

The automotive industry tried to benefit from this public mood. In their (up to this day) only joint advertising campaign of all German firms the industry appealed directly to the people as speed limits had been lifted: 'Now we can decide how safely and responsibly we want to drive our cars. Let us not risk our freedom frivolously. We have to prove that we don't need regulations for everything. Car drivers, this is our freedom, this is our chance. Let us not only warm up our motors before starting, but also our hearts for all the other road users and pedestrians. ... Because: there is no right for freedom without the duty of individual responsibility.'[72] Individual freedom has its limits where the respective interests of the public and of other concerned parties begin – with this message the industry met the socio-political guidelines which the reformers of the social-liberal coalition had put forward since they came into power. That was the basis for the retrieval of the cooperative collaboration between state and industry. Nevertheless, the conditions for the industry did change. The automobile had irredeemably lost its ecological innocence, and the automotive managers had to prepare their communication strategies for a much more complicated and complex exchange of opinions with the stakeholders.

Conclusion: rearrangements of corporate communication

When the automobile received a barrage of social and cultural criticism, the automotive companies not only lost their confidence in the long-established practices of Rhenish Capitalism, but they also started to question the effectiveness of their own communication strategies. A broad consensus about the economic and social benefits of automobility had been a given in Western Germany for years. The apparent harmony of interests, however, seduced companies into thinking that they were able to direct public opinion formation at will by lobbying politicians and cozying up to the press. The scope of their public relations work was too limited to detect changes in their social environment. Accordingly, they were unprepared when new types of stakeholders took up positions in the public arena questioning the social and ecological externalities of mass motorisation. For the first time, the firms did find themselves entangled in a severe public competition between individual and collective interests which have to be considered typical for modern mass consumption societies. They had to learn how to handle these conflicts.

Summing up, two basic conclusions on communicative crisis management must be drawn: First, corporate public relations broadened its horizons and adapted to the changes in the social and political business environment by taking on new assignments and management tools. Even in practice, traditionally asymmetric approaches to communication became substituted with dialogic forms of a mutual communication and at times controversial exchanges of opinions between companies and stakeholders. Strong impulses were given by the automotive association which coordinated the external and internal communication of the industry. The most important problem, as the BMW-press department observed in 1974, was not actually modified public attitudes towards the car, but that the industry lacked suitable instruments to detect social change and to react on it: 'What should be a serious engagement with the social environment is here in this firm and in the whole industry mostly a public relations work stuck in its infancy.'[73] This self-criticism culminated in a call for a change of the communication management. Instead of simple advertising messages, the firms had to focus on an open exchange of information about the expectations of the stakeholders. New and innovative PR concepts of Volkswagen and BMW stressed that the automotive industry had to brace itself for the public demand of objective and coherent communication. This demand, they continued, arises in modern societies due to the anonymity and complexity of the world of consumption itself.[74]

As a result, the companies reflected on the challenges of, as they called it, the 'informed society'[75] and professionalised their strategies of corporate communication.[76] The renewal of the PR activities aimed, on the one hand, at reestablishing the public confidence in the companies' competences and in the expediency of their problem solutions. On the other hand, they tried to enhance public understanding for the common interests of economic and social prosperity, as well as for the challenges companies faced when it came to integrating environmental requirements into the complex process of automobile engineering. While the industry's first spontaneous reaction to the criticism it faced was one of panic and emotion, in the long-run they developed a concise strategy of 'issue management'.

Second, the corporate PR strategists reevaluated the role of the media in the process of public opinion-making. 'The times of champagne journalism are over', stated the BMW press department in 1975, and they combined their statement with a plea for the freedom of the press: 'The press has a public service mission. It fulfils this duty not only by distributing news, but also by taking a stand and by being a critic in order to support democratic ways of shaping public opinion.'[77] Companies now adopted the approach of media 'agenda-setting',[78] which became popular in the communication sciences in the early 1970s. In a growing number of instances, internal company reports referred to the press as the legitimate 'fourth estate' of the democracy. Such acknowledgements could be read to indicate that the companies became part of the process of an inner democratisation of Western Germany, which Jürgen Habermas once called a 'fundamental liberalisation' after 1968.[79] This interpretation holds, despite the fact that corporate public relations was, first and foremost, an instrument of representing the company's individual economic interest as effectively as possible to stakeholders.

The renewal of corporate communication practices, however, was an important prerequisite for the recalibration of a stable relationship between the state, the media, and the industry during the 1970s. Corporate social responsibility, in a proper sense, and the new established modes of confrontational coordination gave Rhenish Capitalism strong impulses to revitalise. Only on the basis of intensified discussions and of mutual consideration of interests were the institutions able to search for new ways of balancing out individual and collective interests in the mass consumption society.

With regard to the further use of the VoC approach in historical research, the empirical findings on corporate communication and public relations work demonstrate that we have to draw a more dynamic picture of the rise and self-perpetuation of Rhenish Capitalism. Its resilience against the challenges of social, political and economic change did not only derive from functional advantages of a stiff institutional setup, which the political economists Hall and Soskice originally had in mind, but also on dominant practices and semantic codes. Former studies focusing on German industrial relations did already show that the mythic social partnership (*Sozialpartnerschaft*) between employer's associations and unions bearded strong traits of a conflict partnership (*Konfliktpartnerschaft*).[80] Mentioning the field of public relations, we find very similar trends towards strategies of antagonistic cooperation in the 1970s, balancing individual and collective interests of shaping the (auto)mobile society. It was the readiness of all actors involved to resume negotiations on necessary institutional rearrangements. Taking the role of institutions as socialising agencies seriously, historical research has to get to the bottom of these continuous processes of change and adaptation, transmitted by the practices of communication.

Notes

1. Streeck, "Beneficial Constraints."
2. Boyer and Freyssenet, *Produktionsmodelle*, 38–45, 97–112.
3. Hall and Soskice, *Varieties of Capitalism*; Hall and Gingerich, *Varieties of Capitalism*.
4. Albert, *Kapitalismus contra Kapitalismus*, 107; Hockerts and Schulz, *Einleitung*, 8, 12.
5. Streeck, *Korporatismus*; Berghahn and Vitols, *Kapitalismus*.
6. See for example Luhmann, *Einführung*, 288–314; Martens and Ortmann, "Organisationen," 435–437.
7. Hundhausen, *Werbung um öffentliches Vertrauen*, 35.
8. Kleinschmidt, *Der produktive Blick*, 206; Reinhardt, "Zeitgenössische Ansätze," 53.
9. Bentele and Liebert, "PR-Geschichte in Deutschland," 228; Kunczik, *Public Relations*, 260–261.
10. Albert, *Kapitalismus contra Kapitalismus*.
11. Hall, "Stabilität und Wandel," 188.
12. Hall and Soskice, *Varieties of Capitalism*, 63.
13. Plumpe, "Ökonomisches Denken", 30–38; Resch, "Neue Institutionenökonomik," 122.
14. *ADAC motorwelt*, 6, 1964, 31.
15. "Vier Räder für Millionen." *ADAC motorwelt*, 12, 1959, 662; Rinn, *Automobil als nationales Identifikationssymbol*, 118.
16. Speech of the Federal Minister of Economic, September 17, 1959, 9, qdt. in Ibid., 133.
17. Klenke, *Freier Stau für freie Bürger*, 37; Flink, *The Car Culture*.
18. Köhler, *Neuvermessung des Automobils*, 82–86.
19. Reichow, *Die autogerechte Stadt*; Schmucki, *Traum vom Verkehrsfluss*, 136–137.
20. "Manifest der Kraftfahrt." *ADAC motorwelt*, 5, 1965, 30–31; König, "Automobil in Deutschland," 127–128; Sachs, *Liebe zum Automobil*, 94–97, 103–108; Andersen, *Traum vom guten Leben*, 168.
21. Klenke, "Pathologie des Straßenverkehrs," 523–524.
22. Tilly, "Die guten Zeiten ... sind vorbei," 214.
23. VDA, *Jahresbericht 1965/66*, 46.
24. Dietrich, "Produktion der Volkswagenwerbung," 82.
25. Hundhausen, *Amerika*, 80; Wischermann, "Unternehmenskultur," 36.
26. VDA, *Jahresbericht 1968/69*, 70.
27. Grunig and Hunt, *Managing Public Relations*, 32.
28. Historical Archive BMW (HABMW), UA 594, Paper of the Press Department, April 13, 1967, 1, 4.
29. Köhler, *Neuvermessung des Automobils*, 497. Kleinschmidt, *Der produktive Blick*, 218.
30. Brauer, *Presse- und Öffentlichkeitsarbeit*, 65; Kunczik, *Public Relations*, 47.

31. HABMW, UA 594, Paper of the Press Department, April 13, 1967, 1.
32. Flach, *Macht und Elend der Presse*, 36–38.
33. John W. Hartman Center for Sales, Advertising and Marketing History (HCD), J. Walther Thompson Collection (JWT), Black Papers, Client Series, Box 2, 1972, Ford T-Plans, Ford in Germany vs. The Automotive Press, 1972, 1.
34. "Public Relations: Werbung in Watte," *Der Spiegel*, July 8, 1968, 32.
35. Hall and Soskice, *Varieties of Capitalism*, 17; Mayntz, "Systemkohärenz," 383.
36. Beck, *Risk Society*, 25; Giddens, *Consequences of Modernity*; Ericson and Haggerty, *Policing the Risk Society*.
37. Flink, *The Car Culture*, 191.
38. Köhler, *Neuvermessung des Automobils*, 163.
39. "Das Gemetzel, das wir Verkehr nennen." *Der Spiegel,* June 28, 1971, 32; "Tod auf der Straße." *Die Zeit,* June 3, 1966, 12; Bode, *Alptraum Auto,* 6; 84–86.
40. Quoted in Möser, *Geschichte des Autos*, 275.
41. Bastian and Theml, *Unsere wahnsinnige Liebe zum Auto*, 92–98; Wanner, *Auto und Umweltschutz*; "Wie löst man das Abgas-Problem?" *ADAC motorwelt*, 5, 1971, 55.
42. Arbeitsgemeinschaft der Verbraucherverbände, *AgV 1953–1973*, 31.
43. Kleinschmidt, "Massenkonsum, 'Rheinischer Kapitalismus' und Verbraucherschutz," 145.
44. Jeschke, *Konsumentensouveränität*, 45–46.
45. Quoted in Wolfrum, *Die geglückte Demokratie*, 315.
46. Hall, "Stabilität und Wandel," 191.
47. Diez, *Handbuch für das Automobilmarketing*, 295.
48. For an overview see: Freudenfeld, *Zukunftschancen*, 245–248.
49. VDA, *Jahresbericht 1971/72*, 103.
50. Köhler, *Neuvermessung des Automobils*, 506.
51. VDA, *Verkehr - Sicherheit - Umwelt*, 14.
52. VDA, *Jahresbericht 1972/73*, 46.
53. VDA, *Verkehr - Sicherheit - Umwelt*, 15.
54. Diekmann, "Verkehr," 134.
55. VDA, *Verkehr - Sicherheit - Umwelt*, 16.
56. "Gesetz zur Verminderung von Luftverunreinigungen durch Bleiverbindungen in Ottokraftstoffen für Kraftfahrzeugmotoren (Benzinbleigesetz)' vom 5.8.1971." In *Bundesgesetzblatt (BGBl)* I, 1971, 1,234.
57. Heaton and Maxwell, Patterns of Automobile Regulation, 33; Köhler, "Small Car Blues," 128–130; HABMW, UA 861, Correspondence of the Executive Board, July–September 1971.
58. Lauritzen, *Der Mensch hat Vorfahrt,* 17.
59. German Federal Archive Berlin (BAB), 102/77728, Statement of the automobile industry, June 12, 1973, 1.
60. VDA, *Jahresbericht 1972/73*, 46.
61. "Überall Gedränge und Geschubse," *Der Spiegel,* May 5, 1973, 54; "Mit Zähnen und Klauen verteidigen," *Wirtschaftswoche*, June 20, 1975, 34.
62. Klenke, *Bundesdeutsche Verkehrspolitik*, 189.
63. Historical Archive Daimler (HAD), Energiekrise 197, manuscript by Jochim Zahn, December 4, 1973, 4.
64. Ibid.
65. Köhler, "Small Car Blues," 133.
66. Ibid., 134.
67. Gasteiger, *Konsument*, 193; Jeschke, *Konsumentensouveränität*, 226–248.
68. Heini, *Public Relations*, 107; Hilger, *'Amerikanisierung' deutscher Unternehmen*, 260–264.
69. Möser, Geschichte des Autos, 267.
70. "Auf die Bremse. Der hitzige Streit um Tempo 100," *Die Zeit,* January 1, 1974, 1.
71. Klenke, *Freier Stau für freie Bürger*, 18.
72. "Auf die Bremse. Der hitzige Streit um Tempo 100," *Die Zeit,* January 1, 1974, 1.
73. HABMW, UA 936, BMW Public Relations. Arbeitspapier 1974, 40.

74. Historical Archive Volkswagen (HAV), Autogramm, Kein X für ein U vormachen. Die Möglichkeiten und Grenzen der Öffentlichkeitsarbeit, February 28, 1975, 6.

75. HABMW, UA 936, Pressearbeit bei BMW, Concept 1975, 11.

76. Köhler, *Neuvermessung des Automobils*, 512–524.

77. HABMW, UA 936, Pressearbeit bei BMW, Concept 1975, 11.

78. McCombs and Shaw, Agenda-Setting, 176–187.

79. Habermas, *Theorie des kommunikativen Handelns*, 26.

80. Müller-Jentsch, Konfliktpartnerschaft.

Disclosure statement

No potential conflict of interest was reported by the author.

References

Albert, M. *Kapitalismus contra Kapitalismus*. Frankfurt/M and New York: Campus, 1992.

Andersen, A. *Der Traum vom guten Leben: Alltags- und Konsumgeschichte vom Wirtschaftswunder bis heute*. Frankfurt/M and New York: Campus, 1997.

Arbeitsgemeinschaft der Verbraucherverbände (ed.). *AgV 1953–1973*. Bonn: AgV, 1973.

Bastian, T., and H. Theml. *Unsere wahnsinnige Liebe zum Auto: Thema Verkehr*. Weinheim/Basel: Beltz, 1990.

Beck, U. Risk *Society: Towards a New Modernity*. New Delhi: Sage, 1992 (translated from the German Risikogesellschaft. Auf dem Weg in eine andere Moderne. Frankfurt/M: Suhrkamp, 1986).

Bentele, G., and T. Liebert. "PR-Geschichte in Deutschland: Allgemeine Entwicklung, Entwicklung der Wirtschafts-PR und Berührungspunkte zum Journalismus." In *Alte Medien — neue Medien*, edited by K. Arnold and C. Neuberger, 221–241. Wiesbaden: VS, 2005.

Berghahn, V. R., and S. Vitols. *Gibt es einen deutschen Kapitalismus? Tradition und globale Perspektiven der sozialen Marktwirtschaft*. Frankfurt/M and New York: Campus, 2006.

Bode, P. *Alptraum Auto: Eine hundertjährige Erfindung und ihre Folgen*. 2nd ed. Munich: Raben, 2, 1986.

Boyer, R., and M. Freyssenet. *Produktionsmodelle: Eine Typologie am Beispiel der Automobilindustrie*. Berlin: edition sigma, 2003.

Brauer, G. *Presse- und Öffentlichkeitsarbeit: Ein Handbuch*. Konstanz: UVK, 2005.

Diekmann, A. "Verkehr, Sicherheit, Umwelt." *Internationales Verkehrswesen* 23 (1971): 133–139.

Dietrich, F. "Zur Produktion der Volkswagenwerbung." In *Das deutsche Auto: Volkswagenwerbung und Volkskultur*, edited by K. Hickethier et. al., 79–88. Fernwald: anabas 1974.

Diez, W. *Das Handbuch für das Automobilmarketing: Strategien, Konzepte, Instrumente*. Landsberg/Lech: Mi-Wirtschaftsbuch, 1995.

Ericson, R. V., and K. Haggerty. *Policing the Risk Society*. Toronto: University of Toronto Press, 1997.

Flach, K.-H. *Macht und Elend der Presse*. Mainz: von Hase und Koehler, 1967.

Flink, J. J. *The Car Culture*. Cambridge: MIT Press, 1975.

Freudenfeld, B. *Die Zukunftschancen unserer Gesellschaft*. Cologne: Deutscher Instituts Verlag, 1983.

Gasteiger, N. *Der Konsument. Verbraucherbilder in Werbung, Konsumkritik und Verbraucherschutz 1945-1989*. Frankfurt/M and New York: Campus, 2010.

Giddens, A. *Consequences of Modernity*. Cambridge: Polity Press, 1990.

Grunig, J. E., and T. T. Hunt. *Managing Public Relations*. Fort Worth: Wadsworth, 1984.

Habermas, J. *Theorie des kommunikativen Handelns*. Frankfurt/M: Suhrkamp, 1981.

Hall, P. A., and D. W. Gingerich. *Varieties of Capitalism and Institutional Complementarities in the Macroeconomy: An Empirical Analysis*. Cologne: Max-Planck-Institute, 2004.

Hall, P. A., and D. Soskice (eds.). *Varieties of Capitalism: The Institutional Foundations of Comparative Advantage*. Oxford: Oxford University Press, 2001.

Hall, P. "Stabilität und Wandel in den Spielarten des Kapitalismus." In *Transformation des Kapitalismus*, edited by J. Beckert, et al., 181–204. Frankfurt/M and New York: Campus, 2006.

Heaton jr, G., and J. Maxwell. "Patterns of Automobile Regulation: An International Comparison." In *Zeitschrift für Umweltpolitik und Recht* 1 (1984): 15–40.

Hilger, S. *'Amerikanisierung' deutscher Unternehmen: Wettbewerbsstrategien und Unternehmenspolitik bei Henkel, Siemens und Daimler-Benz (1945/49 -1975)*. Stuttgart: Steiner, 2004.

Hockerts, H. G., and G. Schulz. "Einleitung." In *Der, Rheinische Kapitalismus' in der Ära Adenauer*, edited by idem, 9–28. Paderborn: Schöningh, 2016.

Hundhausen, C. *Werbung um öffentliches Vertrauen: Public relations*. Essen: Giradet, 1951.

Jeschke, D. *Konsumentensouveränität in der Marktwirtschaft: Idee, Kritik, Realität*. Berlin: Duncker & Humblot, 1975.

Kleinschmidt, C. *Der produktive Blick: Wahrnehmung amerikanischer und japanischer Management- und Produktionsmethoden durch deutsche Unternehmer 1950–1985*. Berlin: Akademie, 2002.

Kleinschmidt, C. "Massenkonsum, 'Rheinischer Kapitalismus' und Verbraucherschutz." In *Gibt es einen deutschen Kapitalismus? Tradition und globale Perspektiven der sozialen Marktwirtschaft*, edited by V. R. Berghahn and S. Vitols, 143–153. Frankfurt/M and New York: Campus, 2006.

Klenke, D. "Pathologie des Straßenverkehrs." *Universitas* 49 (1994): 521–532.

Klenke, D. *'Freier Stau für freie Bürger'. Die Geschichte der bundesdeutschen Verkehrspolitik 1949-1994*. Darmstadt: WBV, 1995.

Klenke, D. "Bundesdeutsche Verkehrspolitik und Umwelt: Von der Motorisierungseuphorie zur ökologischen Katerstimmung." In *Umweltgeschichte. Umweltverträgliches Wirtschaften in historischer Perspektive*, edited by W. Abelshauser, 163–190. Göttingen: Vandenhoeck & Ruprecht, 1994.

Köhler, I. "'Small Car Blues': Die Produktpolitik US-amerikanischer und deutscher Automobilhersteller unter dem Einfluss umweltpolitischer Vorgaben, 1960-1980." In *Jahrbuch für Wirtschaftsgeschichte/ Economic History Yearbook* 1 (2010): 107–135.

Köhler, I. *Die Neuvermessung des Automobils. Gesellschaftswandel und das Marketingmanagement der deutschen Autoindustrie in den 1960er und 1970er Jahren*. Göttingen: Georg-August-University [habilitation], 2012.

König, W. "Das Automobil in Deutschland: Ein Versuch über den homo automobilis." In *,Luxus und Konsum': Eine historische Annäherung*, edited by R. Reith and T. Meyer, 117–128. Münster et al.: Waxmann, 2003.

Kunczik, M. *Public Relations: Konzepte und Theorien*. 5th ed. Cologne: UTB, 2002.

Lauritzen, L. Der. *Mensch hat Vorfahrt: Kursbuch für die Verkehrspolitik. Ein Konzept des Bundesministers für Verkehr*. Bonn: BMfV, 1973.

Luhmann, N. *Einführung in die Systemtheorie*, edited by D. Baecker. 4th ed. Heidelberg: Auer, 2008.

Martens, W., and G. Ortmann. "Organisationen in Luhmanns Systemtheorie." In *Organisationstheorien*, edited by A. Kieser, and M. Ebers, 427–461. Stuttgart; Berlin and Cologne: Kohlhammer, 2006.

Mayntz, R. "Systemkohärenz, institutionelle Komplementarität und institutioneller Wandel." *Transformationen des Kapitalismus, Festschrift für Wolfgang Streeck zum sechzigsten Geburtstag*, edited by J. Beckert et al., 381–397. Frankfurt/M and New York: Campus, 2006.

McCombs, M., and D. Shaw. "The Agenda-Setting Function of Mass Media." *Public Opinion Quarterly* 36 (1972): 176–187.

Mikl-Horke, G. "Neue Institutionenökonomik, kulturelle Komplexität und Wirtschaftsgeschichte." In *Theorie der Firma: interdisziplinär*, edited by G. Mikl-Horke, R. Pirker, and A. Resch, 105–133. Wiesbaden: VS, 2011.

Möser, K. *Geschichte des Autos*. Frankfurt/M and New York: Campus, 2002.

Müller-Jentsch, W. (ed.). *Konfliktpartnerschaft: Akteure und Institutionen der industriellen Beziehungen.* München: Hampp, 1993.

Plumpe, W. "Ökonomisches Denken und wirtschaftliche Entwicklung. Zum Zusammenhang von Wirtschaftsgeschichte und historischer Semantik der Ökonomie." In *Jahrbuch für Wirtschaftsgeschichte/ Economic History Yearbook* 1 (2009): 27–52.

Reichow, H. B. *Die autogerechte Stadt: Ein Weg aus dem Verkehrs-Chaos.* Ravensburg: Otto Maier, 1959.

Reinhardt, D. "Zeitgenössische Ansätze der Marktkommunikation durch Werbung vom Kaiserreich zur Bundesrepublik." In *Unternehmenskommunikation deutscher Mittel- und Großunternehmen*, edited by C. Wischermann, 41–56. Münster: Arday, 2003.

Rinn, G. *Das Automobil als nationales Identifikationssymbol: Zur politischen Bedeutungsprägung des Kraftfahrzeugs in Modernitätskonzeptionen des "Dritten Reichs" und der Bundesrepublik.* Berlin: Humboldt University [dissertation], 2008.

Sachs, W. *Die Liebe zum Automobil.* Ein Rückblick in die Geschichte unserer Wünsche. Reinbek: Rowohlt, 1984.

Schmucki, B. *Der Traum vom Verkehrsfluss.* Frankfurt/M and New York: Campus, 2001.

Streeck, W. *Korporatismus in Deutschland: Zwischen Nationalstaat und Europäischer Union.* Frankfurt/M and New York: Campus, 1999.

Streeck, W. "Beneficial Constraints: On the Economic Limits of Rational Voluntarism." In *Contemporary Capitalism*, edited by J. Hollingsworth and R. Boyer, 197–219. Cambridge: Cambridge University Press, 1997.

Tilly, S. "'Die guten Zeiten ... sind vorbei': Zum Verhältnis von Automobilindustrie, Politik und Automobilverband in den 1970er Jahren." In *Unternehmen am Ende des ,goldenen Zeitalters': Die 1970er Jahre in unternehmens- und wirtschaftshistorischer Perspektive*, edited by M. Reitmayer, and R. Rosenberger, 209–232. Essen: Klartext, 2008.

VDA (ed.) *Verkehr - Sicherheit - Umwelt: Leistungen und Erwartungen der Automobilindustrie.* Köln: VDA, 1971.

Wanner, G. *Auto und Umweltschutz: Erfahrungen, Vorschläge, Maßnahmen des ADAC.* München: ADAC Verlag, 1971.

Wischermann, C. "Unternehmenskultur, Unternehmenskommunikation, Unternehmensidentität." In *Unternehmenskommunikation deutscher Mittel- und Großunternehmen*, edited by idem, 21–40. Münster: Ardey, 2003.

Wolfrum, E. *Die geglückte Demokratie: Geschichte der Bundesrepublik Deutschland von ihren Anfängen bis zur Gegenwart.* München: Pantheon, 2007.

Index

For Product Safety Concerns and Information please contact our
EU representative GPSR@taylorandfrancis.com Taylor & Francis
Verlag GmbH, Kaufingerstraße 24, 80331 München, Germany